INNOCENTS AT HOME

INNOCENTS AT HOME

AMERICA IN THE 1970 S

TAD SZULC

THE VIKING PRESS ● NEW YORK

THIS BOOK IS FOR NELLE MATTHEWS CARR

CONTENTS

AT HOME IN AMERICA

"In the United States all men are to the eye one man, the American. Thus liberty and equality produce moral defects which are not so apparent in other places where the greater part of the people has no chance to exhibit them. What a tumult there would be if those people were suddenly bitten by the same tarantula!"

This rather brutally perceptive and paradoxical comment on America and Americans was produced more than 125 years ago by Domingo Faustino Sarmiento, an Argentine writer-educator and later his country's president, after traveling in the United States in 1847, a time when the American character, personality, and identity had already become fairly established. Señor Sarmiento, who despite his occasional caustic observations felt great affection and admiration for the United States, was only one in a long line of distinguished reporters from abroad to have visited, discussed, dissected, and diagnosed America in the last two centuries. Of course, diagnosing this country and wringing hands over her fate remains to this day a favorite occupation of Americans and foreigners alike.

The roster of memorable foreign commentators on the United States—whether they liked her or not, they all were fascinated by her—runs from Frances Trollope, the mother of Anthony and the prejudiced author of *The Domestic Manners of the Americans,* which she wrote in 1832, just as Alexis de Tocqueville was gathering impressions for *Democracy in America,* to Charles Dickens, who produced his *American Notes* in 1842; Sarmiento himself; Sir William Howard Russell, the great English war correspondent fresh from the Crimea's Thin Red Line in time for our Civil War; Jules Verne, rushing over shortly thereafter; Thomas Huxley, the globe-trotting English biologist; José Martí, the Cuban journalist and patriot, whose home in the 1880s was

3

New York; and, in our time, such social scientists as Gunnar Myrdal; existentialist critics like Simone de Beauvoir; newspaper reporters like Sir William Lewis and Alistair Cooke; and scores of chroniclers, observers, and gossips intensely interested in everything American, from politics to sex, economics to the industrial-military complex, race, space, culture, and counter-culture.

Indeed, uncounted thousands of foreigners have written about America. For the trouble with the country, even (or *particularly*) if you barely know her, is that you want, right away, to write about her. For one thing, the fortunes and misfortunes of the United States inevitably are those of the world, since America's size and power are so predominant. Virtually everything we say, think, or do—whether it is right or wrong—seems at once to affect all of humanity.

I cite the enormous backlog of foreign comment on the United States because after living abroad for many years as an American foreign correspondent—and having turned out a number of journalistic books about foreign lands—I became attracted by the idea of applying the experiences and techniques I used as a reporter to my own country. My notion was to write a book as if I were a foreign correspondent from a faraway country engaged in the process of discovering this land—as I have done so many times in other nations overseas. I first thought of doing this when my family and I returned from Europe late in 1969 after an absence of nearly five years and once more made our home in Washington, D.C., as great and deep changes were shaking American society.

This was a time when massive introspection was the fashion of the day, in this most self-critical of nations. Journalists, publishers, novelists, anthropologists, and social scientists boarded buses and rented cars to crisscross the country, and they promptly let loose with a mind-boggling cascade of varyingly perceptive or shallow essays and books. I tried to read most of them; then I took off on my own.

During the ensuing three years of my American travels—in thousands of casual conversations and formal interviews, and through voracious study of statistics and all kinds of research material—I gained two principal impressions about Americans and the United States.

The first impression is that, by and large, Americans are startlingly ignorant of the facts and realities about their own country. Myths, half-truths, and prejudices abound despite the suffocating news diet supplied by the media and the easy availability of high-quality research. Very few Americans seem to hold a comprehensive view of what is going on in the country. The way we were so dramatically unprepared for the 1973 energy crisis is an example. Naturally, the fantastic complexity of national affairs and each person's unavoidable penchant for concentrating on (or minding) his or her business and family is no help. Clichés make do in the absence of knowledge: "Folks on welfare don't want to work." "The government is too big." "You gotta be a juvenile delinquent if you have long hair." "Whitey wants to keep down the black man forever." "Nixon and his people are a bunch of fascists." Twenty-five years ago, James Thurber said that Americans were wholly convinced of such self-evident truths as "There are no pianos in Japan" and "Foreigners never fish." His words are still true today in America.

On the human level, a man almost literally does not know what his next-door neighbor thinks—even if he knows what he does. In this huge society of more than 210 million (and we are still growing by more than 1.2 million a year), I found what seems to be a breakdown in human communication and, therefore, in understanding and perhaps even in caring.

Possibly this is the price America pays for her demographic immensity: isolation is used as a personal defense against the mounting pressures of the outside world. Different population groups live isolated from one another—and not always because of structured racial, social, or economic forms of segregation. The renewed ethnic awareness of Americans is, consciously or not, an effort at deliberate isolation in predatory surroundings. In fact, the closer Americans live to one another, the less they appear to know about their neighbors, unless they are ethnic kin.

In this over-specialized era, there are fewer and fewer human generalists. Each specialist is hermetically confined to his own area. It is no surprise that whites and blacks, ghetto dwellers and suburbanites, white-collar and blue-collar workers know precious little about one another's problems, anxieties, aspirations. The nation has lost sight of its own ethos.

The second impression I gained is that American trends and patterns change at such breathtaking speed that lasting judgments about this society are almost out of the question. This is as fatal for conventional wisdoms as it is for writers of "definitive" books on the United States. As for myself, I kept rewriting sections of this book every six months or so to make it reasonably up-to-date. Judgments that appeared valid at the outset became useless or outdated before the start of a new year. Our society is mobile, diverse, and change-oriented, and cannot be frozen in place for leisurely observation or formulation of long-range conclusions.

So vast were the changes in recent years that when American prisoners of war returned from North Vietnam in February 1973, the Pentagon thought it necessary to give each man a "catch up" capsule history of the world and a glossary booklet of new American language terms—a dictionary as it were of American "newspeak"—so that he could understand contemporary conversations. Like Rip Van Winkle, the prisoners had slept through a crucial period of American history and culture. They had to be told what was meant by "acid," "Ms.," "gay lib," "a bummer," and

"Jesus freak." The glossary also explained to them what "soul" meant in black American parlance.

In the late 1960s, the youth revolt and the counterculture overwhelmed the American scene—along with drugs and racial explosions in the cities and the antiwar movement. Curiously, while it was a time of violent and destructive crisis it was also a time of joy, innovation, ferment, and the tearing down of ancient social and cultural barriers. The country, when my family and I came back to her, was pulsating and alive. It was a truly revolutionary society in the best and the worst senses.

In the early 1970s, the tide receded and a new mood descended on America, although some of the conquests of the 1960s became a permanent part of the society and its mores. The new mood was sober and reflective, but not necessarily creative. Americans had made the painful discovery that the chief problems they faced were in the realms of poverty, the new social pathology of pervasive work discontent, and their consequences. Unemployment having traditionally loomed as the greatest threat to the working man—shades of the Great Depression—it now became clear that despite relatively stable levels of employment (there were ups and downs in it) and the new technology, millions of those who *do* work are permanently trapped in poverty.

The nation also realized that growth—once the pride of America—simply had to slow down before it asphyxiated the society. Cities and suburbs had grown too large. There were too many people—there were too many cars, too many factory stacks, too many miles of highway, too much pollution. In the 1970s thoughts turned to concepts of "zero-growth" in things and in people. That the Supreme Court upheld anti-abortion laws was one consequence of this trend, as were defensive anti-construction zoning laws in affluent suburbia. At the same time, the modalities and the value of education were suddenly placed in question, along with such other American values as what President Nixon called the old-fashioned "work ethic." But these new challenges stemmed from pragmatism rather than romanticism or radicalism. Inevitably, the 1970s brought boredom and escapism. As a cultural response to the new pressures, football, for example, came to dominate the national interest as few things had before. In 1973, the Super Bowl encounter between the Washington Redskins and the Miami Dolphins, watched on television by 75 million Americans, overshadowed the Vietnam peace agreement.

The energy crisis, hitting the nation late in 1973, deeply affected our lifestyles, shaking up the whole economy, creating unemployment, transforming the mores of the suburban society, changing transportation habits, increasing the alienation between the inflation-ridden average American and the powerful, greedy corporations, and bringing out much of the worst in us. It was a dramatic example on a monumental scale of how abruptly the country can change.

All these shifts of mood make America ever fascinating, and wholly different from every other society I have encountered. Other societies tend to be predictable; the United States is not. She is a nation of surprises, and she keeps surprising herself. And so the study of America continually provides new discoveries. Between the American unpredictability and Americans' own ignorance of each other, we are truly a nation of innocents at home.

This is perhaps why we were so surprised and horrified by the political and financial scandals involving the Nixon administration at its highest levels and threatening our civil liberties and system of justice. The disclosures of secret domestic intelligence plans and political burglaries—set in motion by President Nixon's White House in the name of that elusive concept "national security"—and the accompanying revelations of how Nixon's re-election campaign practiced virtual extortion to collect funds came as such a shock because of our innocent belief that nothing of the sort could possibly happen in America. The "cover-ups" and Nixon's blackmail payments only deepened the incredulity. We saw Spiro Agnew forced to resign to avoid going to prison for taking bribes while serving as Vice President of the United States. We watched Nixon disclosing his new millionaire status and, in effect, acknowledging tax evasion as impeachment pressures grew. But we are both an essentially moral and a moralistic society, which is often forgotten, and Watergate, once discovered, *did* produce a profound reaction. To counteract the conspiracies, we found out, the system still possessed powerful weapons: an outspoken press, an independent judiciary, and a roster of new folk heroes: the Bible-quoting constitutionalist from North Carolina, Senator Sam Ervin; John J. Sirica, the tough Washington judge who was determined to come up with the truth; Special Watergate Prosecutor Archibald Cox, who went to court to sue the President and was fired by him; and uncounted other men and women who simply would not stand still for the White House's cavalier disregard of the rights of Americans. Watergate shook the government as never before, but not the system. And this is what counts.

My first visual—and emotional—reintroduction to America came with the mass October and November antiwar Moratorium demonstrations in Washington in 1969. The huge chanting crowds demanding "Peace Now" in Vietnam, the nocturnal parades of coffins and candles, the helmeted riot police fighting American youngsters (including one of mine) with clubs and tear gas on Constitution Avenue and around the Washington Monument, along with President Nixon's angry pledges that he would not be intimidated by his own Congress and people, clearly revealed a new American dimension. Years later, to be sure, the Vietnam war was still dragging on, although the crowds had vanished, ire giving way to apathy and fatigue. A fragile and incomplete peace was to come only early in 1973, after twelve years of direct American involvement in our longest and most inconclusively fought war. We were out, but our clients in the South were still battling the North Vietnamese in 1974.

What had happened, I asked myself as I came home in 1969, to polarize so many decent and loyal Americans (not all of them young or radical) and pit them against their government and even against one another? It obviously was not the war alone. Too many other tensions and pressures were building up along with the national division over Vietnam. Why, I wondered, were so many young dead set against their parents and the American "system," so disappointed, so bitter, so distrustful? Why were the adults so frightened of their children, why the overall malaise, the growing discontent with the quality of work, the ongoing racial conflicts, the pervading sense of insecurity, futility, the widespread violence, the vicious contest between liberals and conservatives? Why the fear, estrangement, alienation?

Walking on Fourteenth Street, a downtown-Washington thoroughfare, shortly after coming home, I counted burned-out buildings and boarded-up stores in the early autumn chill; other shells of buildings stood in a corner of the black inner city along Seventh Street—a silent reminder of the gruesome violence and arson that swept the ghetto in April 1968 after Dr. Martin Luther King was murdered in Tennessee. I remembered the unbelievable news photos of army troops patrolling Washington streets in jeeps with machine guns at the ready—a sight I knew from Korea, Vietnam, and Santo Domingo but did not think possible in the capital of the United States. And I had always thought our city, 71 per cent black, was relatively free of open racial antagonism. As I write this book in 1974, the charred ruins are still there, a reverse symbol of what the priorities (or nonpriorities) are in the nation's capital. Elsewhere in Washington, right behind the elegant foreign embassies on Sixteenth Street, stand horribly decayed tenements, some of them condemned and abandoned, which are the preserve of drug addicts, criminals, and oversize rats. Packs of wild dogs roam the neighborhood. With the elimination of many federal poverty funds in 1973, the outlook for improvement here seems nil. And a similar state of affairs prevails in dozens of other American cities. As it turns out, the first priority in Washington is given to expensive high-rise apartment and office buildings, and a new multimillion-dollar headquarters of the Federal Bureau of Investigation, with which we, the Washingtonians, have been graced during these years. Only in 1973 did the administration give the city a commitment that $38 million in federal grants would be available during the year to rebuild the inner city.

In Washington and New York, already in my first weeks back home, I saw the citizens' terror of mounting crime, so much of it committed by underprivileged against other underprivileged people, and so aggravated by the Congress' stubborn refusal to pass strong gun-control laws. People were shot, knifed, and mugged in streets, parks, homes, hallways, and elevators. Policemen were ambushed and killed in cities around the country.

The heartbreak of drug addiction had reached epidemic proportions in the years I had been away—through the massive use of heroin among the very young and the very poor. In the emergency room of a Miami hospital one night I saw a seventeen-year-old boy a few minutes before he died from an overdose of heroin. His young face was rigid in agony, a sight etched forever in my memory.

But the much-touted war on narcotics by law-enforcement agencies (there is a quasi-mathematical ratio between drug addiction and crime for it may cost up to sixty dollars daily to maintain the heroin habit), the rehabilitation programs, free clinics, and Methadone treatments moved slowly. New York City alone had over 100,000 hard-core heroin addicts. National totals, including the returning veterans who contracted the habit in Vietnam, could only be a ghastly guess. In 1972, there were 1746 narcotics-related deaths, and we had 10 million alcoholics. Hundreds of millions of dollars worth of heroin somehow entered the country; the crime syndicates distributed it, the pushers sold it, and ghetto children, welfare mothers, unemployed men, discontented blue-collar workers, bored middle-class youths, and everybody else who was unhappy or disturbed shot it up. And this was not just pot—still illegal but a virtually accepted part of the culture. Only deep national distress, I thought, could explain the demand for such a volume of drugs and alcohol.

As I studied basic American statistics—the first thing a reporter should do before he faces the human beings behind the figures —I incredulously learned that the number of poor people in America (defined in 1972 by the official poverty level of an annual income of $4137 for a family of four; the national median family income was $9590) had risen from 24.2 million in 1969 to

25.5 million in 1970, a jump of 1.3 million in one year. It was to stay at about that number in ensuing years, representing in 1973 over 12 per cent of the population of the United States. They were poor in the most actuarially drastic sense. This total included 7 million "working poor" whose earnings fell short of assuring survival. (Only 7.3 per cent of all American families had incomes of over $25,000 in 1972.) Adding up all the federal programs, the cost of supporting, aiding, educating, and keeping healthy these 25.5 million poor Americans was around $30 billion in 1972. Direct welfare costs were only part of the bill.

Once upon a time one talked about "pockets of poverty" in the United States: in the 1970s poverty was recognized as a widespread phenomenon, rampant in the northern cities as well as southern countryside.

In a striking comment on the contradictions in American society, the Census Bureau said that the 5 per cent rise in poverty between 1969 and 1970 was "the first time that there has been a significant increase in the poverty population"; yet the national wealth went on growing. (The number of poor people had gone down between 1966 and 1969.) The "mini-recession" of 1970 could hardly have been responsible for this quantum jump; the best available research suggested that we were witnessing a widening gap between the affluent and the poor, evidently a sign of deep social distortion in our technological society.

Traveling across the country during the next four years, I saw the face of American poverty from Washington's inner city to the slums of Harlem, the Salt River Bed area of Phoenix, Arizona, the Roxbury shanties of Boston, and the Mission-Fillmore skid row of San Francisco. Statistically, these were America's most destitute areas—and they were more than mere pockets of poverty. Humanly, this poverty knew no color: it festered impartially among blacks, whites, Chicanos, Puerto Ricans, and Indians. Its only common denominator was despair.

I also noticed—first in the statistics and then in my travels—
that more than a third of that 1969–70 poverty increase affected
black families whose "heads of households" were women, a
tragic ghetto phenomenon. (In all, 5.5 million American
households are headed nowadays by females—this being under
10 per cent of all households in the nation.) Another way of
looking at this evidence of family breakdown is to cite the bare
statistic that in New York City only 72 per cent of youths under
the age of eighteen lived with *both* parents in 1970 (a decade
earlier it was 83 per cent), and among black youths, only *half.*
The American family, then, was being not simply eroded but
downright ruined as a basic social institution—with obvious implications for the emotional and educational stability of our children. It stood to reason that welfare rolls had to increase, as they
did, at an extraordinary rate in the late 1960s and early '70s.

In 1969, when I began my reporting on America, over 12 million Americans—almost half of the officially poor people—were
on welfare. In 1972, when I started to write this book, the total
exceeded 15 million (the latest reported high point was 15.1 million in August 1972) in this most affluent of nations with an
annual gross national product running well above a *trillion* dollars. (Ironically, the welfare problem was worst in California
and New York—especially in New York City, where every sixth
person was on welfare—the most affluent states, and 75 per cent
of the welfare cases were in the big cities.) By 1972, direct welfare at the federal, state, and local levels cost the United States
the fantastic figure of $19.1 billion, slightly below 10 per cent of
the federal budget. Subsidized medical care for the 22 million
elderly was another $12 billion. Thirty million Americans de-
pended on social security benefits, receiving about $45 billion in
1973. In submitting his budget for fiscal year 1974, President
Nixon asked for $115 billion for total "income security"—43 per
cent of the national expenditure. There was something quite

amiss, I thought, in the American social structure—and the unanswered question was how much worse did the situation have to become before we devised rational means of coping with it?

After an extensive exploration of this problem, I have come to believe that the solution, if there is one, lies in removing the causes of poverty and social distortion rather than in simply doing away with welfare, as some Americans have proposed in their adherence to an ill-conceived "work ethic." Unquestionably, "welfare is a mess"; there have been grave abuses, incredible overpayments to doctors in the Medicaid program for the poor, and vast political and bureaucratic confusion. A whole welfare bureaucracy has grown in the shadow of the multibillion-dollar programs.

But the overwhelming fact, running counter to the established myth, is that the vast majority of poor Americans on welfare *do want to work.* This point was established by social researchers who participated in the massive study on *Work in America,* issued in 1972 by the Department of Health, Education, and Welfare, as well as by such independent social scientists as the Brookings Institution's Leonard Goodwin. Having interviewed some two thousand welfare recipients, blacks and whites, in six major American urban centers, Goodwin concluded that "welfare recipients, whatever their race or time spent on welfare, have essentially the same work ethic and aspirations as do employed middle-class people."

The need, then, appears to be to create, or make available, the kind of jobs that not only constitute incentive to work but offer reasonable income and a sense of self-esteem as well. This, of course, requires a fundamental rethinking of the American work ethos, the removal of racial discrimination in employment, and the understanding that a job ought to provide self-respect rather than take it away—which so often is the case on the assembly lines and in menial ghetto occupations. Nixon's defunct plan for welfare reform—killed in Congress in 1972 by a coalition of liberals and conservatives—provided for a combination of earned income and complementary welfare payments, a highly rational approach. But, in the end, what seems to be required is a fresh cultural attitude by Americans toward their poor.

In 1870, the Code Relating to the Poor of the state of New York provided that "every poor person who is blind, lame, old, sick, impotent or decrepit, or in any other way disabled or enfeebled, so as to be unable by his work to maintain himself, shall be maintained by the county or town in which he may be." The Code also set up county poorhouses for "paupers." This was the welfare philosophy of a century ago. Vast progress, of course, was achieved in the last one hundred years. But poverty in America has many dimensions. Thus, several hundred thousand migrant workers, with seasonal employment from coast to coast, usually live in appalling misery and virtual bondage, as I observed in a Florida camp twenty miles south of Nixon's luxurious compound on Key Biscayne. The situation was so bad when I was there in June 1972 that a typhoid epidemic broke out in the camps and six camp operators at Sun City, near Tampa, were arrested by Federal Bureau of Investigation agents on charges of holding five farm workers in "involuntary servitude," an unbelievable state of affairs in America of the 1970s. Two years later, the migrant situation had not improved.

With malnutrition rampant in the central cities, the rural Southwest, and Appalachia, nearly 30 million persons—15 per cent of the U.S. population—were receiving food stamps, school breakfasts and lunches, day care, and surplus food for families in institutions at a cost of $2.8 billion. A Senate report in May 1973 said that 12 million Americans remain undernourished. Shades of the Great Depression! The report *Hunger—1973* added that between 25 and 30 million Americans are eligible for food assistance, suggesting that "the hunger gap is far from closed either for the country or for the individuals concerned." Given the enormous rise in the cost of food, the Senate report said, "the food stamp program offers less than $1 per person per day. . . . The average value of foods distributed is only about $7 per month, or 23 cents per person per day."

The total food-stamp subsidy, by the way, in 1971 (a not unrepresentative year) was 10 per cent more than the amount the United States spent on medical research, and nearly half of the year's investment in new public and private hospitals and health facilities. And this was before President Nixon decided to cut back on federal funds for health and medical research programs and hospital construction as he went about dismantling the government's big social programs.

In June 1973, nine American Nobel Prize winners, speaking for eight thousand members of the Federation of American Scientists, protested the administration's reduction of funds for basic medical research (other than cancer and heart disease) from $210 million to $120 million in fiscal year 1974. Oddly, what seems like a lot for welfare seems like a trifle when it is spent on medical research designed to prolong lives and diminish suffering. Heart disease and cancer still kill, multiple sclerosis and arthritis cripple, and sickle-cell anemia decimate our black population.

But so improbable had the U.S. social system become—or was it turning into a mockery of a social system?—that welfare families in New York City were housed at the city's expense, at one point, at the Waldorf Astoria Hotel on Park Avenue, that plush symbol of capitalist affluence. In New York City alone, with 1,275,000 recipients, the annual cost of welfare and Medicaid was running at 2.56 billion dollars during 1972, though by 1974 welfare rolls in New York City had dropped below one million as procedures were tightened. In other cities, the homeless stayed that way, in festering, condemned structures.

And, supreme irony, President Nixon in 1971 vetoed legislation providing funds for child day-care centers whose existence would have allowed welfare mothers to work: the plan was too "socialistic." Later, Congress killed the administration's relatively sensible welfare-reform plan—such are American contradictions—and the "welfare mess" went on. In 1973, the President countered by dismantling basic social programs still further—abolishing, for instance, the Office of Economic Opportunity.

The U.S. tax system continues to be inequitable, to say the least —favoring big corporations and the rich at the expense of middle- and lower-income groups. Mortimer Caplin, my neighbor across the street in Washington and a former Internal Revenue commissioner, wrote in the *Indiana Law Journal* that despite the 1969 Tax Reform Act, "it is quite likely that there will continue to be large numbers of high income individuals paying little or no federal income tax." Caplin worked out an example showing that a man with an annual income of a half-million dollars would pay only $32,000 in taxes, the minimal rate, because, if he had oil and gas and real-estate investments, he could deduct depletion, intangible drilling costs, paper real-estate losses, charitable contributions, and personal deductions to the point where he had no taxable revenue. The normal rate in this man's income bracket should have been $250,000. Tax exemptions on municipal bonds are another fantastic loophole, and countless other tax havens are possible for a rich man. Home owners can deduct the interest on mortgage payments. But none of this is available to poor or strapped Americans who own little to begin with. Tenants receive no deductions on their rents. The oil industry, the principal beneficiary of the loophole system, in 1970 paid only 8.7 per cent in federal taxes on a total net income of $8.8 billion for the nineteen biggest companies. In 1972, the four biggest oil companies paid 2.6 per cent on the average on earnings totaling $7.3 billion. A billion-dollar corporation in the Midwest paid less than 40 per cent in taxes on more than $100 million in profits for 1972.

Revenue-sharing programs between the federal government and the states and municipalities—a plan to distribute about $6 billion in tax revenue annually—served as an insouciant political football between the White House and Congress before it was finally approved in 1972. In any event, the new system has already proved totally inadequate, with most of the money going to law enforcement and only a tiny fraction to social programs.

Government low-cost housing projects, chiefly for blacks, were meanwhile collapsing and central core cities were dying a cancerous death, although three out of every four Americans lived in urban areas, including the suburbs and "new cities" that had sprouted since the mid-1960s.We have 153 cities with populations over a hundred thousand, plus their vast suburban "fringes." Meanwhile, the exodus from the countryside, especially in the South, keeps on, as farm towns literally close up, one after another, like factories going into bankruptcy. The arriving poor fill the inner cities while the more affluent flee to the suburbs. Between 1960 and 1970, the suburban population grew by 44 per cent to 54 million.

One of the most shocking sights I can remember was contained in television films of a relatively new housing project in Saint Louis, Missouri, being blown up with dynamite by city authorities because tenants had deserted the dwellings, refusing to live in such unfamiliar and constraining vertical ghettos—high-rise rabbit warrens with a special kind of criminality marking them (muggers, rapists, and dope addicts lurked in the empty halls and stairways). The refugees from the Saint Louis housing project, like similar refugees in other American cities, preferred the relative tribal safety of old tenements where slum landlords gouged them for exorbitant rents to total alienation in the less costly and theoretically better-equipped projects. (In mid-1973, Saint Louis gave up altogether on the Pruitt-Igoe project, expelling the remaining two thousand tenants and boarding up the last six buildings that were still occupied. Built in 1956 at a cost of $36 million in federal funds alone, Pruitt-Igoe had once housed ten thousand people.)

The reason for this return to the traditional ghetto remains generally ignored by government housing planners—bureaucrats and cost accountants—who consider that the urban problem can be solved simply through the construction of x new dwellings for y families without any regard for their cultural condition. For blacks, Spanish-speaking people, and other poor ethnic groups, all of whom have traditions of strong family bonds, even the worst neighborhood slum may offer a sense of physical, emotional, and cultural safety. The neighborhood is the tribe, or the village, with its own peculiar safety mechanisms built into the church, the familiar grocery, or the social club. Individuals and families know and constantly see and hear one another, share a common life in the streets and the intimacy of warm-weather conversations on the stoops. Codes of behavior and precisely defined sexual mores are rigidly enforced. Each neighborhood—whether Polish, Italian, Irish, Puerto Rican, or black—offers a haven from the hostile outside world.

No wonder, then, that the ethnic groups, like the blacks, are asserting their identity and origins as they have not done since the great waves of migration which brought them to the United States at the turn of the century. To uproot them without any kind of social and cultural transition is, in effect, to smash their family and tribal structures and hurl them into anonymity and disorientation. Anyone who has ever gone through a low-income housing project after dark knows the pang of fear one senses in the deserted, silent, evidently lifeless buildings and their surrounding grounds; it is not what one feels in a crowded, throbbing slum neighborhood. For my part, I feel considerably safer on the streets of East Harlem or Washington's Shaw-Cardozo area, in the midst of people, than in a housing project.

Of course, I am not making a case for the perpetuation of the urban slum. Instead, I am suggesting—on the basis of countless conversations with people who live in the ghettos, with social workers, priests, ministers, and cops—that it is harmful, if not downright impossible, to transform overnight a close-knit "culture of poverty," as the late anthropologist Oscar Lewis called it, into an artificial pseudo-modern society without inducing destructive alienation. Lewis's own superb research of family patterns among New York's Puerto Ricans makes this point clearly.

I had the occasion of observing the same phenomenon in Rio de Janeiro and Caracas in the late 1950s and early 1960s. There, too, families abandoned spanking-new housing projects, first smashing the elevators, toilets, and windows, to stream back to the Rio *favela* and the huts at the foot of Caracas' Avila mountain. It took Brazilians and Venezuelans long years of social and cultural experimentation to attempt the transition away from the "culture of poverty" again in a humane way. Curiously, the United States, so advanced in so many ways, seems to have not yet quite comprehended the human aspects of this housing problem. In any event, the Nixon administration disposed of the whole complex matter in one fell swoop when it froze all new federal funds for low-cost housing in 1973. It must have seemed easier to forget the problem than to face it.

If we tend to lock the poor in an artificial society of estrangement, we do even worse with the ones we have condemned to our unbelievably oppressive prison system. For a society that prides itself on its concern with the rights of the individual, the United States all too often allows sentenced prisoners (and those awaiting trial, sometimes for months and years) to be treated almost in a concentration-camp fashion and with an awesome and sadistic denial of most rights and personal dignity. In New York City, for example, out of 11,653 jail inmates in August 1972, 8087 were simply awaiting trial, were not yet convicted of any crime.

A few months later, a man named Ralph Garcia was acquitted of a double murder charge after spending over two years in New York's Tombs prison. A week after that, the state Court of Appeals announced that it would start a massive release of defendants from jails unless speedy trials could be assured.

The federal prison system, which handles only a fraction of the prison population, tries to operate with relative decency, but horror reigns at state and municipal institutions. I have gone to visit prisoners at San Quentin in California, the Tombs, the D.C. jail in Washington, and elsewhere, and the conditions are reminiscent of those under a retrograde police state or in a Dickens novel about nineteenth-century England. Chancing upon a report by inspectors of New York State prisons in 1870, I was shocked to see that basically neither the problems nor the methods have changed greatly in a hundred years.

Blacks, Chicanos, and Puerto Ricans who, for reasons and with results I shall discuss further on, constitute the bulk of the inmate population bear the brunt of man's institutionalized cruelty to man in this land. It is impossible to avoid the conclusion that plain racism on the part of wardens and guards is a major element here. A dramatic case in point was shown in the New York Board of Corrections' report to the mayor in August 1972 charging that "the number of suicides and attempted suicides in the city's correctional institutions continues at an alarming rate," that "the custodial facilities presently used for the housing of mentally disturbed prisoners are themselves the cause of suicide attempts because of their oppressive, dehumanized environment," and that out of the nine suicides in New York prisons in the first half of 1972, six were of "Hispanic background." One can only speculate about the depths of misery that mark the alienation of these minorities.

In California, conditions in the state prisons are aggravated by a system of "indefinite sentence," under which felons are made to serve terms from one year to life at the often capricious discretion of parole boards. What this does to the morale and psychology of the inmates—and of the wardens and guards, for that matter—requires no elaboration. Numerous other states also have laws resulting in terrible and corroding uncertainty for the prisoner over his future, if any. Robert Sommer, a professor of psychology at the University of California and an authority on penal problems, has written that much of the tension in the California prisons results from ethnic and ideological factors. "A 'militant' inmate, particularly if he is black or brown, is sent to another institution and placed in isolation. Unfortunately that policy spreads militancy to institutions that had previously been quiet. . . . Following the pattern set by black activists and the students, prisoner militancy will abate only when prisoners have some voice in making decisions that affect them."

There is nothing new, to be sure, about what goes on inside American prisons. Volumes have been written about it. But both Congress and public opinion have always looked the other way, ignoring this American opprobrium—almost in the way in which Germans once pleaded ignorance of concentration camps in their midst. Only when sectors of public opinion on the one hand and many prisoners on the other became highly politicized, as they did in recent years, did Americans begin to be aware of the horrors they had tolerated for so long. The violent uprisings in the early 1970s at California's San Quentin and Soledad prisons, New York's Attica prison, and New York City's Tombs, to mention the most famous ones, served to sharpen this awareness. But serious remedial action is still to be taken. A friend of mine who has been talking to parole boards has reported that a key factor in evaluating a prisoner is still whether he is a "good Christian."

In my observation of the contemporary U.S. scene I also learned that while millions of Americans cannot afford to get enmeshed in our judicial system, many millions more cannot afford illness or even death. The staggering cost of doctors, hospitals, medical services, and burials has pushed them into a class of social luxuries—indeed, the whole concept of national health and death is regressive. In 1973, Americans spent out-of-pocket $80 billion on their health—eleven times more than they spent in 1945 and 14 per cent more than in 1970. Medical- and hospital-insurance plans—such as the big federal government plans, Blue Cross, Blue Shield, and those plans run by labor unions and ethnic community groups—are largely inadequate to meet the people's medical needs. (Military plans, which cover 2.3 million servicemen and dependents, are an exception, in part because of the Defense Department's extensive medical facilities.) Usually, civilian plans cover about half of a doctor's surgery bill, for example. A majority of Americans, about 80 per cent, are theoretically covered in some form by these plans, usually under group programs at their place of employment, but much of this is illusory. To an estimated 25 million Americans, not employed by the federal or local governments or by big and medium-size corporations, even this relatively cheap coverage (for example, I paid about nine dollars a month for the whole family, and the newspaper that employed me picked up the balance of the forty-dollar monthly premium for comprehensive coverage under the labor contract) is not available. They cannot afford the more expensive private plans to which one must subscribe individually. The average annual cost had gone up in 1973 to $300 per family. This amount of money is of course out of the question for the 25.6 million Americans who live below the poverty level. Other millions, who are protected by some group plans, are eligible for only limited benefits because they cannot meet the high premiums required for full-fledged coverage. And there are limits, too, on hospital benefits after a certain number of days, leaving a family unprotected in a prolonged illness. There is such a thing as "using up" one's health insurance.

To be sure, cheap or charity care is available for indigents. The federal government's Medicaid program, which cost $6.5 billion in 1971, looks after the very poor. But its quality is debatable at best, as is Medicare for citizens over sixty-five. There is also the matter of human dignity of the indigent patient and his family in a society which places its stamp of approval on affluence and begrudgingly, almost contemptuously, dispenses charity. Interestingly, the poorer countries I've known—Brazil, Chile, Mexico, or Spain, and the socialist countries of Eastern Europe—have long provided better social services, and without the destruction of human dignity.

All these problems loomed large for me recently after my daughter was injured in an automobile accident and required delicate plastic surgery for deep facial lacerations. She received superb care at a university hospital, and no financial problems arose because we had automobile insurance as well as a decent income level. But what if we had not been so well protected? Her hospital bills for three days of confinement, including surgery, totaled $1429.57, of which semi-private room and board was $258, the use of the operating room for three hours $635, and so on. In addition, the surgeon's fee was $550. With medicine, it all came to a cool $2000. What, I wondered, would an uninsured black or Puerto Rican worker (who might also have been unemployed) have done, even if some of the costs were waived, unless he chose to be a charity case? And would the quality of the care have been really as good as that given my daughter? And what if an American below the poverty level has a long illness, such as cancer, in his family?

Hospital administrators have told me of the immense and ever-rising costs of running their institutions and of the difficulty of raising funds despite federal and state aid and charitable contributions. I am also aware of the growing problems of operating hospitals in big cities. (Not long ago, for instance, doctors at New

York's Lincoln Hospital, caring mostly for black and Spanish-speaking patients, went on strike demanding better protection from criminals roaming the institution's corridors in search of narcotics or just plain money. Lincoln in the end had to hire extra guards to keep the doctors and their staffs safe, thus increasing its operating costs. In 1973, an incredible hospital-staff strike affecting most of New York City forced the closing even of emergency wards.) One can only conclude that hospitals *have* to go on charging more and more for their services—unless a better national system is devised—or face collapse. Physicians, too, have become a major financial problem for the American patient. Citing overhead expenses—office rents, nurses, technicians, and equipment, and, more candidly, their determination to collect with a vengeance for their six or more years of medical education—doctors charge exorbitant fees, especially in the big cities. This is why allowable medical-insurance benefits under the major plans frequently meet less than half a doctor's fee—even for surgery. Insurance overpayments are rampant.

The New York Death Review Board, concerned with causes of death among the city's prisons' inmates, noted in a 1972 report that full-time physicians in the correctional facilities start at $30,000 annually in the "voluntary hospital sector," but that their pay must be raised if the level of medical services is not to deteriorate further. In the private sector, medical fees other than in charity practice are, literally, what the traffic will bear. In Washington, consultations in the doctor's office run between ten and twenty dollars, a charge which is usually not covered by insurance unless it relates to a major illness or accident. Psychiatrists charge forty dollars an hour or more for consultation or therapy, and only a few major-medical insurance plans in the country cover psychiatric care. Untold numbers of Americans must forgo the help they desperately need until it is too late. An orthodontist of my acquaintance grosses about $150,000 annually (dental work is not covered in most major insurance plan), and a Washington surgeon I know can afford a private luxury aircraft for pleasure flying. A famous heart surgeon in Minnesota was convicted in 1973 for a $250,000 tax evasion. At the same time, more and more physicians refuse to participate in insurance plans because of the red tape and delays involved in the collections. Health-plan subscribers complain that they have difficulty obtaining appointments from doctors who give priority to private patients. In small towns and rural areas, physicians' fees and availability are, perforce, more in phase with the possibilities of their communities. But the big cities attract the best doctors.

Medicaid can be profitable for the physician: More than a dozen Washington doctors earned over $60,000 each under the plan in the first eleven months of 1972. An obstetrician who made over $200,000 from Medicaid in 1972 was a ghetto doctor; his case is an illustration of the incredible abuse of blacks by blacks in the American ghetto, where everything from medical care to medicine and food costs more than in white neighborhoods—the paradox is that the poorer the family, the more expensive are the necessities of life.

How does our affluent society propose to deal with the health crisis? It took years before Congress approved in 1966 the federally financed Medicare hospital program for persons over sixty-five years of age, and this over the angry protests of the American Medical Association, one of Washington's most powerful lobbies. Medicaid, too, was fought. But the medical lobby has succeeded for years in blocking a general national-health program—relatively limited as it is in comparison with, say, the British plan—by again invoking the threat of "socialization" as if, indeed, medical care within everybody's reach were not an elementary social function. Many doctors likewise oppose the broadening of existing health plans to avoid losing their private practice. The argument I have so often heard in discussions with doctors—that by overcharging the affluent (and what is affluence in this over-taxed and inflation-ridden society?) they are able to provide free care to indigents—seems hardly convincing in a modern nation. And it brings out the medical profession's ingrained patronizing attitude of dispensing charity or quasi-charity, overlooking the social responsibility to look after the sick without depriving them of dignity. In mid-1970, however, it finally appeared possible that the Congress would approve compromise national-health-insurance legislation linked to the social-security system.

Paying for death in the United States is as hard as paying for health. Having had the responsibility in recent years of taking care of two family funerals, I know from experience that even a modest burial may run from $1500 to $2000 (a fairly plain casket may cost $500), without counting the cemetery lot. The ghoulish joke of "Die Now, Pay Later" is an unfortunate American reality with poor families left behind to pay the funeral bills of their deceased kin. Social security is not much help.

The social state of American health, as I found it, was also highly disturbing in the 1970s. Venereal disease was soaring for the first time since World War II—across the country as many billboards warn against VD as against drug addiction—an extraordinary commentary, it seems to me, on a society that regards itself as educated and civilized. Three prostitutes interviewed on a recent television talk show argued very professionally and righteously (and perhaps correctly) that the rise in venereal disease resulted not from prostitution, but from the avid discovery of the American "sexual revolution" by careless young people. Venereal disease is now an upper-middle-class affliction. Scientists at the National Institutes of Health in Washington told me that the incidence of tuberculosis, a malady normally associated with poverty, backwardness, and malnutrition, was mounting again because, inexplicably, uncounted thousands of families gave up having vaccinations. The same phenomenon was occurring with polio, although the vaccine

was available everywhere for the asking. My NIH friends speak
of a cultural breakdown among people who know, or should
know, better.

It is clear to any explorer of the current American landscape
that effective school desegregation has faltered more in the
North than the South, while Americans are pitted against each
other over the issue of busing of their children to school in the
name of "quality education," often a euphemism for continued
racial segregation. At the same time, they vote down school-bond
referendums, thus denying money to improve this education.
The notion of raising the salaries of teachers, among the most
underpaid creative Americans, is anathema. In 1972, for example, the average teacher earned $13,500 annually in New York
City, much less elsewhere. Teachers' strikes of varying duration
hit New York City, Saint Louis, Washington, D.C., Philadelphia,
and Cleveland in the 1972–73 academic year. And the more affluent the district, the greater the opposition to school-bond issues
and better salaries for teachers.

I saw this when I visited Arlington, Ohio, a rich suburb west
of Columbus, in 1970. There the parents (many of them well-paid
professors at nearby Ohio State University) voted against a $7.9
million issue to finance pay increases for teachers, ignoring the
efforts of their own children, who rang bells door-to-door in support of the proposal. And I saw it again in 1972 in Fairfax County,
Virginia, a bedroom area serving Washington, D.C., and distinguished for its expensive homes, air-conditioned shopping centers, two-car families, and horse hunts. (Fairfax has one of the
highest median family incomes in the United States.) In June
1973, however, Fairfax voters finally approved a $24 million
school-bond issue, largely because affirmative votes came from
new suburban residents whose children lacked schools altogether.

According to the records of the U.S. Office of Education, less than half of 1086 school-bond issues were approved across the country in the 1970–71 fiscal year, as compared with an approval rate of almost 75 per cent in 1965. Was this caring about one's children? This refusal to spend more tax money meant that additional schools could not be built, which in turn necessitated the growing reliance on busing that many affluent white parents battled so angrily. Money was simply drying up for schools. Recent reductions in federal education grants forced a cutback in library programs. I know elementary schools where teachers have to buy their own red pencils. And seven million American children require special education programs because of physical, psychological, or mental handicaps.

From my own experience I know that the total annual cost per child of a private school in an average American city can run close to $3000—three-quarters of the yearly income of a "poverty level" American family—and even if parents do have the money, overcrowding poses major enrollment problems. On top of that, I have serious doubts whether private schools necessarily offer better education than the public school system. For one thing, they are hermetically isolated from the real life outside their manicured gardens, oblivious of the strife and struggle of everyday life.

The catalogue of America's social ills extends to her old people, for whom we seem to have neither time nor money. Statistics for 1972 show that some 27 million Americans were over the age of sixty-five, and more than 5 million lived below the $4137-a-year family poverty level. The lucky among the other 22 million could count on maximum social security payments of around $4850, retirement or pension plans, or savings. Only a fraction, the truly rich, were the very lucky ones who could afford luxury retirement in Florida or elsewhere in the sun, or on world cruises.

Because we have a national propensity for empty grandiloquent phrases, we call our old people "senior citizens." This is presumably intended to denote respect for them. In truth, the overwhelming majority of them are treated neither as senior nor as citizens. Given the American deification of youth, we tend to grow impatient with anyone showing signs of age (not just senility), discard them, and consign them to oblivion. Average longevity now stands at 66.6 years for men and 74.1 years for women, but the new tendency is to bring the normal retirement age of sixty-five down to sixty-two and, in some cases, to fifty-eight. In practical terms, the American dream of retirement is more often a nightmare and a resigned wait for death. Old people who live alone are battered by inflation which, running at a 15 per cent annual rate in 1974, shrinks the value of their fixed social-security or pension payments (although in the past two years Congress, conscious of their voting power, raised social-security benefits and added a minimal cost-of-living provision for automatic increases in the future) and destroys their savings. And pension plans themselves are not only inadequate but also downright pernicious.

Recent studies indicate that only 35 per cent of all American workers are covered by private (as distinct from government) pension plans and that 70 per cent of the participants will not receive payments of any kind upon retirement. The reasons for this bleak prospect range from being laid off (a growing reality in the American economy) after a lifetime of employment with a company that goes out of business, to people being cold-bloodedly fired on the eve of retirement or the employee having once or more times changed jobs for valid human motives. The end of a job, for whatever reason, means the end of participation in a pension plan. The benefits, of course, are calculated on the basis of length of service to a single company. There are no "portable" pension plans. Severance pay, when given, rarely approaches full retirement benefits. So the senior citizen winds up high and dry.

The same studies show that half of those who will receive

pension benefits, perhaps three or four million persons, will get less than $1000 annually. Even combined with social security, a maximum income between $7000 and $10,000 a year is hardly a bonanza for a man and his wife. At the same time, the corporations and labor unions that control private pension funds hold $150 billion in them (more than half the national annual budget) for investments, frequently of a questionable nature. The contributor to the pension fund to which he belongs has no say, naturally, as to how his money will be used nor does he benefit from the profits. And without the pension funds, according to my friends in brokerage houses, Wall Street, and much of the business financed by it, would come to something like a grinding halt. It is both grotesque and sinister.

The most gruesome aspect of old age in America is the nursing home. Most of these establishments are a rich source of revenue for their owners, but the services they offer often are an abomination and a national shame. Senior citizens are frequently ill-treated, mistreated, or left to vegetate in boredom. To complicate matters, an estimated 30 per cent of our hospitals and nursing homes—often a euphemism for human junkyards—dropped out of the Medicare programs by the end of 1971. Thus some 5000 hospitals and homes for the elderly no longer accept patients under Medicare payments. Senior citizen be damned. I have visited nursing homes where a cheap transistor radio is the only link with reality. So the transistor becomes a precious possession jealously guarded from stealing or over-borrowing. Almost daily, newspapers across the nation report violations of every kind—sanitary as well as medical—in these nursing homes. Five million elderly people were expected to be hospitalized in 1973 under Medicare for actual illness. So many of the inmates (I am using the word advisedly) and the sick become in time empty-eyed zombies bereft of self-respect, whose physical death is eagerly awaited by the families. And emotional blackmail is prac-

ticed on the elderly by the nursing homes in the hard-sell advertising pitch that "you don't want to be a burden to those you love."
What, I wondered as I traveled across America, is this society
doing to itself?

Still freshly arrived in the United States, I began meeting
young militant blacks, their splendid Afros rising in defiance,
some of them convinced that the gun and knife were the only
tools they could use to carve out living space in dignity for their
people—11 per cent of the population—in what they saw as a
racist nation. Some of them were guerrilla-trained Vietnam veterans—the supreme irony of American policies—threatening to
turn on those who first taught them to kill. Those were the snipers of Detroit, Newark, and Washington of the riots of the 1960s,
and the Black Liberation Army who in the 1970s turned to ambush killings of policemen. Black-white racial conflict was also
deepening in the armed forces. Black and white soldiers fought
in Germany and aboard navy ships. White officers were
"fragged" with grenades by black soldiers. A lot of black patience
and moderation died with Martin Luther King though, as I saw
in time, a lot did survive.

Despite enormous progress in ostensible racial equality since
the early 1960s, blacks unquestionably remained in inferior positions—either because of actual or hidden discrimination or because our society had historically denied them the education and
preparation to compete on equal terms with the white American.
Census figures emphasized the chasm between the status and
incomes of white Americans on the one hand and blacks and
Spanish-speakers on the other. Overall unemployment in 1972
hit 4.6 per cent of the work force but 9.8 per cent of the black. And
a 1972 survey by the Bureau of Labor Statistics found that unemployment among black high-school graduates was twice that of
white graduates. The Bureau commented drily that "these differ-

ences may reflect discriminatory hiring practices and, for Negroes, possible differences in the quality of schooling available." White graduates, when employed, often earned considerably higher wages than the blacks for identical work. In New York City, the Census Bureau found the median white family income to be $10,378 in 1970, the black family's $7150, and the Puerto Rican's only $3811—just $68 above the official poverty level that year.

It can probably be argued, as I have heard it argued, that impatience and anger alone cannot solve basic social problems. While some militant groups demanded immediate action, even with gun in hand, other black leaders chose moderation at the risk of being reviled as Uncle Toms by their more impatient constituents. Working through the system, such as it was, blacks had risen to the mayoralty of Washington, D.C., by presidential appointment and of Cleveland, Newark, Gary, and a number of other cities by election. The greatest black success came in May 1973 when Thomas Bradley, a one-time black policeman, was elected mayor of Los Angeles, easily beating incumbent Sam Yorty who injected racism and charges of radicalism against his opponent in the campaign. And Los Angeles was the city where the Watts riots in 1965 had sparked a nationwide wave of black unrest. Bradley won nearly half the white vote and nine out of ten black votes. But in 1973 there was only one black senator out of 100 and only 16 black congressmen out of 435, hardly enough to represent 11 per cent of the population if some concept of proportional representation seems valid. The Democratic party, a political pioneer in relative American terms, did come up with fairly proportional representation for blacks (along with other minorities) among the state delegates to its 1972 presidential convention. And about the same time, the Black Panthers themselves turned back to the system, with several of their leaders seeking elective offices.

Still, the racial problem was far from resolved. In some ways, it became aggravated in the 1970s as increasing numbers of young blacks chose self-segregation over social integration in white society. (Between 1960 and 1970 mixed marriages had increased by 63 per cent—but this was virtually meaningless, since the total amount accounted for only 0.7 per cent of the 44.5 million American marriages.)

Through my daughter, then a highly radicalized college student in Washington, D.C., I began in 1969 to meet other young people—chiefly whites—who were desperately nonconformist, desperately hungry for believable ideas, and desperately wanting to be understood and, yes, loved—even if a few chose, in those days of rising alienation, to be bomb-planting, police-hating "Weatherpeople" of the radical Left and others became involved in the formless "Movement" of protest and change. For one thing, they were aware of American injustices and problems that we, the Establishment people, chose to overlook.

Classically, these young people came from the enlightened and guilt-ridden middle class, and they were a small fraction of the 40 million Americans between the ages of fourteen and twenty-four. Revolution seemed possible only in affluence. The working-class youth, aside from the militant blacks, generally ignored the new revolt. Young workers, better educated and more exposed to ideas than their parents, still remained by and large conservative. (The Nixon landslide in 1972 proved it beyond question.) I was reminded of the bitter saying of the 1930s: "The working class can kiss my ass, I'm the foreman now." But on the issues of working conditions and alienation from the assembly-line syndrome the young worker was turning into a different kind of rebel, as rising industrial sabotage, wildcat strikes, and the sharp increase in absenteeism made abundantly clear.

Curiously, the bourgeois revolutionaries' heroes were Ché

Guevara, Patrice Lumumba, and Charlie Chaplin rather than Marx, Lenin, or even Mao Tse-tung. The romantic easily overshadowed the ideological. The accent was on "doing one's thing" and, in a more deeply American way than these young people perhaps realized, on a need for individualism and independence so deep as to reject any form of leadership. This may have been one reason why the youth's political efforts never found an effective doctrinaire expression, dissolving in ennui when the 1970s rolled around. And thereby also hung the destiny of the American Left, old and new.

But in 1969 (it now seems eons away), Woodstock had just happened, and the youth culture was hard upon us (complete with smuggled whiffs of grass), right in our quiet northwest Washington house, in the ghostly shapes of Herman Hesse, poetry, and long hair; Herbert Marcuse and philosophy and blue jeans and beads; and tragic Janis Joplin and the guitar and acid rock.

Taking stock of all these impressions, I remembered Mark Twain writing about Americans who had gone to other countries and continents completely innocent of any knowledge about what and whom they were seeing. But, it struck me that many of us, myself very much included, were just as innocent about the new (and even old) realities at home in America. Being a politically oriented reporter, the state of liberty and equality in the United States was inevitably on my mind—with all its broad implications for the American democracy—as was the question of those "moral defects" of which Sarmiento, the Argentine visitor, had spoken in 1847 but which still plagued us. I did not know at the time that Nixon's White House was launching a domestic intelligence plan in deep secrecy, largely out of fear of young radicals. Even in 1973, when this plan surfaced as part of the Watergate horror, the national leadership still believed that it had been right. It still did not understand the people it was supposed to govern.

Yet, perhaps most important of all to me was to find out how the problem of freedom in the United States on the one hand and the society's moral defects on the other might be perceived by my own children (as, for example, they watched the emergence of political trials in the country for the first time in postwar history) and how this growing conflict affected them. As I was to discover, my daughter, nineteen years old when we returned home in 1969, and my son, then thirteen, helped me over the ensuing years in a much more profound way than I thought possible to shed the mantle of innocence at home. They were very clear-eyed and rebellious when we, the early-middle-aged liberals, still tended to defend the American system as essentially good, take the easy way out, and look the other way. Like Pangloss, American political leaders, strangely oblivious of the country's terrible social distortions, insisted that all was well in these United States. But the tarantula was out to bite us all.

Professional reportorial instinct at first, then exposure, and finally the actual work of reporting for the next three years convinced me that the 1970s were bound to be completely distinct, a time of greater fundamental change in American life than anything my generation had seen, experienced, or imagined. Americans were changing, as rebel college students of the late 1960s grew into young professionals of the new decade; as embittered and disoriented veterans returned from Vietnam (over the

ten years of the war there were 3 million young men who had
served in Indochina) seeking work and understanding from a
nation that had sent them to fight so far away and so much in
vain; as the country searched its soul over the quandary of
amnesty for those who refused to go to war. A whole new culture
was blossoming, re-evaluating the rights and roles of men and
women, producing new concepts, new art, and conquering new
frontiers—from newly accepted social behavior on earth all the
way to outer space and the moon.

This social revolution was responsible, among other things, for
the fact that women filled two-thirds of all the new jobs open in
the country between 1960 and 1970. The American woman became *almost* liberated. She flew airline jets, helped to run the
U.S. economy from the White House, drove New York subway
trains, ran major corporations, served with the police and the
FBI, and held ambassadorial posts. (The Supreme Court had, in
effect, legalized abortion on demand—a million women were expected to take advantage of it annually—though the Roman
Catholic church and other groups fought it tooth and nail.) To be
sure, there was no liberation in sight for ghetto women and welfare mothers. And, from my own observation at the other end of
the spectrum, it was not all that certain that affluent suburban
women wanted to be liberated. There, the rhetoric was louder
than acts.

With the change in the American people, their institutions, too,
were changing—their politics, mores, morals, tastes, habits, and
life styles. There were new fads—acupuncture, for example, became fashionable, along with Satanism—and new morality
standards, under which explicit sex movies were hailed as pure
art and some of them actually deserved this recognition. Best-
seller lists accentuated the American readers' voracious interest
in sex. American society displayed in many ways much more
real freedom than it had ever enjoyed before: chiefly personal
freedom to think, act, work, dress, and make love as it wished.

And all this was happening despite the inroads made by technology and overcrowding that, almost by definition, called for uniformity.

But there was a price to be paid. Social and cultural change brought resistance and fear from the guardians of the status quo. The freer the society was becoming, the greater became the pressures for repression, surveillance, and invasions of privacy on the part of the Establishment. Government and private intelligence data banks, not to mention wiretaps, were a pervasive threat to the new freedoms. So were the new restrictions on the operations of the news media. All in all, I realized, a completely different America would be the home of my protesting children. Alexis de Tocqueville observed 140 years ago, speaking of America, that "nations do not grow old as men do, and every fresh generation is a new people ready for the care of the legislator."

As the 1970s opened the nation was deeply embroiled in the Indochina war, split asunder by it, and in a situation of moral self-flagellation. The My Lai massacre, coming on top of all the bombings and defoliation missions over Vietnam, hit public opinion with the savage force of a sledge hammer, although Americans in time learned to assuage and discard this guilt.

The racial conflict, changing in character and sometimes becoming more subtle, seemed to deepen instead of moving toward reasonable solutions in which whites and blacks (and Chicanos, Puerto Ricans, Indians, and Orientals) could live and let live. In 1970, the blood of all these American colors was still being shed in sneaky assassinations and ghetto shootings. The Indians were increasingly on the warpath. The treatment of migrant workers continued to be a national scandal. Affluent whites were fleeing in droves from the impacted cities to inexpugnable suburbia, while poor blacks were left behind to fester in urban ruin.

New York City is a prime example of the flight of white affluence, fat rats abandoning a rotting, leaking ship. According to the Census Bureau, the number of the city's black and Spanish-speaking inhabitants increased from 1.8 million in 1960 to 3 million in 1970, although the overall population remained at a fairly constant level of some 7.5 million. This meant that 1.2 million black and Spanish-speaking people had been born in New York City, or migrated to it during the decade, while roughly 1.2 million whites had turned over their Manhattan, Bronx, and Brooklyn neighborhoods to the new dwellers.

But those new tenants were never given a chance to keep their homes in adequate condition. A walk along, say, East 124th Street just off First Avenue, tells the story of Spanish Harlem in a spectacle of half-ruined tenement houses, piles of rotting garbage, scampering rats, abandoned cars without tires or windows, and children playing in the filth of rain puddles. This is an area where the median family income hovers below $4000, unemployment is around 10 per cent, and the sub-employment rate is 33 per cent, meaning that one-third of those who work do so on a part-time basis. The same sights were on display on the Lower East Side, along Tenth and Eleventh Streets off Avenue A, as well as in Newark, Elizabeth, and Hoboken across the Hudson River in New Jersey. And this urban misery is paralleled in the slums of San Antonio, Phoenix, and New Orleans.

Youth, with its counterculture and screaming defiance of the generation in power and the old order, was up in arms, as no younger generation I had ever seen before in the United States. The older people, uncomprehending, screamed back their fear of youth and change, though in time they began to come to terms with it. Rather unbelievably, the average middle-aged and otherwise rational American reacted to long hair as a bull to red cloth: with blind rage. Deputy sheriffs in Georgia and Mississippi arrested boys on loitering charges only because they had long hair.

In Arizona, a gas station attendant would not service the car in which my daughter was traveling because she had long-haired companions. A minor *cause célèbre* in New Mexico in 1970 was the shooting of a youth who lived with a girl in a cabin in the mountains, because the local authorities disapproved of their morals. Around Taos, kids living in communes armed themselves against the police (and, ironically, against the local Chicanos, who feared for the value of their land). But I also know of parents who offered their sons a hundred dollars to have a haircut—God forbid they should embarrass the parents in their "nice" neighborhoods—or who threatened dire punishment if they failed to go to the barber. It was ridiculous.

Intelligent people, whether parents, judges, or legislators, quickly associated long hair, beards, beads, jeans, or peasant blouses with marijuana and heavier drugs along with free love and revolution. Pot and sex, to be sure, were much in evidence, but the insecure adults made hasty judgments as to the probable behavior of their children on visual suspicion rather than tangible proof. Peace symbols irritated them, and so did the new slang —"far out," "out of sight," "Right on!"—because they implied some vague threat to adult authority. Serious ideas were seldom seriously discussed because this, too, enervated the guardians of the Establishment. At almost every dinner or cocktail party I have attended for the last four years, I have heard parents criticize their children and deplore their life styles, behavior, and ideas—as they chattered away clutching their martinis and scotch-and-sodas. The country around them offers a spectacle of corporate and individual greed and carelessness—the environment destroyed, the air and waters polluted, the fish poisoned, natural beauty done away with, the landscape littered, the ecological balance disturbed, and citizens caring not a hoot for one another—but they do not seem to see that it is no wonder that their children become obsessed with the protection of the environment, presumably desiring to save the country for themselves and *their* children.

Every summer since we returned to the United States, we have lived through smog and pollution alerts along the eastern seaboard. Elderly people and those with respiratory diseases are told to stay home as a matter of actual survival. Almost every time I went to New York, I saw a filthy yellow-gray haze hovering over the city, too thick to be pierced by the rays of the sun. Los Angeles smog had become as proverbial as London fog. It was with a sense of deliverance that I sat beneath a glacier high in the Colorado Rockies in July 1970, breathing pure air as I read a newspaper story about the worst pollution alert in history affecting the East Coast. In the summer of 1972 the administration reported to the nation that despite official efforts, the pollution of rivers and lakes was getting worse rather than better (it had belatedly discovered that farms, especially the huge mechanized agribusiness latifundia, were as bad water polluters as industries). One still could not swim in the Potomac, the Delaware, the Hudson, or San Francisco Bay. The official target for cleaning waterways was set for 1985—more than a decade away. Air pollution had lessened, we were told, but the citizen was hardly aware of it. In fact, the Environmental Protection Agency said early in 1973 that sulphur standards across the United States were inadequate, causing respiratory diseases that cost between $1 billion and $3 billion annually in health care. Late in 1973, the energy crisis pushed environmental controls toward oblivion: sulphuric fuel was better than none.

Another predictable American spectacle was the auto junkyard—the broken cars like unburied corpses. (The worst such cemeteries I have seen are north of Baltimore and along the strip between Scranton and Dickson City in the once-rich and now depressed coal country in eastern Pennsylvania. They made me think of the work of a demented giant sculptor in junk steel and iron.) And of course America was also polluted by grim crime and the terrible drug scene. (There were no effective gun-control laws except in Maryland.) And, the ultimate insult, giant corporations, contractors, and the elusive TV repairman had joined in an unholy alliance to dupe and mortify the American consumer through dishonest advertising and failure to meet standards, commitments, and needs.

It was the age of the rip-off. Breakfast cereals, once the byword of American children, were revealed to be made of little more than artificial additives and, in one case, sawdust. A major food company could not prove to the satisfaction of the Federal Trade Commission that its bread, as advertised, built "the body twelve different ways," whatever they are. Automobiles were so carelessly built that between 1966 and 1972 the manufacturers had to recall 36 million cars for repairs. Early in 1973, the Ford Motor Company was fined $7 million for tampering with its cars undergoing pollution tests under the Clean Air Act. All auto makers fought the government over the deadline for installing pollution-emission-control equipment on new cars.

But the consumer was learning to fight back—through legislative pressures, legal group actions, and boycotts—pitting himself against the conglomerate, big business, and big government in myriad guerilla skirmishes. As a Washington-based writer on consumer affairs said, "If you play your cards right, you can scare the hell out of the big corporation." People were getting sick and tired of being mere dots on sales charts.

But it seemed to me as I visited our cities and small towns that, citizens' protests notwithstanding, there was little caring about America by Americans—and by Americans about other Americans—and little compassion; in the end, something had to jolt the people if they were to start to care again. Later, I discovered that the sense of caring had not altogther vanished, and that the nation was being jolted more than I had realized and that it was beginning to respond, albeit slowly.

But the reportorial questions were clear. What is the American

Revolution? Is there an American Revolution? Should there be a new American Revolution?

On a windy April day in 1971, I drove from San Francisco to San Quentin State Prison to interview George Lester Jackson, the black "Soledad Brother" who was probably the most celebrated prisoner in the United States, officially serving an indeterminate sentence for a gas-station robbery. Jackson, who was killed four months later in a still-unexplained shoot-out in the prison yard, impressed me as a man of unusually high intelligence (he became during his years at Soledad and San Quentin a self-educated intellectual), and as a totally dedicated black radical militant. As it happened, Jackson considered himself a communist. But after reading his superbly articulated books, listening to him for an hour in the tiny visiting room, and observing the prison conditions he lived under, I could well understand why a black or Chicano inmate would quickly turn into a political extremist. Indeed, my visit to San Quentin made me realize why and how much minority prison inmates in America were becoming radicalized.

At the suburban home of an old newspaper colleague in Omaha, Nebraska, who was running for Congress (he was a Democrat and lost), I spent a long evening with a group of Chicano leaders. They all were in their middle forties, several were veterans of World War II, and until recently they accepted with relative resignation their status as second-class citizens in the United States. But on this summer evening the tone and the mood was of rebellion. They spoke of job discrimination because their skins were brown and their cheekbones high and their names Spanish. They admired César Chávez, the farm workers' organizer in California, and Reies Lopez Tijerina, the Chicano militant leader who had raided a courthouse in New Mexico to claim rights for his people.

In Akron, Ohio, an uneasy mid-America city of rubber workers, I had lunch with a conservative lawyer who had gone to high school with my wife in the 1940s. This was in July 1970, two months after four students were killed by National Guardsmen on the campus of Kent State University, on the outskirts of Akron, during an antiwar demonstration set off by the United States "incursion" into Cambodia. Staring stolidly at his plate, the lawyer told us that he could not really blame the Guard for the shootings: law and order had to be enforced, he said, and it was just a shame that Akron was put on the world map by this kind of incident. He was clearly uncomfortable with us—liberal interlopers from the East—and our farewells were hurried. Later that day we drove to Kent and its midsummer silence.

I visited with college deans in Princeton, New Jersey, and Cambridge, Massachusetts. This was just after the height of student rebellions in the country, and the universities' administrators were running scared. But the men I met were keeping their cool, as the saying went, and they were far from convinced that the rebellion they were witnessing necessarily meant the death of the American system of higher education. I went twice to Berkeley, California, both to visit my daughter there and to learn something of its rampaging counterculture and "new politics." Four "radicals" had been elected to the City Council, and their program ranged from lowering rents and controlling the police under a community program to the refusal to pay allegiance to the Stars and Stripes. I had long conversations with each of the four, and I found it hard to disagree with many of their ideas on how a college town like Berkeley should be run. I chatted at length with an English-born professor of criminology at the University of California who had devised the police-control plan and was at some pains to explain why the city's voters had rejected it. For good measure, I was caught in a riot on Telegraph Avenue. My son, then fourteen, was enthralled, and we talked about the riot far into the night at the commune-type house where my daughter and her husband then lived.

I kept encountering all kinds of remarkable individuals everywhere I went. In Washington, D.C., I spent an afternoon with the disconcertingly young director of the city's narcotics' rehabilitation center, who had become the target of major controversy because of his reliance on Methadone treatments. Even in the 1970s it took certain courage to look for new ways of dealing with heroin addiction. But the young doctor was relaxed and full of confidence. And I talked to a personal friend just released from a federal prison in Pennsylvania, where he had spent nearly two years as a draft-resister. (One of our links was that I had stored his furniture in my basement during his incarceration. His wife, pursuing her career as a lyric soprano, had not wanted to be burdened with furniture and bric-a-brac while he served his sentence. Their first weekend together after his release was spent at the summer music festival at Tanglewood.) A former Roman Catholic seminarian, he refused as a matter of principle to invoke his rights as a conscientious objector or flee to Canada as so many opponents of the Vietnam war had done. As we chatted about his prison farm experiences, he was free of any bitterness and recounted laughingly his inmate acquaintanceships with well-treated famous criminals.

In New York I often saw an old friend, a white woman who doggedly stays at her volunteer job as a social worker in a Spanish Harlem school even though someone once fired a gun into her office, barely missing her. "Someone has to do it," she says.

Back in Washington, one of my friends is a one-time senior Central Intelligence Agency and State Department official who has spent several years running a mental-health program associated with the Children's Hospital in the middle of the black ghetto. He has also found time to serve on a police community project and on the Washington council against drug and alcohol abuse. (The council, by the way, is directed by the high-born niece of a former New England senator who once was an Embassy Row society columnist.) A retired admiral of my acquaintance has become an articulate opponent of the huge Pentagon spending programs. And among my other friends is a young white Roman Catholic priest in charge of a ghetto church and parish school, who in 1972 was elected by black voters to the District of Columbia Board of Education. One day, when I visited his house, where doors are always open to all neighborhood kids, I asked him why he thought he had been elected. "Oh, I guess because Jesuits treated the blacks right, way back in colonial days," he said airily.

As I look through my notes, I find references to scores of equally dedicated men and women I met everywhere in the United States. These, of course, are the kinds of people who remind one that, after all, America is the most extraordinary of countries, no matter what one may say about Americans not caring as they should about each other.

As part of my American research and reporting, I tried to go everywhere and meet everybody. But, above all, I wanted to see America. So I took many memorable walks.

In the slums of upper Manhattan and South Bronx—incredibly depressed areas of ghastly urban poverty, drug addiction, crime, and sadness—decay of a city and decay of a society were the overwhelming impressions. And it was the same in the Williamsburg section of Brooklyn, in Newark, and on Chicago's South Side. In Chicago, I stared down at the brightly lit city from the lounge of a private club atop one of the Loop's tallest buildings. It looked beautiful and peaceful: the shore of Lake Michigan, the light-studded outlines of the streets, the moon shining over the city. The next morning, I counted the shootings, muggings, and rapes listed in the crime section of the newspaper; it all had happened under cover of night as strings of lights shimmered over the nearly empty streets.

In Washington, I was a frequent visitor to the inner city—only minutes away from my own home on the *good* side of Rock Creek Park—meeting with community leaders, clergymen, cops, and the merchants who always kept a gun at the ready under the counter. There, in the ghetto, my teen-age son made me proud when he served as the only white volunteer tutor at a black youth center.

When I came to Santa Fe, New Mexico, on one of my driving trips, I chanced upon an evening of Indian lore at a local college. The old culture was being revived and the dances and the chants had a mystical quality and an intensely sexual content. (But Washington had little interest in Indian culture. In 1973, the Nixon administration cut from the budget $600,000 for the preservation of Indian archeological sites in the country.) And I spent a week visiting Polish communities in Pennsylvania—Port Richmond in Philadelphia, the industrial sections of Pittsburgh, Scranton, Wilkes-Barre, and Dickson City. These were ancient cultural islands in the mainstream of contemporary America—islands not only retaining but also rebuilding their identities. The purpose of this tour was to report for my newspaper on political trends before the presidential primaries, but, speaking Polish as I do, I was quickly drawn further in. I had dinner at the home of a wealthy newspaper publisher in Scranton, a beer with a funeral director in Port Richmond (they say in Philadelphia that you will find a funeral home and a tavern on every street corner in a Polish neighborhood) who reminisced about the old country. I went to a Polish grocery to buy a foot-long kielbasa to take home. In Scranton, I was half seriously offered the editorship of a Polish weekly published by a fraternal insurance chain. In Pittsburgh, I drank whiskey with a Polish-American advance man for Senator Edmund Muskie who told me—quite accurately, as it turned out—that the Polish vote would split between George Wallace of Alabama and President Nixon.

During the summer of 1970, I happened to hit Cheyenne, Wyoming, during the annual Frontier Days rodeo. Ranch folk from all over the state had come down to watch the rodeo riders, shop, drink, meet friends, and have a good time. But the worried talk in Cheyenne was all about outsiders buying up Wyoming land for development, spoiling the natural beauty, and driving up prices.

In a motel in Albuquerque, New Mexico, I ran into a college-educated law-enforcement specialist from Los Angeles. We talked at length about many things, and I found my companion to be unusually compassionate. Albuquerque has a well-respected police academy, but it has neither enough local crime nor enough money to pay its graduates, so police departments from all over the West do quiet recruiting in Albuquerque. (My other experience with western law enforcement was in the sleepy Texas town of Shamrock, where I was arrested for speeding. Shamrock has a highly sophisticated speed trap: I was immediately taken to the courthouse, where a judge in green shirtsleeves, sitting in front of a huge ledger, automatically fined me twenty dollars.)

I saw other faces of America—at Colonial Williamsburg in Virginia, where my wife and I meditated about the past during a rainy November weekend, and in the upper-crust exclusivity of Southampton, Long Island, where the rich remain enormously rich and little old ladies are driven around in Rolls-Royces. Inevitably, I partook of life in the upper-middle-class suburbia along the East Coast—a sociological phenomenon quite apart from the rest of American life. I visited artist friends in the quiet Housatonic country in Connecticut. One Saturday in November 1971 I nearly froze (despite hip flasks) watching an Army-Pittsburgh game at West Point.

Needless to say, I watched television, faithfully listened to the car radio everywhere (in the dulling monotony of interstate highway travel, the local broadcasters provide an excellent introduction to the states, counties, and towns one crosses, though the outside world is hardly acknowledged), and went to the movies. I read Establishment newspapers and the once-lively underground press. In Washington, as a correspondent for my newspaper, I was, of course, a full-time witness of the doings of the Nixon administration and the Congress—which is quite an education in our political mores and the prevailing power *modus operandi,* including that of the lobbyists armed with limitless expense accounts. I was a close observer of the Watergate scandals in 1972 and 1973—I even found out my home phone was tapped by the White House "plumbers."

Having done, seen, and heard all these things, I surfaced with the strong impression that, all the appalling appearances and frequent offenses and contradictions notwithstanding, Americans still basically cared, or wanted to care, about their country and their fellow citizens. The degree of stubborn self-help and compassion even in the most blighted communities (it makes up for the benign and not-so-benign neglect from Washington, the state capitol, and city hall), the dedication and the courage of many individuals—ranging from the hirsute, unkempt "street people" to ghetto school principals and young local administrators, from churchmen of all faiths to Black Panthers—and the enormous capacity for self-examination and imaginative remedial action are significant proof of the fact that Americans do care.

If something does not work in a society, it will be discarded sooner or later: whether it is exaggerated school busing, a damaging "track" system in public schools, inequities in welfare, the forced resettlement of Indians from their reservations to the cities, or the construction of airports, bridges, highways, and pipelines harmful to the environment. And an awful lot of discarding and new creativity will be required in the 1970s if we are to regenerate ourselves. But the old town-meeting spirit survives and is resurrected in communities across the country. New needs and concepts of religion are emerging—even in the far-out form of Billy Graham spectaculars, Jesus freaks, teen-age Hindu "Gods" commanding the attention of tens of thousands of Americans, and Children of God communes. Despairing as one may often be about injustice and the quality of life, one finds vast reserves of idealism among the "doers" and an abiding faith that American society is a decent society. This, I believe, is America's indestructible puritan and fundamentalist heritage, now further strengthened and leavened by the youthful rebellions and a humanistic conscience.

Not surprisingly, grass-roots politics have acquired a new importance. Local elected officials now face tough scrutiny from their constituents. A county supervisor, for instance, may be rooted out of office if he does not go after the local utility or the mainstay industry to force them to curb pollution, or does not try to put some order in the welfare operation. In the old days, really not so long ago, the utility or the industry frequently helped the cooperative candidate to assure themselves of a powerful friend in the local government. But now, as I saw it happen in numerous cases in Maryland, New York, California, Florida, West Virginia, or Arkansas, the politician is often elected only if he is on the side of the angels—that is, with the citizenry and the environment—and may the utility or his local industry be damned, even if it does provide the jobs. This is consumer politics with a vengeance, and on the grass-roots level it could not matter less who is a Democrat and who is a Republican. Hip young politicians nowadays closely study local election patterns and the interests of the independent voter—who, already powerful locally, will before long start deciding national elections. Ralph Nader, the consumer crusader, and his "raiders" probably carry more weight than most federal officials. The old Consumer Union is no longer a voice in the wilderness. The great belated discovery is that consumers are voters too, and that they have had enough of big-business and big-government tyranny and neglect.

To wit:

• Acting on their own, New York state authorities raided (and fined) storekeepers who sold national brand-name detergents containing more than 8.7 per cent of phosphates, the maximum permitted under a 1971 law. The state legislature approved this law to protect rivers, lakes, and bays from phosphate pollution (phosphorus being a nutrient, it stimulates the growth of algae to proportions that choke off all other forms of life). Miami's Dade County did likewise, and so did scores of other communities across the nation, forcing the huge detergent industry to meet the new standards, regardless of cost, if they were going to stay in business.

• Student Vote, a national organization seeking to register students after the Twenty-sixth Amendment in 1971 lowered the voting age to eighteen, quickly related politics to environment and consumerism in full-page magazine advertisements proclaiming, "Our 11 million votes can make sure your mother's wash comes out clean. . . . Or make sure our lakes and rivers do."

• In the May 1972 primary elections, coal strip-mining was the overwhelming issue in West Virginia, where the voters elected candidates pledged to the abolition of this traditional practice, despite the opposition of the $200-million-a-year industry and United Mine Workers' Union chieftains.

• In California, the principal issue in the 1972 primaries was Proposition Nine, drastically curbing industrial pollution.

• In Idaho, the Republican governor was defeated in 1970 because he actively supported the American Smelting and Refining Company's plans to develop a vast open-pit mine for molybdenum in the unspoiled White Cloud Peaks mountain range.

• A San Francisco group known as the Friends of the Earth led conservationists in the 1971 campaign to keep Congress, in the name of clean environment, from approving funds for the SST, the supersonic airliner. It joined with other groups to kill plans for a jetport in Florida's Everglades National Park (it would have served Disney World, a commercial venture) and the Cross-Florida Barge Canal, and to dissuade the administration from authorizing the building of the trans-Alaska oil pipeline though the energy crisis led late in 1973 to congressional approval of the construction. Sierra Clubs, organizations of conservationists, acquired their own political clout.

• Communities everywhere fought against land developers and more growth, often successfully. Howard County in Maryland, which already has an artificial "new city," blocked the efforts by a Washington-based hotel chain to build America's biggest amusement park.

• Kentucky, Delaware, Washington, and Georgia set up toll-free "hot lines" for irate consumers to call state agencies for help.

All this suggests that America is capable of creative wisdom and positive change, and that, in the best sense, she remains perhaps the world's only truly revolutionary society, always in flux and open to new ideas. Europe's most perceptive observers speak of the United States as a basically revolutionary society. The Soviet government worries over the effect of the American dissent on its own new generations.

Curiously, the giant government and corporations are not being challenged so much by ideologically minded youths—the feared "radiclibs" or "leftists"—as by pragmatic-minded consumers and taxpayers. Besides, the ideological challenge seemed to wane after 1972—until the next cycle.

Peter Weaver, a nationally syndicated columnist on consumer affairs and a close friend, put his finger on the politics of consumerism when he wrote late in 1971 that "politically conservative consumers become wild radicals when their car, their brand *new* car of just two weeks, gets what is called a 'wall job.' A wall job is when you bring your new car in under warranty because the engine goes 'thunkity-thunk' and the right door won't completely close. You get a 'ticket' written up. You are promised your car will be ready that evening (you've had to appear at dawn to bring it in). You come back that evening. Smiles. Your car is ready. You get to the first corner outside the dealer's garage and the engine is still going 'thunkity-thunk.' Your blood begins to pound. Sure enough, you check the door and it doesn't work either. That's a 'wall job.' You bring it in. They park it against the wall all day. You come and fetch it. No hits, no runs, no errors. So, when this kind of thing happens (there's another equal syndrome involving color TV sets with pictures that look like psychedelic light shows) many consumers become instant radicals. To the wall with the president of the automobile company . . . to the wall with the TV dealer. That's why many of them can be for Nader and Agnew combined."

Not illogically, then, the Federal Trade Commission slowly became an advocate of consumer interests, so much so that its strict enforcement of laws and its new rulings and interpretations set off mounting anger in the business community and the Nixon administration, which had appointed the present FTC commissioners in the first place. Neither the businessmen nor the White House had imagined that the once stodgy and bureaucratic FTC would become a crusading agency with fighting young lawyers. As he began his second term, President Nixon dropped the FTC chairman, but the new chairman, and his commissioners and staff, were just as aggressive.

These new confrontations may produce greater weal than the

artificial consensus which followed the Great Depression, the New Deal, and the Second World War. The society was neither dogmatic nor doctrinaire, despite its inevitable resistance to change until it was good and ready to absorb it—as usually is the case. The "Now generations" are naturally impatient, but it takes time, education, and effort to move a nation of 210 million persons.

Yet, the nation does move. The gradual acceptance of school integration in the South (where bloodshed was once feared if blacks and whites were forced to sit together in the same classroom) is an example. So is the beginning of the blacks' movement to suburbia and the growing awareness that they must be accepted in these white enclaves. Selma, Alabama, site of the great civil-rights battles in the early 1960s, elected black city councilmen for the first time in its history. The ten million Spanish-speaking Americans, too, were finding a voice along with the 800,000 American Indians. And while it is true that blacks and other minorities are still getting the short end of the stick in the American economy, their median family incomes had doubled during the 1960s (to be sure, from an infinitely lower base).

The awesome problem of communication among Americans remains, however. This is what makes it so painfully difficult for people to work together in the Great American Revolution of the 1970s. The technical means available to the country—so superbly equipped with satellite transmissions, cable and color television, and the now ever-present cassette—have nearly frozen our human capacity to hear one another in the unabating din of of our public civilization.

Shortly after the nationwide convulsions triggered by the invasion of Cambodia and the shootings at Kent and Jackson state universities, I drove nearly seventeen thousand miles in my battered black convertible over much of the United States, covering nineteen states from Virginia to Iowa and Wyoming and from Colorado, New Mexico, and Texas back to the American South through Arkansas, Tennessee, and North Carolina, looking at the sights and listening to the sounds. At different times during that summer journey, my wife and either of my two children (they took turns with me, although in the West we all managed to be together) accompanied me; they were in charge of operating my tape recorder, without which this book probably could not have been written.

Driving from Washington, D.C., to the Rocky Mountains and back over long lazy loops, first through northern and then southern United States, we quickly began absorbing the culture of the Great American Highway and what lies beyond it.

Off the multilaned interstate speedways—slashing the American continent east-west and north-south, so that this nation may always be on wheels—we found the great beauty of upstate New York, the Rocky Mountains, the Appalachian Trail, and the serenity of the great empty midwestern prairies which made one think of Carl Sandburg. We discovered neat, little-known national and state parks tucked away in pockets of woods not far from the highways—in Colorado and Nebraska, one in Oklahoma, a couple in Arkansas, one or two in North Carolina, and the ones atop the Virginia ridges—and every discovery was a cool delight during the hot days. In Colorado I had my birthday lunch in the snow under a glacier. We swam in unpolluted lakes and rivers and slept safely at tent sites. We did not have to worry about muggers and robbers, but only, if anything, about hungry black bears such as the four-hundred-pounder my son Tony and I encountered one night outside our tent in a park off the Skyline Drive in Virginia. I suppose it is easier to deal with bears than with aggressive humans, and one need not harm the animals. "My God, how beautiful America is," I could not help saying, again and again.

But I *never* said this when I dealt directly with the Great American Highway Culture. It is entirely possible to cross the United States from one end to the other without actually realizing that one has done so. To accomplish this feat, it is sufficient to stay on, say, U.S. Route 66, one of the Interstate 95s, or any of their multilane tributaries, never deviating more than a few hundred yards for food, gas, or lodgings. The good driver who keeps his eyes steadily on the road, as a good driver should, will see no palpable indication (except for his map and the green-and-white road signs) that he is driving on the outskirts of Cleveland, between Indianapolis and Peoria, on his way from Oklahoma City to Little Rock, or cruising at a safe speed from Memphis to Nashville. He sits in his car like an aviator flying on automatic pilot. The scenery outside his window does change some, of course, but in an air-conditioned car (mine was not) and with the radio turned on high, his awareness of anything that is not the gray ribbon of the highway ahead of him dims quickly. Observing the license plates of the other cars on the road is about the only clue as to where one is: a predominant number of Illinois plates, for example, would suggest that one is in Illinois. Night need not be different from the sameness of the day.

A reasonably affluent traveler, as many of them seem to be nowadays, will readily find a Holiday Inn, a Howard Johnson's, a Ramada Inn, or what-have-you chain motel in time for a weak drink, expensive bad dinner, and air-conditioned sleep. The less-well-off and more adventurous families or the kids have campers (the number of campers had risen from two million to more than four million since 1965) or sleeping bags or tents, so they can dispense with the trappings of affluence and get to see a little bit of the country. It is sad that the energy crisis is now doing away with the gas-guzzling campers.

After a week or so on the road, the traveler sees the inns blur into one unified vision of the cocktail lounge and the fake-elegant dining room with yawning waitresses, the fenced-in little swimming pool out front, the neon WELCOME sign (or NO VACANCY below it), the color TV set, and the Hollywoodish bed. It is all very comfortable and easy—machines in hallways dispense ice cubes, soft drinks, candy, cigarettes, sewing kits, and an infinity of other useful and useless products. The trip becomes a weird dream, the same reel being played over and over again until he gets home.

If the traveler decides to penetrate the American city, rather than bypass it by staying on the Interstate, he is in for culture shock. The air in Akron, Ohio, still smells of burning rubber from the big plants as it did when my wife was a little girl there. Amarillo, Texas, is unbelievably impersonal and dull despite its growing wealth as a trading and communications center in the Panhandle. Fort Smith, Arkansas, baking in the sun astride the Oklahoma state line, exudes for some reason an air of indefinable but unmistakable hostility toward the visitor. Buffalo and Niagara are tourist-oriented eyesores. In New York, Chicago, Los Angeles, Washington, Miami, or Dallas, one is swallowed by traffic in daytime and let loose at his own risk at night. The American city is perplexing and shocking because it tends to reject the visitor, perhaps because it is too suspicious of strangers and too preoccupied with its own problems and has time only for quick and superficial business with the intruder.

You enter the average American city along interminable neon-lit strips—this is where most of the business with the visitor is transacted—with cheap motels, postage-stamp swimming pools, topless bars, burger joints, pizza parlors, ice-cream stands, used-car dealers, and gas stations. Past this garish entryway, the heart of the city is locked up and deserted for the night. For me, this was among the most depressing experiences I had on my return to the United States. (Another discouraging way to arrive in an American city is by train. One example is the approach to New York City from the south through the immense garbage dumps of New Jersey and among the phalanxes of oil storage tanks. I know nothing uglier in America.) In city after city—Akron, Columbus, Philadelphia, Washington, Baltimore, Chicago, Des Moines, Omaha, Tulsa, Denver, Memphis, or Nashville—the downtown streets were eerily empty except for an occasional police cruiser or prostitute. One felt uneasy when stopping at a red light, often alone on the whole block, and one craved for the safety of the Holiday Inn.

As we traveled around the country, it did not take long to realize that America had infinitely more to offer than the sights and sounds and smells that greet the casual visitor. We found very quickly that the extent of moral and spiritual soul-searching was great, cutting clear across social groups and generations—a lot of individual courage and dedication to principle. There was something enormously refreshing about young Americans with a sense of commitment, like a cool stream on a stifling day, and one immediately sensed the promise that in the end they will prevail, they will overcome.

It was so in Warsaw, New York, a quiet upstate farming center in the Wyoming Valley, not far from Attica Prison. (We stopped there en route to Buffalo principally because I was born in the *real* Warsaw and was curious about this one.) An old town, Warsaw seemed devoid of excitement or, for that matter, of any ideas not pertaining to crops and trading. It struck me as America at her provincial dullest and most conventional. But I was wrong; this is the country of surprises. There is a weekly newspaper in Warsaw, and I read one issue over a Coke at an ice-cream parlor on the nearly deserted Main Street. A lead article concerned the fate of American Indians, one of whose confederations still spreads over upper New York state. And the other main feature contained the texts of speeches at the graduation exercises at Avon Central High School. A graduating student named Pat Phillips asked the assembled parents and teachers of Warsaw whether, at this time of "radical dissension," "we [shall] decide on adopting the safe middle-of-the-road philosophy, or shall we commit ourselves to answering the challenge of conscience?"

And in Rock Island, Illinois, another deceptive-looking farming center famous for its tractor industry, we were told about one Jerry Janecke, a high-school teacher who had publicly attacked the local library's board of trustees for "censorship" after it banned the Los Angeles *Free Press,* an underground youth newspaper, because of its generous use of the four-letter word. In his statement, duly printed in the city's Establishment newspaper, Janecke asked this basic question: "If teachers will not defend intellectual freedom, the right to read, the right to know, and the right to comment on the crisis in civil liberties, who will?" No immediate answer appeared to be in the offing for Mr. Janecke, but I thought it was important that his protest was being made publicly in Rock Island, one of the outwardly staid Quad Cities on the Mississippi, and not routinely, as might have been expected, in a cosmopolitan eastern-seaboard metropolis or in California.

In Davenport, Iowa, across the river from Rock Island, Van der Veer Park was allowed to be a quiet haven for bearded freaks and their blue-jeaned girl friends. The Davenport police—which, incidentally, offers pistol target practice to the citizenry—evidently did not consider it necessary to interfere with the young people in the park. And an advertisement in the newspaper pleasantly proclaimed: "Make Wine, Not War. Send for Free Catalog." (Most of the small-town South and Southwest, as we were to discover later, did not possess the Iowa equanimity. Southern and southwestern policemen and sheriffs were determined to keep out the "freak plague" by all the means at their command, including jail and, when needed, the bullet.)

Judicious reading of local newspapers is one of the eye-opening pleasures for a roving journalist, as any experienced reporter knows. News articles and editorials, letters to the editor, and ads all provide useful clues to what an unknown town is all about, and I had the newspaperman's habit. I faithfully bought, read, and clipped every paper I could get my hands on. Among other things, this exercise helped me to understand that truly there was no such thing as a "silent majority" or a "Middle America" —but simply human beings across the nation who may hold distinct views on everything under the sun, and who resent having patronizing labels slapped on them, even if they hold out for some form of the status quo. This was true of the Nixon "new American majority" in the 1972 election as it was true of all other majorities—majorities tend to be ephemeral. But in the summer of 1970, these myths, so beloved of American editorial writers, commentators, and amateur social analysts, were very much alive, artificially dividing the citizenry.

Still, it was obvious, if one took the trouble to observe it, that geographic Middle America was as much part of the ongoing national process of change as the East and the West coasts. *Everybody* was concerned about souls, destiny, decent jobs that did not dehumanize, a proper life style, and the environment. They certainly did not fit the facile stereotype of reactionaries or even rock-ribbed conservatives. This, too, went for the "hard hats" (another label of the day), who were immediately classified (such is our national compulsion) as hawkish intransigents after a New York City Hall demonstration of construction workers against young antiwar people responsible for burning an American flag during a protest. But everywhere in the country I have seen young "hard hats" with long hair, beards, and mustaches, whose life styles—and ideas—were not far out of tune with their more rebellious (and wealthier) peers. These young workers were the ones who began to rebel against the monotony of the assembly line to the point of engaging in widespread industrial sabotage—a gesture of defiance that Charlie Chaplin understood forty years earlier.

Many Middle Americans, whether in soft hats or hard hats, displayed the Stars and Stripes in the days of "flag battles"—when young rebels childishly tore and burned Old Glory as a symbol of what they saw as phony patriotism, and the red-white-and-blue sprouted in the lapels of men's suits, on women's dresses, on buildings, on car antennas, and on window decals. This was because they were traditional Fourth-of-July Americans. Yet it is important that one not mistake this gut patriotism for blind political conservatism; Americans of the Middle West and much of the Southwest have for years sent notorious liberals to their state legislatures and to the Congress in Washington. As an Iowa congressman once expostulated to me, "Damn it, why do you people always forget our great populist tradition in the Middle West?"

So, while Washington commentators in 1970 wrongly worried about Middle America turning reactionary, we were reading the graduation speeches by boys and girls in Warsaw, New York, hearing of the good fight led by Mr. Janecke, the Rock Island, Illinois, teacher, and discovering in Iowa this surprising letter sent in July to the Davenport *Times Democrat* by a gentleman named Herbert B. Denger:

"I am an old man who has watched three generations of children grow from the crib to maturity and, believe me, the youth of today have my deepest sympathy. For 25 years, the span that has brought forth our youth of today, the fathers and mothers of this nation have been on a binge of greed with one objective: material gain. . . . Now these parents have the audacity, when their children make a simple demand, to condemn them for the very thing they taught them to do: to want, to demand, to strive for the things they want. . . . These are wise children, our youth of today. Parents should begin to show them how not to strive for material things alone, but for the love and consideration of their fellow man."

Alecia Kessinger, a fifteen-year-old student from Bettendorf, Iowa, wrote to her local newspaper on July 4, 1970: "I imagined it was July 4 in 1920. I heard people laughing, clean jokes told, the quiet of a place happy and full, and the crackling of wood in the campfire with marshmallows roasting by the side. . . . But when I think of July 4, 1970, I imagine a different scene. Instead of a backyard full of happy people, I see a deserted, dirty, grassless open lot with slums behind me. Instead of hearing people laugh, I hear a son and a father screaming profanities at each other. Instead of clean jokes told by adults, I hear gross remarks passed between children. The serenity of a happy place was not there. Instead, I heard a radio belching the latest music we pride ourselves on. . . . The TV newsman emotionally telling of the weekend deaths and putting his heart in a sobering commercial. Instead of a place full of security, I see deserted shacks empty of the life that should occupy it . . . nothing but junk and bugs. Instead of the crackling of the firewood I hear a can of beer popped open. I think it is sickening."

We stopped for a lunch of Polish kielbasa at a college joint in Iowa City, a university town, to learn with some surprise that the area had been under curfew just a few weeks earlier because of the students' intense antiwar demonstrations after the Cambodian invasion. Later, we heard on the car radio a broadcast of the proceedings at the Des Moines City Council, where proposals to authorize the police to shoot to kill at looters during riots, and to order judges to imprison all rioters for thirty days, were defeated after noisy clashes among the councilmen. Des Moines was still recovering from the trauma of a dynamite explosion at the main police station on May 13 and a blast at the Chamber of Commerce a month later. The mayor, Thomas N. Urban, spoke clearly about all these issues: "The whole law and order appeal is built on the unsaid assumption that the police should punish. This is not American justice as I know it. It is a myth more akin to romantic cowboy westerns and sheriffs' posses than to good, sound law enforcement. I do not see the police as hired guns or clubs to bring order out of chaos. Once a police force loses its control, law and order have lost any but the most primitive of meanings, and the police will have earned the undying hate of the community they were trying to protect." Yet, less than two months later, Mayor Urban joined eight other mayors at a secret conference in Omaha to sign a mutual-assistance pact against bombers and revolutionary groups. Omaha; Des Moines; Madison, Wisconsin; Minneapolis; Tulsa, Oklahoma; Sioux City, Iowa; Lincoln, Nebraska; and Denver were represented.

Only two months earlier, in May, students had been killed by National Guard and police fire at Kent and Jackson. We drove around Kent, on the outskirts of Akron, and both the town and the campus were still dazed. On July 21, two days before the Des Moines City Council confrontation, a radical student was killed by the police in a street affray at Lawrence, Kansas, a college town not far from the Iowa state line. The boy was a leader of Lawrence "street people" and something called the Lawrence Liberation Front.

In Chicago, as we heard it on the car radio, black snipers fatally shot two policemen. Countless such ambush incidents were to follow in cities across the land. In Madison, Wisconsin, a researcher was killed in the explosion of a bomb set in a university laboratory by a young white radical. Another explosion damaged a Wisconsin military installation. There had been a bomb scare at an elementary school near Elmira in upstate New York a week before we came there searching for Mark Twain memorabilia. A bomb scare at the State House in Santa Fe, New Mexico, was reported just as we were approaching the city from Taos, the artists' community. There was a shoot-out, with fatalities, between black militants and the police in Houston, Texas, about the time we reached Amarillo to the northeast.

Shortly before we arrived in Colorado Springs, a local jury had quickly acquitted a white soldier from nearby Fort Carson for having shot and killed a leading black educator during a gas-station altercation. This was briefly a *cause célèbre* in Colorado, but after a while only the blacks remembered bitterly the professor's murder. While we were spending several days at Boulder, another lively college town, the local police were busily hunting down hippies, freaks, and marijuana peddlers, just as Selective Service headquarters were being fire-bombed. The Denver Police Department was advertising on the radio for Spanish-speaking policemen, offering high pay and fringe benefits. Chicanos and Spanish-surnamed people in general were becoming a factor in the political life of the Southwest, but the white Establishment's instinctive response was mainly on the law-and-order level. It seemed more important to enforce the law than to eradicate the causes of crime: job, housing, and education discrimination against the Chicanos, the ghastly situation of the migrant workers, and the neglect of the Indians.

Our peregrinations showed, to my surprise, the very considerable extent of unrest all over the United States. Living in Washington or New York and reading big-city newspapers, one could be unaware of the pattern of revolutionary-type violence that recurred across the country. Only major incidents and disturbances were reported, creating the impression that they were fairly isolated acts. But travel, a perusal of local newspapers, and random conversations revealed how unexpectedly widespread was this American violence. Hardly a college or university avoided some form of bombing, riot, "trashing," arson, or confrontation in 1970. The University of California at Berkeley, which had special community problems of its own, and the University of Wisconsin at Madison received the brunt of the attacks along with the burning of ROTC buildings on scores of campuses. Scientific installations engaged in defense work, military posts, banks, industrial plants, corporate offices, government buildings, and police stations were fire-bombed everywhere. High administration officials, invited as speakers, were chased off the campuses, harassed and booed if their views differed, as they had to, from those of the militants. The FBI reported 1785 college and high-school demonstrations in the 1969–70 academic year.

All these actions were fueled by the Indochina war, but, instantly, they were related to other political, racial, and social grievances at home. The war seemed to have unleashed all kinds of pent-up emotions and resentments. I was becoming aware (sometimes courtesy of my children and their friends) that quite a few young people had concluded (as it turned out prematurely and altogether erroneously) that the time had come for "armed action" in the United States to create a prerevolutionary climate. This may have been a romantic idea, but the number of "urban guerrilla" incidents, largely ignored in Washington, was astounding during 1970. Manuals on the manufacture of bombs and on urban sniping techniques were available for the asking. Throughout the summer, weapons and ammunition were regularly stolen from military port terminals in California and depots elsewhere, sometimes with the help of disgruntled antiwar GIs. Racial clashes and street snipings were continuous, but the daily tension—like the unabating black-white confrontation in Cairo, Illinois—went almost unrecorded.

The Senate Subcommittee on Investigations reported 4330 bombings in the United States between January 1969 and April 1970. *Scanlan's* magazine claimed proudly in a special issue on "Guerrilla War in the USA" that there were 546 "guerrilla acts of sabotage and terrorism" in the country during 1970. The General Services Administration estimated the loss of $2.2 million in man-hours in the first half of 1970 as the result of 130 evacuations of workers from government buildings due to bomb threats. The Secret Service counted a total of 35,129 bomb threats in the United States between January 1, 1969, and April 30, 1970.

A cooling-off period had set in, at and around the campuses and the cities, by 1971, with a sudden lowering in the level of militancy and violence. In fact, Americans seemed downright apathetic as the Vietnam war wound down, though it did not end, and the economy was beset with unemployment, shortages, and inflation. National attentions were riveted, following President Nixon's example, on the outcome of college and professional football games—even radicals were rabid football fans. And presently, the nation took to the fads of Ping-Pong, chess, religious revivalism, and pornographic movies.

Yet so mercurial are Americans that the pendulum could still swing back toward protest and violence. In 1971 the bombing of the Capitol in Washington in March and the subsequent May Day riots there (twelve thousand persons were arrested when the "May Day Tribe" came to town) may have been only temporary last gasps. In January 1972, time bombs, apparently planted by a man with a doctorate in psychology, were found in banks in New York, Chicago, and San Francisco. At the Republican National Convention in Miami Beach in August 1972, several thousand demonstrators turned out to harass the Nixon people. But by 1973 the violence was gone completely—only the protest remained. Some fifty thousand persons gathered in Washington on Inauguration Day, 1973, to show their disapproval of Mr. Nixon, even though the Vietnam peace agreement had already been worked out. Fifteen thousand turned out at the Washington Cathedral on the evening before inauguration to hear Leonard Bernstein conduct Haydn's "Mass in Time of War." And after all, very few, if any, basic problems affecting American society had been resolved. If anything, old problems were becoming worse. New ones, like the returning Vietnam veterans who could find no jobs, were exploding around us. While the returning prisoners of war from North Vietnam were receiving deserved red-carpet treatment, statistics showed that early in 1973, some 250,000 Vietnam veterans between the ages of twenty and twenty-nine (out of a total of three million) were unemployed. Among black veterans, the unemployment rate was 9.5 per cent, almost double the national figure. Sarmiento's venomous tarantula was still in our midst.

I first came to live in the United States in 1947, at the age of twenty-one, having been born in Europe and educated in various places around the world, according to the fortunes of war. In 1948, I married a girl from Ohio. In ensuing years, I set foot in thirty-six out of the fifty states of the Union, including Alaska and Hawaii, and, of course, the District of Columbia. I actually lived, however, only in New York and Washington. As a reporter or lecturer, I spent some time in virtually every major American city. I lectured at nineteen universities, from Yale and Columbia to Nebraska and Colorado and Stanford, as well as at Navy and Air Force academies and the National War College. On all these different errands, I crisscrossed the United States by plane, train, bus, and car. I had *seen* the country, its cities, its resorts, and its countryside. But I had taken only a superficial interest in the problems of the places I happened to visit, only idly relating them to the wider scheme of America. Until my family and I set out on our big trip in 1970, I had never made a special effort to study the United States professionally, searching for trends and patterns. But now the long motor expedition served as a backdrop for specific and systematic research. As we drove from state to state and from city to city, I watched out for significant patterns as well as for the small detail and the vignette that so often and suddenly will lock everything in perspective. I kept my eyes open for visible pollution and for the way the highways and the streets of America looked—and survived. I watched the young people, so much part of the permanent American migration, and I saw the way the local cops and state troopers watched them: as if, indeed, they were America's alien enemies and not her children. I made detours in many a town to inspect the slums and the "inner cities."

At night, after watching the local TV news, I sat up late reading editorials, news stories, letters to the editor, and ads in the newspapers, never failing to come up with nuggets of unexpected and illuminating discovery about American life. To wit:

• The Little Rock, Arkansas, chapter of the Women's Liberation Front held its first public meeting and was told by a young woman, "I'm pregnant and not married, but I don't feel oppressed by the boy.... I feel oppressed by the men in my family."

• The Woolco Department Store in Fort Smith, Arkansas, offered the "discriminating hunter" a real bargain for $64.88: "A Mosburg–508, 12 or 20–gauge pump shotgun, offering very good smooth action, perfect balance, automatic disconnecting trigger, positive top safety, cushion recoil pad, fine walnut stock, holds six regular of five 3–mm. magnum shells." Needless to say, firearms' control is not a welcome topic of conversation in Fort Smith any more than it is anywhere in the West. Outside Amarillo, Texas, a highway sign proclaims: "When guns are outlawed, only outlaws will have guns."

• The Wauwis Trading Post urged in the Milwaukee *Journal* to "Make This a Handgun Christmas," offering a Blackhawk 357 Magnum at $79.95, a Colt Trooper Magnum at $115, and a Smith & Wesson Magnum also at $115 as well as seven other choice models. (So powerful, indeed, is the western dedication to guns —the government estimates that there are 100 million guns of all types in 60 million American homes—that three of the Senate's most outspoken liberals voted in August 1972 against a bill banning the cheap "Saturday Night Special" handguns. They did so even though Alabama's Governor George Wallace had only three months earlier joined the roster of famous Americans victimized by assassination attempts. (Governor Wallace survived, though paralyzed for life.) Limited as the handgun legislation was, it was finally passed over the opposition of Majority Leader Mike Mansfield of Montana, Frank Church of Idaho, and Mike Gravel of Alaska, idols of American liberalism. The shooting of Mississippi's Senator John Stennis by teen-age robbers in front of his Washington home early in 1973 likewise brought no new pressure for tougher laws.)

• Wilbert Montel Brown, a twenty-five-year-old citizen of Tulsa, Oklahoma, who "claims he is a Black Panther," went to jail to serve a thirty-day sentence for uttering "obscene language" while delivering a speech in the fall of 1969. He and his lawyers lost appeals arguing that the 1910 Oklahoma obscene-language statute violates free speech and that Brown is a pauper entitled to equal protection under the Fourteenth Amendment. Said Brown as he entered the Tulsa jail: "This is an example of injustice to me and to all oppressed people."

• James Todd, president of the Afro-American Students' Union at the University of Oklahoma, told a human-relations panel, "You have taught the black youth to think and that's your mistake. . . . You have taught the black American and the Indian to pull himself by his bootstraps when he has no shoes."

• William Richardson, a fifty-one-year-old former professional football player and currently minister of the United Methodist Church, walked 1100 miles from Missouri to Tahlequah, Oklahoma, to repeat the "trail of tears" trek by Cherokee Indians forced by federal troops out of their Oklahoma homelands in 1838. The Reverend Mr. Richardson, known as "Pitcher Billy," collected $1500 during his walk and then sent the money to the Space Age Circuit Riders Association, Inc., which is said to grant scholarships to young American Indians.

• Bill Light, of Milan, Tennessee, wrote to the Memphis *Commercial Appeal* that "the only second rate people we have in the South are Senator Gore and Senator Fulbright." (Senator Gore was defeated in the 1970 elections.)

• A comment on "tokenism" delivered at a teacher-student workshop on racial problems in Memphis schools: "Some people feel they have done their good deed for the whole black race by saying 'hi' to two black students. It's bound to make the blacks mad."

• The police in New Brunswick, New Jersey, admitted they imposed a two-day curfew after Euclid J. Taylor, a man with a record of twenty-two arrests, convinced them he was a New York City policeman and that he knew that armed Black Panthers had infiltrated the city. The information was false and Police Commissioner William J. Cahill ordered an investigation to find out how a man who was arrested seven times for impersonating a cop was allowed to work with the New Brunswick police during racial disorders.

• A three-judge panel in Eric County, Pennsylvania, issued an injunction against a rock festival scheduled there for August 8 and 9, 1970, because it "would have constituted an atmosphere that would have been detrimental to the health, safety and welfare of the townspeople." Memories of Woodstock were dying hard.

• Albuquerque, New Mexico, shifted to the use of plastic garbage bags to expedite collections, as other cities have done, but a local resident warned in a letter to his newspaper that "plastic garbage bags is part of the Communist plot to make the streets of Albuquerque look like a garbage dump and so demoralize its citizens that the Communists can take over the city's vital functions and make them ineffective." (A New Mexico newspaperman offered me this explanation for the furor over plastic garbage bags: "Albuquerque is on the fringe of the Bible Belt, and from there on south and east what can't be attributed to Satan *has* to be the vicious machinations of Communists or liberals—and I don't think they make much distinction between the last two.")

• Gene Trimball, chairman for information of the Ogalala (Nebraska) Sioux tribes, said in a formal statement on June 25, 1970: "Ninety-four years ago today at this hour the Sioux Nation with the Northern Cheyenne and Arapahoes brought General Custer and his Seventh Cavalry down in total defeat. . . . We will no longer stand by like defeated people and watch the government and private interests take lands that were given to us by treaty. We say to the United States government that great governments and great men must keep their word."

A lot of this was sublime in its own special American way, and a lot was frivolous and downright silly. But, it seemed to me, it all added up to a reaffirmation of the American tradition of intensive involvement in the affairs of the society on every level. As Tocqueville noted in his day, "If an American were condemned to confine his activity to his own affairs, he would be robbed of one half of his existence; he would feel an immense void in the life which he is accustomed to lead, and his wretchedness would be unbearable."

What Tocqueville saw as an American obsession with "the cares of politics"—he remarked that "almost the only pleasure which an American knows is to take a part in the government, and to discuss its measures"—has evolved into such concepts as participatory politics or, as consumerism militants now do so aggressively, "working through the system." This desire to be involved and express viewpoints, popular or not, which I found everywhere, encouraged me to think that, after all, the 210 million of us are not as deeply foundering in uniformity as some of the "in" social critics, who seldom leave home, would have us believe. Even militant actions outside the "system" are a form of involvement and participation in society. Civil-disobedience movements in the late 1950s and the early 1960s unquestionably did more to bring compliance with racial-equality legislation than all the hortatory efforts by the government; this is how society was jolted into a rational response over civil rights. Similar political activism in the 1970s, one assumes, can provide another jolt forcing Americans to show again that they are capable of caring and absorbing change. The 1972 Democratic National Convention at Miami Beach was, I think, a case in point, regardless of the Democratic defeat in the national elections.

The 1960s gave us a legacy of many parts: an almost overwhelming sense of crisis, the inexorable rise of the minorities, the youthful rebellion, the steady self-assertion of women, the new politics, consumerism, the caring for environment—and, above all, the hunger for discovery and experimentation. As I said before, my expedition in the summer of 1970 introduced me to these many aspects of the American crises and tragedies, and to situations I thought I wanted to explore more deeply. But it was the sight of American youth on the move—and the insight into the actions and reactions of the young people that my children helped me to gain—that set the tone for my final approach to our innocence at home.

YOUTH
IN AMERICA

"A vast number of Americans of the younger generation . . . find themselves born into a race that has drained away all its spiritual resources in the struggle to survive and that continues to struggle in the midst of plenty because life itself no longer possesses any other meaning. The gradual commercialization of all the professions, meanwhile, has all but entirely destroyed the possibility of personal growth along the lines that our society provides and, having provided, sanctions. Brought up as they have been to associate activity almost solely with material ends, and unable in this overwhelmingly prosperous age to feel any powerful incentive to seek these ends, acutely conscious of their spiritual unemployment and impoverished in will and impulse, the more sensitive minds of the younger generation drift almost inevitably into a state of internal anarchism that finds outlet, where it finds outlet at all, in a hundred unproductive forms. Our society, in fact, which does everything by wholesale, is rapidly becoming a race of Hamlets the like of which has hardly been seen before, except perhaps in nineteenth-century Russia. . . . A national faith we had once, a national dream, the dream of the 'great American experiment.' But if it had not been sadly compromised, would the younger generation find itself adrift as it is today?"

Van Wyck Brooks, a very thoughtful and very angry American essayist, offered this diagnosis of the problems of young Americans in an essay on "Letters and Leadership" written in 1918, some half-century before my adult (or parental) generation faced the present youth crisis.

I bought Van Wyck Brooks' essays in a secondhand bookshop in New York City in 1947 (they were written between 1915 and 1927, and republished in 1934), shortly after I came to live in the United States. I was in my early twenties. In those postwar years, young people in America were essentially unassertive but not really adrift. If anything, my impression of my more-or-less peer group in my new country was that it was *too* serious, *too* purposeful (in the sense of aiming for gain and status), and, in truth, too dull. I thought that Brooks was deliberately exaggerating so that he could make his aesthetic and ideological points. There was nothing in and around New York in 1947 to make one believe that America could ever have bred or would breed a "race of Hamlets."

On the contrary, I thought in my own young impatience that this pragmatic country could use both a dose of some kind of mild anarchism and a few Hamlets; it needed new energizing intellectual and emotional dimensions. One evening, over a bottle of cheap California wine, I conveyed to a Columbia University professor of my acquaintance my reactions to Brooks' writings, venturing the opinion that his views deserved at least some attention from contemporary students of literature and educators. The professor winced and answered me with a quotation from Alexander Pope: "Dullness! Whose good old cause I yet defend."

I came across Van Wyck Brooks again late in 1969, as I was unpacking my books at our new home in Washington, D.C. For some reason, *Three Essays on America,* the small volume in the pale-green jacket that I had not opened in more than twenty years, suddenly caught my attention. I reread it at one sitting because it suddenly began to make sense.

I still doubt that Brooks was an entirely accurate reporter of the trends and moods in 1918, but he did prophesy in an uncanny way what was to be the American youth ethos fifty years later. His essays speak for the generation of the late 1960s and early 1970s much more clearly than it has been able to do for itself. Brooks wrote that "we of the younger generation . . . find ourselves in a grave predicament." I wondered why the spokesmen for the New Youth, so concerned with the legitimacy of their counterculture, failed to discover good old Van Wyck Brooks and make him a prophet of the Movement. I suppose if they had any, it was Bob Dylan. But in any event, American youth was clearly in a "grave predicament" in those October days of 1969.

Our daughter, Nikki, then nineteen and very much part of this "predicament," played a considerable role in my own process of comprehending the phenomenon of the new American youth. My son, Tony, then going on thirteen and sidetracked at a private boys' school, had not yet become politically conscious and concentrated his attention on his neighborhood Boy Scout troop, whose scoutmaster, a retired naval intelligence officer, took the simple view that all opposition to the Vietnam war smacked of communism. He was not the only one to think so in those days. But stirrings were already noticeable in Tony. It came as no surprise when he soon served for a time, until his interests evolved in other directions, as our in-house Maoist, resigning in intellectual contempt from Troop 595 and convincing us to let him attend a public school. On his own time, he studied the history of the Chinese Communist party along with Marx and Lenin. Later, at fifteen, he saw no contradiction between his revolutionary interests and a deepening involvement in church community affairs through his friendship with a progressive young minister. Tony played his guitar at church services and recited his own poems. Here is one of them, written when he was fifteen, and which I cite because, at least to me, it conveys the thoughts of *his* generation:

Masked in prejudice and sin,
The human god won't reach in
To the compulsive betrayal of the naked truths,
Bred by fear and hailed by satisfaction.

The self-hatred he doesn't want to know
Is drenched in perfume of other souls,

Which are chastised by the many for being too few,
For holding the responsibility of their actions.

The armies of pencils and pens,
They worship the conformity of men.
Their enemies are minds, with dedication to change,
Misfits fat from freedom
The few who are strong,
The ones whose halos melt in the rain,
And who fight back with love for each other.

The money that runs through their veins,
Is made to buy away all the pains
That are there because
Feelings are still in their souls.

Emotions which live lives of dying coals
That are tossed by guilt into forgotten holes,
Which are the homes of the masters of fate.

Nikki was a full-fledged activist at the time we came to Washington. She had already taken part in at least two "heavy" actions —the student assault on George Washington University's Sino-Soviet Studies Institute and the protest against the construction of Three Sisters Bridge over the Potomac—during which she faced the police. Soon she tangled again with the police at antiwar demonstrations in Washington and Berkeley, but these early incidents were her initial exposure to the power of the Establishment and the first defiance of its authority. She was arrested briefly on October 15, 1969, the day of the first big antiwar Moratorium in Washington, and then in the course of the affray over the proposed Potomac bridge.

Whether liberal or not, *my* first reaction to the notion of *my* daughter participating in street riots against the police and actually being arrested was one of horrified inner shock. It was one thing for her, I thought, to preach revolution to us and to predict a dire and dark future for what remained, she said, of our system, but it was something else again to get herself arrested. Such is bourgeois ethics, and such is the bourgeois, American, law-abiding response. But on reflection and second thought—and I hasten to report that it took quite a bit of reflection before the second thought came—I faced the reality that in a changing society it is both unwise and probably impossible to apply absolute traditional ethical concepts.

To the mid-century liberal, it was pretty much of an absolute concept that one simply did not use violence to advance one's views no matter how right one knew them to be. Put another way, the liberal stopped at the water's edge of real militancy, with its implications of risk-taking. He preferred to reason, and rejected *a priori* the notion of violating or breaking a law (or regulation, or ordinance, or police officer's order) even if he knew it to be absurd. He applauded resistance to foreign dictatorships, of course (he was *for* the Soviet dissident and the Greek, Spanish, and Brazilian opposition leaders in or out of prison), but inasmuch as the United States was a democracy, not a police state, he believed staunchly in working through its system and abhorred open challenges to its authority.

For my part, I had approvingly reported over the years the battles of Latin American, Spanish, and Czechoslovak students against their oppressive governments. I remember writing a magazine article late in the 1950s contrasting the highly politicized and sophisticated Latin American student with his counterpart in the United States, then chiefly concerned with his future career (or panty raids), oblivious to politics and ideology. In my newspaper dispatches, I often cited the prison backgrounds of the new Latin American leaders, for whom prison was a badge of honor: Cuba's revolutionary Marxist premier Fidel Castro, liberal democrats such as President Rafael Caldera of

Venezuela, Fernando Belaunde Terry of Peru, and so on. But the thought of young North Americans battling North American police over politics and being jailed for it had not entered my mind. The Anarchists and the Wobblies of a half century earlier somehow did not seem like a precedent, perhaps because the comfortable liberal never felt much real affinity with those working-class rebels of an earlier American age.

To be sure, traditional liberal inhibitions began waning in the late 1950s as the civil-rights movement waxed. The 1954 Supreme Court decision on school desegregation served, among a great many other things, to raise basic questions about whether established local authority had to be respected if it came in conflict with the Constitution, the laws of the land, or just plain moral laws. With the advent of the Montgomery boycott against segregated transportation and the Birmingham lunch-counter sit-ins by local blacks, civil disobedience as a political weapon became a fairly common occurrence. Black and white activists joined in challenging state authorities in the South over every conceivable aspect of racial segregation. Martin Luther King, a minister of the church, emerged as a national leader of this new crusade. Young people of both colors launched the Student Non-Violent Coordinating Committee, though SNCC soon turned to violence and radicalism. Soon it was "in" for respectable ladies and gentlemen, to say nothing of clergymen of all faiths and militant students, to be arrested in the cause of racial equality. I remember when the daughter of friends of ours, who were in Europe at the time, was arrested in Selma, Alabama, along with other students on Freedom Rides from the University of Michigan and other northern schools. After the girl's parents failed to reach her by telephone from Geneva, my wife succeeded in doing so from Washington by calling the Selma city jail with what I recall as considerable uneasiness. But the jailer was casual and pleasant: "I'll get her for you," he said. The girl, then on a hunger strike with her companions, was happy and proud of herself (she later married a fellow Selma detainee student), and I found myself telling her parents over the transatlantic telephone that they should be proud of her too.

But, as I said, getting arrested on a civil-rights charge was in the vein of upholding the spirit, if not always the letter, of the law. We liberals accepted in this instance the concept of defying constituted authority (the local one) in the service of higher principles and laws. But by 1969 I quickly learned that what I had once regarded as American society's absolute concepts were falling by the wayside—and not even selectively.

I said that I was shocked by the news that Nikki, my daughter, had been taken down to police headquarters after the Potomac bridge protest. I was even annoyed and angry, although she got off with only a ten-dollar forfeiture of collateral. But it is pertinent to observe here that white kids like Nikki from reasonably affluent families, even if arrested, were almost never caught in the inexorable and enormously unfair system of criminal justice which in cities like Washington was and is stiffly imposed on poor blacks charged with disturbing the peace. Our children were reprimanded or lightly fined by local magistrates, normally without acquiring a police record. Ghetto kids, on the other hand, were seen in a different social light—a deeper criminality was at once assumed in their case—and the police and the courts as often as not dispatched them to reformatory or jail, thus saddling them for life with a criminal record. This may have something to do with why blacks have always stayed away from the great white protests and demonstrations, from rock festivals to anti-war movements. To be sure, most blacks do not identify with white causes (despite the high number of black draftees in the army in Vietnam) or white counterculture (they prefer to develop their own). But, as a black lawyer I know in Baltimore observed, "For a black kid to be grabbed in a peace demonstration or something like that would be two strikes. . . . Who needs it, man?" (In 1973, the John Howard Association, a private group in Maryland, reported that judges in that state tended to refer most white children to juvenile courts while black youths accused of crimes were sent down to state training schools, a euphemism for reformatories. The Association found that 70 per cent of children referred to Maryland's juvenile courts were white, but 54 per cent of those committed to the training schools were black. "There is discrimination. . . . Black children are more likely than white children to be committed to training schools and are more likely to be committed as delinquents." White children, it said, are usually classified as Children in Need of Supervision so that they can avoid being sent to predominantly black institutions.)

In my daughter's case, quite aside from the possible legal implications of her acts, it struck me after a while that her political and social involvement had a certain degree of ethical logic. And looking back at the events of the late 1960s, I wish that more of us adults had been more emotionally and intellectually honest with ourselves when our kids took the path of rebellion. As it was, I suspect, we were too scared of the children's defiance to analyze the phenomenon with sufficient intelligence and detachment. And, worse, most of us refused support. Yet if the young people will not question the status quo, who will do it?

With almost all these youth movements, the kids were vindicated or, at least, proved right by subsequent events. It certainly was true in the case of the Vietnam war, their deep suspicions of Richard Nixon, and their denunciations of corporate power. But I hadn't fully realized this in the autumn of 1969 as I made my brusque re-entry into the tense atmosphere of American society. And I was even less convinced of the wisdom of Nikki's participation in protests against the construction of new bridges. Moreover, I took exception (as I still do) to the invasion of the offices of the Sino-Soviet Studies Institute where scholars' files and records, product of many years' work, were destroyed by radical students. I do not believe in the burning of books or manuscripts because one does not happen to like what they say. Fascism of the Left is not any more acceptable than the fascism of the Right.

Young people opposed the idea of the Three Sisters Bridge, which would have spanned the river between Georgetown and the Virginia shore, on both ecological and social grounds. In the first instance, as they saw it, the new bridge would have further damaged the Washington environment—the beautiful Potomac had already been turned into a sewer of pollution—and filled precious wooded spaces with more concrete for the required approaches and additional superhighways. Anyway, there already were seven bridges between metropolitan Washington and Virginia (the latest, the Theodore Roosevelt Bridge, had been inaugurated only a few years earlier). Yes, there were horrendous rush-hour traffic jams on these bridges, but, I thought, this was the price suburban commuters had to pay for their bedroom-towns' luxury and the "one car, one man" mentality.

Actually, the Washington commuter situation was a grotesque example of the state of affairs in many cities in the United States. And it was a vicious circle. The suburbanite insisted on driving his own car to work in the city (the more two-car families, the fewer car pools) because the mass-transit system was totally inadequate; this required more cars, more highways, more bridges; and few cities could develop mass transit because of the powerful opposition of the highway lobbies, which claimed in perfect sophistry that available federal and state transportation funds should be used for more roads, rather than for subways or bus lines, in view of the mounting automobile traffic. (All this, of course, was happening before the 1973 energy crisis reshuffled all the national priorities.) In Washington, one of the most incongruous results was that thousands of employees of the Health, Education, and Welfare Department, a huge government complex in southwest Washington, began arriving as early as two o'clock in the morning for their 9:00 a.m. jobs in order to secure precious parking space, sleeping or reading in their parked cars until time to report to work.

The second objection to the new bridge was that it would force the removal of numerous lower-middle-class families, many of them black, from an area southeast of Georgetown to make room for a new freeway approach. Washington faced a serious low-cost housing problem, as all major American cities did, and it seemed frivolous to aggravate it for the sake of a new bridge favored principally by well-off Virginia commuters. Some time earlier, I knew, Virginia residents in the Great Falls area—a wealthy sprawling upriver suburb—had prevented the damming of the Potomac some fifteen miles north of Washington and the construction of a bridge *there* because it threatened their bucolic environment. They preferred downtown bridges.

As I learned subsequently, numerous Georgetown community groups had sought to block the Three Sisters Bridge, but their objections were ignored. Required public hearings had not been held. So, as construction gangs were preparing to start preliminary work late in 1969, the students swung into action. The kids, who first symbolically occupied the Three Sisters islets in mid-Potomac, now faced the builders' bulldozers on the Georgetown shore. The police were called, tear gas was fired, and arrests were made. But in the end, the students triumphed—the ethical logic was with them—as increasingly aroused citizens demanded public hearings, the courts upheld the opponents, and, finally, the bridge project was quietly dropped. The highway lobbies turned their attentions to plans for new freeways elsewhere, and their congressional friends moved to freeze funds for the $3 billion Washington Metropolitan subway unless additional highways were built as well. Similar situations arose all over the country. (Eventually the highway lobbies had their way. A "sleeper" provision in the Federal Highway Act of 1973 called on the District of Columbia to build the Three Sisters Bridge, voiding the earlier court ruling. But years were likely to elapse before this became a reality—new studies were required and, suddenly, we had the energy crisis.)

The Washington incident was significant, I believe, in proving to conservatives and liberals alike that young people are not always wrong when they take to the streets. The citizens' right of petition is guaranteed in the Constitution, but the way things are these days, a petition is sometimes better heard from the street.

There was another important aspect of the Three Sisters episode. This was the question of urban aesthetics and of who may pass judgment over what should be built—and how—and what may be torn down in our cities.

The new Potomac bridge plan was resented in part because it would have spoiled some of the beauty of old Georgetown and the river. The Washington landscape was already burdened with the aesthetic drawbacks of the Kennedy Center for the Performing Arts (though we remain eternally grateful for its existence and the superb acoustics of its halls), the *nouveau-riche* architectural excesses of the adjoining Watergate apartment–office–building–hotel complex, and the ungraceful, aggressive modernity of the new Federal Triangle downtown. The mammoth headquarters of the Federal Bureau of Investigation on Pennsylvania Avenue and a scattering of new office buildings there, all apparently conceived by the same monotonous mind, clashed with the city's neoclassical architectural tradition.

Because Washington is a federal city, its Fine Arts Commission is responsible in theory for its urban aesthetics. But no concerned citizens were consulted over the blueprints for the Kennedy Center (national architecture critics hollered only when its inauguration came in 1970) or the downtown renewal. Elsewhere in urban America, there are few fine arts commissions, and the arbiters of American urban taste are usually City Hall bureaucrats, uninspired architects, hungry building contractors, and the ever-greedy builders of superhighways, freeways, and overpasses. My own impression from my travels is that Pittsburgh, for example, acted unusually in its wise and attractive renewal of the river waterfront (though it did little else for the inner city). Atlanta is another example of aesthetic wisdom in urban redesign. Chicago's new downtown section is on the whole pleasing to the eye. But Akron featured an empty space along its main thoroughfare, when we visited there in 1970, in preparation for the erection of a modern-office-building complex that, to judge from the maquettes, bore little relationship to the rest of the area. San Francisco, despite its growth, still retains charm and a sense of ensemble, as do parts of Boston. Los Angeles is shapeless, and Dallas predictable. For unfathomable reasons, American cities found it easier to destroy old landmarks than to create new ones. Every city has witnessed battles, most of them losing ones, over the preservation of important buildings against profit-oriented real-estate operators and builders. New York goes through this trauma continuously. In Washington, the federal government succeeded in saving and renewing the lovely old houses on either side of Lafayette Square, facing the White House, but a beautiful eighteenth-century house in Georgetown was razed in 1971 to make room for a revenue-producing property despite efforts by community historical societies. Its recent owner, one of the city's leading real-estate operators, could not be persuaded to be somewhat less businesslike and more civic-minded about his investment. And so on.

My daughter's activism (and that of her companions) had other repercussions and ramifications that I found interesting.

Several months before our return from Europe, Nikki had contrived to get involved in political activities that, she feared,
might lead to her arrest. I think the incident at the George Washington University's Sino-Soviet Studies Institute had something
to do with it. In any event, she sought emergency advice from a
friend of ours who is a senior partner in one of Washington's
most prestigious law firms.

Nikki received advice, all right, but her visit to the law offices
also served to arouse our friend's interest in how young people
without means or connections may fare in overcrowded local
courts in political-type cases. Presently, our friend, a specialist in
corporate practice, began appearing in District of Columbia
courts on behalf of arrested demonstrators, radical SDS members, and a variety of other youthful hell-raisers who were out to
give the system a jolt. His concern, of course, was whether the
accused had the benefit of the due process of law, something that
has become increasingly casual. At the same time, his law firm
encouraged its young lawyers to donate free time to this type of
case. All this was a novelty at the time, but soon it became the
proper thing for a well-established young lawyer in Washington
to allot about 15 per cent of his time to the defense of young
radicals. The young people no longer had to rely exclusively on
busy court-appointed attorneys, the harried Civil Liberties Union, Legal Aid societies, or the government's own lawyers for the
poor. (Sadly, court-appointed lawyers were sometimes guilty of
incredible abuses. One Washington lawyer received $70,312
from the federal government in 1972–73 for defending indigent
criminal defendants. The new ceiling in the District for annual
earnings by court-appointed attorneys is $18,000, but the city was
quickly running out of money even for these payments.) The
same phenomenon surged in other American cities. This, it
seemed to me, was a pertinent illustration of the capacity of the
American system to renew itself.

Another novel way to provide the protection of the law in communities as well as for individuals lacking means to retain attorneys was the federal government's legal-aid program, run by the Office of Legal Services of the Office of Economic Opportunity before its demise in 1973 decreed by President Nixon. This federally funded program operated through nine hundred local law offices in three hundred American cities and used the services of 2500 lawyers, mostly young, who handled 1.2 million cases in 1971, winning the bulk of them.

The "poverty lawyers" or "neighborhood lawyers," as I came to know them in a number of different states, sued the federal government along with states, counties, and municipalities on issues ranging from health services to the protection of the environment, from new freeways to consumer interests, from the rights of ex-convicts to equality in providing community facilities in the South to blacks and whites alike. They could not, under the statute, handle criminal or political cases (this is where the private volunteers come in), but they were free to act in civil and personal cases (such as divorce) for millions of underprivileged Americans. By 1972, poverty law was taught in most of this rich country's law schools.

But as with the Federal Trade Commission, whose attorneys challenged the Establishment on behalf of consumers, the poverty lawyers, active since 1965, came under fire from conservatives who felt that things were getting out of hand if almost everybody was free to sue the powers that be. Spiro Agnew and California's Governor Ronald Reagan became the most outspoken critics of the federal law program, and the White House itself twice killed legislation to expand the program into an independent National Legal Services Corporation. In the end, the Nixon administration came up with a compromise proposing an independent Legal Services Corporation whose charter would be considerably more restricted than the former activities of the poverty lawyers.

In all these ways, my daughter's interests and activities provided an excellent link for me with the thoughts and moods of
her generation. Nikki and I saw a great deal of each other, we
argued and fought over ideas, but I think we were able to accomplish some reciprocal teaching. It is possible to learn much from
one's children—if one cares. I met many of Nikki's friends—and,
independently, other young men and women—and I hope I developed a bit of insight into their lives and life styles. Some of them
were impressive in many ways and others were freaks. (The
latter then inhabited the streets around Washington's Dupont
Circle. The stretch of Twenty-first Street, Northwest, between
New Hampshire Avenue and P Street, a quiet neighborhood of
lovely old houses, was for a while the city's revolutionary Rialto.)
As I gradually came closer to them, I saw what a perplexing,
often tortured, uncertain and self-damaging, but brilliant, perceptive, and on the whole well-intentioned generation we had
spawned—possibly despite ourselves.

2

I am not sure I know precisely what aroused American youth in
the 1960s to become a rebel generation. These boys and girls,
born during the beginning of the cold war and the Korean war,
were reaching adolescence and young adulthood and replacing
the "silent generation" of the 1950s, the last children of the Great
Depression and the first war babies. (Nowadays, this "silent generation" is fully parental and at the threshold of middle age. I
daresay they were as perplexed by the emergence of the rebels

as we were in our somewhat more advanced age.) It was an astonishingly varied and multifaceted phenomenon, particularly when one considers that it was carried out by a minority of the nation's youth, perhaps just a few million of them.

Yet the youth rebellion had an enormous influence on America's thinking and policies. It pushed the political parties into a new round of social concerns and commitments—the 1972 presidential campaign made this quite evident, even if after his reelection President Nixon backpedaled on the nation's social problems—and forced the first fundamental changes in the philosophy of higher education since the days of John Dewey, along with a major cultural revival.

Young Americans questioned the authority of a government that ill-governed and cared not enough, that was lost in an endless Asian war and its own bureaucratic bigness. They questioned the power of corporations and the relevance of teachers who did not teach and considered little about anything except their own tenure and the compulsion to "publish or perish." At first, these youngsters were perceived as destructive; in time it dawned on a great many people that, disorderly as it seemed, their protest was an essentially constructive process. Thus the young gained a voice in the fashioning of their own destinies.

Like everything in America, the youth rebellion had a touch of the sublime and a touch of the ridiculous. It reeked of contradiction, it was dizzyingly mercurial, it abhorred any form of leadership, it displayed intellectual brilliance and deep naiveté, and, inevitably, it blended inspiring idealism with cheap and irresponsible opportunism. It had to shout out everything "like it is," leaving nothing to imagination. It was irreverent and enamored of freedom, if not of duty. It talked incessantly of love, its members were "brothers and sisters," yet it was cruel. There was nothing quite like young Americans anywhere in the world—and they were quickly imitated everywhere.

Everything overlapped. The youth revolt had something for everybody, but not always enough for most. The rebellion was politics when it came to the Vietnam war or racial relations. It was "student power" and the rejection of the "irrelevant" in education. It was the need to "relate" to people in an alienated society. It was attire, hair, sex, drugs, the discovery of nature and beauty and art and natural foods, new life styles without end. And, of course, the young were used by anybody who had any kind of axe to grind.

The initial political position taken up in advocacy of the civil-rights movement touched off a national youth rebellion which, in short order, turned against the Vietnam war and then against the entire structure of the American state. So short-circuited had the pattern of ideas become that support for the Vietcong and North Vietnam—expressed in adolescent chants about "Uncle Ho" and the defiant hoisting of red-and-blue Vietcong flags—was quickly transmuted into ideological positions taken up against American "imperialism," "corporate state," and capitalism. Hence bomb and arson attacks on banks, police stations, corporate offices, ROTC centers, and armories—the "centers of imperialism." Strongly influenced by the SDS, the only seriously structured movement to emerge briefly from an otherwise unorchestrated political rebellion (SDS split in 1968 into the armed-action Weatherpeople faction and the quasi-Maoist-Marxist-Leninist Progressive Labor faction, rapidly losing its national influence), uncounted thousands chaotically joined New Left and neo-New Left groups. There were Yippies, factions of rampaging "Crazies," and, later, "Zippies." The large Socialist Youth Alliance, key in the antiwar movement, quarreled with the pro-terror Weatherpeople and the class-conscious "Revolutionary Marxists."

Support for blacks at home soon extended to all minorities and, quickly, to the "Third World" and to an infatuation with revolutionary Cuba and every "liberation movement" in the world. Several thousand young Americans traveled to Cuba individually or as members of the "Venceremos" brigades to cut cane and harvest vegetables for the Cubans, gain ideological indoctrination, and, allegedly but unprovably, receive guerrilla and sabotage training. It is a matter of record, however, that a number of those who had gone to Cuba were later implicated in bombings and other terrorist acts at home. (The National Committee of the Venceremos Brigades was a dedicated and highly ideological extreme leftist group. Its members bought, sold, and read *Granma,* the Cuban government's official newspaper—it could be obtained openly in New York, Berkeley, and elsewhere—and disseminated propaganda in favor of revolutionary Cuba.)

In this affinity with the Third World, an old American humanist tradition was present, though probably not consciously accepted. Defenders of Asian, African, and Latin American freedoms were the heirs to the Americans who had once gone overseas as missionaries, doctors, and nurses. Their immediate forerunners were the Peace Corps volunteers whom John F. Kennedy had energized into helping the poor and the sick abroad in an American mission for humanity. It made absolute sense to me that in 1965 the Peace Corps volunteers actively aided the rebels in the Dominican Republic against right-wing military forces and the U.S. troops sent there to back the generals. I saw them at work in Dominican hospitals (one of them was a blind volunteer) under air and artillery bombardment, and I was never so impressed by a group of young Americans as in those grim days in Santo Domingo.

The great political battle fought by the young rebels in support of Senator Eugene McCarthy during the "Days of Rage" at the Democratic National Convention in Chicago in 1968 was the most violent and the ugliest American confrontation between kids and Establishment. The youthful workers for Senator George McGovern in 1972 were the calmer and more pragmatic successors of the Chicago warriors. But now, having talked to scores of Chicago veterans, I have my doubts as to what extent those young people really wanted McCarthy nominated back in 1968. I'm inclined to think that the convention simply provided them with a perfect setting for protest against the war and the Establishment. Would they, I wondered, have worked in the campaign for Robert Kennedy had he lived and been nominated? Chatting with McCarthy late in 1971, just before he announced his short-lived candidacy for 1972, I found him so totally detached and aloof from his one-time constituency that it was almost impossible to visualize him as their champion only three years earlier.

In any event, the Establishment, which has a demonstrable talent for overreaction and overkill, played right into the hands of the rebels by having them brutalized by the Chicago police and staging politically motivated trials against their seven more mature leaders. This proved to young people (and to many others) that brute force is the only response of which the Establishment is capable when it is challenged—which, of course, it was. Other challenges came at Berkeley's "People's Park," Kent State, and Jackson in 1970, bringing deaths to students at the hands of those charged with intelligently maintaining peace and order. Chicago, Berkeley, Kent, Jackson, Lawrence, Baton Rouge, and so many other events of these years deepened their cynicism and alienation. Their political candidates had been defeated, the government would not end the Indochina war, racism could not be eliminated overnight, the government went on ignoring misery and injustice and applying maximal police power against dissidents in the streets. So the "pig"—the policeman—became the official enemy of the young, and, inevitably, the harried police perceived the young as their enemy.

The Weatherpeople (they were first called Weathermen but changed the name in deference to their activist women) had gone underground by 1969 to dedicate themselves to bombings. They were a tiny minority, maybe only five hundred kids, but the underground press glorified them in describing feats that represented a totally new experience for middle-class Americans. The violence in the United States earlier in this century was the work of anarchists, enraged trade unionists, or Trotskyites: those were barely known to the new generation and certainly not regarded as part of their history. The Weather Underground (which had developed a strong link with the LSD cultists of Dr. Timothy Leary as well as with the most militant Black Panthers) and their friends and imitators tried to establish a psychological climate favoring guerrilla warfare, evidently believing that New York or Berkeley and the Rockies and the Catskills could be the Algiers or Havana or Sierra Maestra of the United States.

But, as Van Wyck Brooks remarked in 1915, the "importation of radical ideas and the ferment of radical ideas which have been imported scarcely touch, it seems to me, the centre of the American problem. So far as we are concerned, the sea-crossing, to begin with, has a very dampening effect on the gunpowder contained in them." This, I think, remains true today.

The tragic and romantic flavor of the handful of America's new *guerrilleros* comes across well in the Weather Underground's "Communiqué No. 1" issued on May 21, 1970, as the "Declaration of War." Taped in hiding by Bernardine Dohrn, the group's best-known leader, it proclaimed:

"Black people have been fighting almost alone for years. We've known that our job is to lead white kids to armed revolution. We never intended to spend the next five or twenty-five years in jail. Ever since SDS became revolutionary, we've been trying to show how it is possible to overcome the frustration and impotence that comes from trying to reform this system. Kids know that the lines are drawn; revolution is touching all of our lives. Tens of thousands have learned that protest and marches don't do it. Revolutionary violence is the only way.

"Now we are adapting the classic guerrilla strategy of the Vietcong and the urban guerrilla strategy of the Tupamaros to our own situation here in the most technically advanced country in the world. . . . The alienation and contempt that young people have for this country has created the ocean for this revolution. . . . The parents of 'privileged' kids have been saying for years that the revolution was a game for us. But the war and racism of this society show that it is too fucked up. We will never live peaceably under this system. . . . We fight in many ways. Dope is one of our weapons. The laws against marijuana mean that millions of us are outlaws before we actually split. Guns and grass are united in the youth underground. Freaks are revolutionaries and revolutionaries are freaks. If you want to find us, this is where we are. In every tribe, commune, dormitory, farmhouse, barracks and townhouses where kids are making love, smoking dope and loading guns—fugitives from American justice are free to go."

This was heady rhetoric, and, as I found out during my trip around the United States a few months later, at least some young radicals were responding vigorously to it. The Weather Underground's "Communiqué No. 2" on June 10, 1970, took credit for that day's bombing of New York City police headquarters. "The pigs try to look invulnerable, but we keep finding their weaknesses. Thousands of kids, from Berkeley to the U.N. Plaza, keep tearing up and ROTC buildings keep coming down. . . . Every time the pigs think they's stopped us, we come back a little stronger and a lot smarter. . . . They build the Bank of Amerika, kids burn it down. They outlaw grass, we build a culture of life and music." The astounding thing is that the Nixon White House took it all so seriously as to convince itself that the very destiny of the Republic was at stake and that the Weatherman kids had it in their power to destroy national institutions. Presently, Nixon set in motion his domestic intelligence plan that led to the creation of the White House "plumbers" unit and, finally, to Watergate.

These exploits and rhetoric now form part of the legend of the American youth rebellion. But a footnote should observe that only a small number of the revolutionaries were ever caught (there were seventeen indictments in 1970), despite intense efforts by the FBI and local police departments, the interrogations of countless "freaks," and the stake-outs by federal agents in the vicinity of "freak" homes. Last time I was in Berkeley, a young acquaintance unerringly spotted and pointed out to me the unmarked FBI cars parked here and there in the town. The occupants of the cars certainly *looked* like stake-outs. Late in 1973, the government dropped its case against fifteen Weatherpeople rather than disclose how it had obtained its evidence.

Another major ingredient of the youth rebellion was concern with environment and ecology. Young people who were aghast over the erosion of moral values in America—they believed these were being destroyed by the ruling generation's materialism, opportunism, and obeisance before the almighty dollar—now came to believe that for decades the country was being physically fouled by every conceivable type of pollution of land, water, and air. They became aware that much of the United States was being turned into a gigantic garbage dump, that the nation's beautiful land and seascapes were being mutilated by urban honky-tonks, gray impersonal superhighways, and overwhelming works of industry. They saw the huge open-pit mines in the midst of wilderness, offshore drilling rigs, oil spills on the beaches, and fluvial transportation canals slashing across wildlife preserves. They saw the rats in the streets of the ghettos, and dead fish and dead birds on the beaches.

Defense of the environment and of ecological balance became, at least for a while, one of the loudest battle cries. Consumerism was another popular cause, intimately related to the protection of the environment. And all these concerns fed into the overriding opposition to the bigness and impersonality of American corporate and political structures.

It is obviously impossible to draw with any accuracy a portrait of American youth in the early 1970s. There were about 40 million Americans between the ages of fourteen and twenty-four in 1971—15 per cent of the total population—and this mass was so diverse that any attempt at generalizing would be downright foolish. There is no such thing as an average American youth— which is presumably good for the country—and it would be unconvincingly artificial to create a composite picture.

Neither of my two children, who lived abroad extensively, is typical of their generation, and anyway there are huge differences between them. Nor is my nephew Matthew, a product of upper-middle-class New York suburban life, who in a very few years succeeded in packing these experiences in: playing the cello to please his mother, acting in Shakespeare, organizing for Eugene McCarthy, dropping out of college, living as a vegetarian, working on a construction site in lower Manhattan, de-sexing chickens at a kibbutz in Israel (without being Jewish), driving a taxi, and, finally, returning to college. Not typical, either, is the son of a rich Washington lawyer I know who enlisted in the Marine Corps and later went for a while into the trucking business instead of following in his father's steps at Princeton and the Yale Law School (although in the end, he enrolled at the University of Virginia). Just thinking of children of my friends and acquaintances, there is—atypically—the young man who first refused to take his graduate degree in 1970 in protest against the Cambodian invasion, but later became one of the youngest assistant deans at a major university; the internationally educated daughter of a well-known Washington journalist who spent two years working with VISTA in Houston and New Orleans slums; the son of a senior diplomat who took up sky diving instead of college, but then found his vocation as a free-clinic volunteer and orderly in a mental hospital; the son of a New York publishing executive who opted for the life of a ski bum; the two sons of an Italian-born railroad worker who aspire to remain just where they are and who belong to the National Guard; a Boston girl who moved from an exclusive college to a California commune; the son of a nationally respected writer, who became a heroin addict; and so *ad infinitum*. The good, the bad, and the indifferent.

Turning once more to statistics (the Census Bureau is a treasure trove for American sociology), I discovered that of the 40 million young Americans in 1971, 34 per cent worked full time, 30 per cent were in schools, 25 per cent went to college (and tended to drop out less than their predecessors two or three years earlier), 6 per cent were in the armed forces, and 4 per cent were unemployed. But I was surprised to learn that despite their youth cult, Americans in 1971 were on the average older than they had been sixty years earlier: the nation's median age was 27.9 compared with 24.1 in 1910, presumably because longevity had increased while Americans were having fewer and fewer children. (On the other hand, there were more *young* people in 1971 than in 1960, because the last of the postwar baby boom was still inflating the statistics.) If the present trend is to continue, including the new concern for demographic "zero growth," aided by legalized abortion and birth-control pills, we may be witnessing in the years to come an increasingly older U.S. population.

It is equally impossible to sketch a clear *political* portrait of young Americans. The conventional wisdom seemed to suggest that *all* youth was liberally if not radically oriented. The protests, the violence, the counterculture life styles, the physical appearance, and the whole pattern of defiance long fed this myth. A case in point is Charles A. Reich's judgment in *The Greening of America,* a runaway best-seller in the early 1970s, that with the "New Consciousness" and the new culture being rejected by the older generation, "a fraternity of the young grew up, so that they recognized each other as brothers and sisters from coast to coast." At the time Reich was writing his book at Yale, I would have been in absolute agreement with him. Three years later, I no longer see his observation as valid. It has been overtaken by events. The "fraternity" has largely come apart, although we have retained a great many emancipating ideas from the crucible of the 1960s and passed them on to the generation coming out of secondary schools now. After all, American society as a whole accepted and appropriated forever many fundamental values of the counterculture, white and black.

At the outset of this book, I remarked on the dizzying rate of change in American moods and patterns. This holds true of the young just as of the old. My own children, having religiously read Reich's book, have not turned into Establishment reactionaries, but they have evolved more subtle approaches to the crises of society. They feel, I believe, that important conquests were made and many more still challenge and await them. They no longer seem to think, however, that all the answers are to be found in the ways suggested during those bygone days. The mood has changed on the campuses; the underground press has gradually disappeared. I regret to see it all go, and I would hate to see another "silent generation" in my time.

But even at the height of the youth turmoil, for each protester, white or black, there was at least one or more status-quo youth, white or black. In the colleges, there were students who simply wanted to study, just as there were sports-oriented "jocks" and kids who wanted to be amused for four years before embarking on careers and marriage. Beyond the campuses there were noncommittal factory and office workers and young farmers. Only a small fraction of the few millions in the armed forces were disaffected GIs fragging their officers, joining antiwar "coffeehouses," and turning later into activist veterans-for-peace. The majority's problem, if that is what it was, stemmed from low visibility and a low noise threshold. But, then, a middle-class minority historically leads most great movements toward change. Unlike the earlier trade-union campaigns in the United States, also responsible for basic changes in our society, the youth revolt was almost elitist in character.

In 1972, both Democrats and Republicans tirelessly courted the 11 million new potential voters added to the rolls after the passage of the Twenty-sixth Amendment lowered the voting age to eighteen. At first sight, these new voters appeared to be solidly for the Democrats. But when the nominating conventions came, it turned out that a lot of kids had swayed to support President Nixon, to defend the status quo and his brand of patriotism. In 1970, James Buckley, a staunch conservative, was elected to the Senate from generally liberal New York in part because of the superior organization and work of the Young Conservatives. At the Republican National Convention, a thirteen-year-old boy, put up to deliver his state's votes for the incumbent President, declared theatrically that "Virginia is for lovers, and Virginia loves Richard Nixon." In the end only a fraction of the new eligible voters came to the polls, a sure sign of political passivity, probably explaining the extent of Senator George McGovern's defeat.

Still, certain generalizations were permissible, I thought. The first generalization goes back to Van Wyck Brooks' assessment that America was possessed of a "systematic optimism." To him, this meant "a complete revaluation of values" and the enthronement of "truth upon a conception of animal success the prerequisite of which is a thorough-going denial of emotional experience." This "revaluation of values," I felt, was a continuing

American process. Even the "know nothing" conservatives of the new generation were forced to keep revaluing the status quo. In the early 1970s, a wholly different dimension of protest and unrest emerged among young workers, uninvolved in the earlier ferment but now attacking the dehumanization of work.

My second generalization—related to the first one and made more obvious by our new technological resources—had to do with young America's incredible mobility, which I saw as the search for every type of experience, emotional or otherwise. This cut across all social strata. The Census Bureau reported that 26 per cent of the 40 million Americans between the ages of fourteen and twenty-four (exclusive of those in the military) changed addresses between March 1970 and March 1971. A fantastic migration! Students (or dropouts), freaks, new professionals, and young families filled the highways in their campers and cars and motorcycles, crowded trains and buses, and helped to keep the airlines in business. To those 10 million or so who changed homes between 1970 and 1971, one could add uncounted other millions who simply traveled for briefer periods: vacations, rock festivals, camping trips, or simply getting away from home.

One sobering aspect of this vast movement was that in 1971 about a million juveniles had run away from home. And while in 1963 the average age of the runaway was sixteen or seventeen, it dropped down to eleven to fourteen in 1971. The FBI, which keeps track of runaways because it is a police function to grab them and return them home, reported in 1971 that runaway arrests increased by 60 per cent over the previous five years. In New York City, for example, there are twenty thousand teen-age runaways at any given time. Arrests result in police records and, the FBI said, the young runaways were thus "drawn into the criminal justice system." Why runaways should be saddled with criminal records is beyond my comprehension. And half of them, we are told, are girls.

Berkeley, California, has long had a policy of arresting juvenile runaways and sending them home, mainly because the city cannot physically and financially afford their presence. A ranking Berkeley police official told me that one of the principal functions of his department during the summer is telephoning parents all over the country (reversing the charges whenever possible) to request funds for their children's repatriation. When the parents or guardians refuse the money, the Berkeley police pay for the one-way ticket home. But one of the demands of the April Coalition, the catch-all political group that elected a radical slate to the Berkeley City Council in 1971, was the repeal of the anti-runaway policy. They insisted that Berkeley should be open to all. The Washington Runaway House (headed by a one-time juvenile runaway from New York) handled about three thousand runaways annually. Matters reached the point where the Senate considered appropriating $10 million for temporary shelters throughout the United States under a proposed Runaway Youth Act.

William Butler Yeats wrote at the beginning of the century that "the fiddles are tuning as it were all over America." Van Wyck Brooks commented a few years later that "under the glassy, brassy surface of American jocosity and business there is a pulp and a quick, and this pulpy quick, this nervous and acutely self-critical vitality, is in our day in a strange ferment. A fresh and more sensitive emotion seems to be running up and down the old Yankee backbone, that rarely blossoming stalk."

During my 1970 journey, I came upon a fascinating document at the Nebraska State Historical Society in Lincoln, showing once more that there was little entirely new in the thought of young Americans of my time. It was an article in an 1877 issue of *The Hesperian* (the name means "Western"), a publication of the University of Nebraska, written by F. M. Lambert, a graduating student. Lambert (who later became a deputy collector of internal revenue in Harrison, Arkansas) had this to say: "Mankind must yet be free, free not merely in the sense of our Constitution and Declaration of Independence, but free from those unfeeling fetters which bind a man to a party and these rags that smell of the prison chambers. . . . Hence freedom is the first condition of reason and thus personal freedom becomes a private condition of personal perfection. . . . No bondage can equal mental bondage, no freedom can equal mental freedom.. . . The time has past when government must be formed for government's sake. . . . Personal freedom comes through like a Good Samaritan to the good politician. But in these latter days he has fallen among thieves. He must again learn to value his own dignity and be master of his own opinions. Conservatism will then go down; it is a dead mummy that serves only to corrupt the old mortal things of the past. . . ."

The long-forgotten F. M. Lambert, along with Yeats and Brooks, was saying in his day, it seemed to me, just what the protest generation was hoping to express in my time. The fiddles were indeed tuning all over America.

Veterans of the youth rebellion whom I asked to name the principal milestones in the history of the Movement (young people still say the word with a capital *M*), both political and cultural, seemed to agree on the foundation of the SDS in 1962 and the Free Speech Movement launched at the University of California in Berkeley in 1965. The birth of the SDS was the first major step toward a wider politicization of the campuses. And the Berkeley Free Speech Movement was an important expression of the need for personal freedom—it went much deeper than simply the unfettered use of a four-letter word—and it was one of the bases of the counterculture. It was also in Berkeley, five years later, that the young people waged a bloody but losing battle to turn a university-owned parking lot into a "People's Park." The first student member of the youth revolt in the United States to be killed by the authorities died on Telegraph Avenue in 1970 during that affray. (I was in Berkeley the following year when a lively riot marked the anniversary of his death.) After many of the youthful hopes for a better America died with Kennedy—and the Vietnam war was being escalated by Lyndon Johnson and Richard Nixon—diverse political and cultural strains came together; in the end, they were virtually inseparable.

Many young people with whom I discussed the genesis and the history of their amorphous Movement agree that the appearance on the scene of The Beatles, the British rock-music group, had much to do with launching the new youth culture. The Beatles influenced a whole generation of Americans (and others throughout the world)—and, as it developed, not only the young ones. Quickly, physical appearance turned into a visual expression of something deeper. The country became populated by millions of young men with long hair and beards and mustaches of every description. Young women literally let their hair down. The attire for both sexes was *de rigueur* simplicity and deliberate casualness. It was a colorful world of blue jeans and Levi's and peasant blouses, lumberjack shirts and surplus military fatigues, boots in the winter and sandals, moccasins, or just plain bare feet in warm weather. The more disrespectable the kids looked from the viewpoint of their elders, the more assertive they thought themselves to be in their defiance. In the end, however, this attire became as much of a uniform as the button-down shirts and the gray flannel of an earlier generation. Those who revolted against America being a nation of sheep found the answer in looking like a nation of unshorn sheep. Still, for young whites to wear tattered clothes was a conscious or unconscious identification with America's past and her rural poor, though the affinity seldom went further. To Charles Reich, the "earliest sources" of the new culture were Thoreau, Joyce, and Wallace Stevens as it returned to "the earlier America" of "Myself I Sing." The bandanas and leather thongs holding back the hair of young men and women alike were imitations of old American Indian customs. It was not coincidental that groups of young people thought of themselves as "tribes." The old Indian culture was forcibly if superficially revived in the nomenclature of antiwar and other militants who, calling themselves the "Mayday Tribe," sought to "shut down" the government in Washington in May 1971, in the last massive demonstration in which twelve thousand "Indians" were arrested. One of the best-known underground newspapers was the Berkeley Tribe. A college publication in Oklahoma, which has a real Indian population, was the *Comanche*. Indian-type bracelets and costume jewelry, much of it produced by young people, were another visible sign of the newly discovered attachment to a tribal past.

For reasons that also apparently stemmed from hunger for a "pure past," thousands and thousands of young middle-class people set up rural communes or urban collectives all over the country. (Their fad for "organic foods" was a logical consequence.) But, by and large, the communes were short-lived, never attracting more than a handful of young workers or farmers.

Counterculture politics found sartorial expression in military fatigues, berets, and beards. Here, American rebels were romantically seeing themselves as replicas of Castro's Cuban guerrillas, as they paraded their "uniforms" along Washington's Wisconsin Avenue in Georgetown, Berkeley's Telegraph Avenue, or

New York's East Village. The underground Weatherpeople, needless to say, refrained from displaying military-type attire. Black Panthers, Puerto Rican Young Lords, and other minority militants were impeccable in guerrilla garb. There were black berets and brown berets. But, overwhelmingly, young blacks, in contrast with the whites, chose flamboyant and elegant dress. They did not need to affect the uniform of poverty: poverty was their reality.

Peace symbols, first introduced by students, were soon adopted by everybody who opposed the Vietnam war. They were worn on chains around the neck, painted on walls, made into car stickers (a favorite American form of political expression), and stuck into lapels. I know a bank branch manager in Oakland, California, who wore a peace symbol in his lapel when he left the office, just as "straight" young people changed into sartorial "freaks" after working all day in Establishment offices.

Counterculture and politics blended, too, in the new music. The Weathermen took their name from the lyrics of a Bob Dylan song which proclaimed, "You don't need a weatherman to know which way the wind blows." Dylan, Joan Baez, and other bards of the counterculture were highly political. Antiwar rallies were incomplete without rock groups. At times, one could not tell a peace rally from a rock festival. The Jefferson Airplane, one of the best-known (and financially most successful) rock groups, was a feature at antiwar rallies just as "Peace Now" speeches were commonplace at gigantic rock festivals. Sex and drugs went along with antiwar politics and deafening hard rock wherever young people congregated in large numbers.

It should be recorded in passing that enormous fortunes were made by quick-witted adults who catered to this counterculture, much as many of them might have deplored it in the privacy of their homes. Organized crime and drug peddlers tapped a gold vein. Recording companies earned millions from records and tapes by Dylan and Baez, the late Jimi Hendrix and Janis Joplin, the Jefferson Airplane, Led Zeppelin, the Doors, Cream, The Band, the Youngbloods, and countless other groups. The performers themselves cashed in. Festival organizers did extremely well in some cases (but lost money on others, especially when local authorities banned scheduled programs—as happened during 1970 in county after county from Oklahoma to Connecticut —fearing too much sex, too many drugs, and too much disorder). Guitar makers and manufacturers of blue jeans, boots, and camping equipment struck it rich. The Hollywood company that filmed the Woodstock festival found itself boycotted by the youth who belatedly concluded that they had been victimized by an Establishment which transmuted the counterculture into gold. I remember seeing in the summer of 1970 the virtually empty drive-in theater in Hickory, North Carolina, where young people simply stayed away. Ironically, *Woodstock* was also being shown in downtown Kent, Ohio, two months after the shootings at the nearby university. When we drove past the theater, not a soul was at the box-office.

The counterculture's principal internal communications network was the underground press and, to a lesser extent, local radio stations. But the underground press was neither illegal nor really underground. Sold at street corners by volunteer hawkers (often harassed by the police but seldom prevented from selling) and available by subscription, the underground newspapers were designed as an alternative to the "straight" media which the young totally distrusted. They served the essential function of offering political propaganda—they never made any bones about openly urging revolution and violence, and the government never sought to stop them—and service to their local constituencies. They also provided links among communities across the country. The Underground Press Syndicate and the Liberation News Service served as clearing houses for nationwide dissemination of important items of news and opinion.

Starting with the appearance of the Los Angeles *Free Press* in 1964, the "alternative" publications blossomed; they were colorful, stridently and violently written and edited, irreverent, uncompromising, unforgiving, but immensely dedicated. They could be bitter, when attacking the Establishment, or tender, when writing about the freaks and revolutionaries. They were often funny and amusing in that severe cruel way in which revolutionaries cut down the world they detest, but, as is always the case with single-minded revolutionaries, they were incapable of pure humor or of laughing at themselves or their causes. I suppose my principal criticism of the counterculture—and its newspapers exemplified it here—was that it lacked a sense of humor so necessary for the preservation of sanity in a mad world. Which meant, I thought, that it was just as self-righteous as its adult foes.

Early in 1971, the Underground Press Syndicate estimated that there were seven hundred underground newspapers in the United States with a total circulation of 20 million. Exact or not, there was no question that the circulation *was* massive. *Fortune* magazine, which could not be accused of partiality toward the underground press, estimated a circulation of 5 million in 1968, when there were only one hundred such publications. The Twentieth Century Fund recognized their importance by ordering a special study of the counterculture press. By 1973, however, the underground press shrank dramatically both in individual circulation figures and in number of newspapers. Fewer people bought them and advertising (yes, advertising by "straight" clients who wanted a share of the counterculture's commercial business) dried up. In August 1972, Washington's three-year-old *Quicksilver Times,* in its final issue wrote that it was closing down "primarily because of a number of interrelated money and staff problems. . . . We always were a communist newspaper, though our politics and understanding of communism matured as we published. . . . In the community, we tried above all to organize around local issues and problems first while pointing out that no solution could ever become effective without the complete destruction of the most basic concepts that control this country—those concepts fostered by capitalism—concepts of imperialism, racism, and sexism."

The Washington paper's farewell profession of faith was similar to the philosophy of the other underground papers. In its heyday, the radical press—one must include in it the SDS *New Left Notes,* New York's *Liberated Guardian, East Village Other, Ramparts* magazine, and briefly *Scanlan*'s, along with the other underground newspapers—was a powerful anti-Establishment voice, and its gradual disappearance left a political and cultural void in a society returning to relative conformism.

Samples from my collection of underground newspapers convey the flavor of what once was. The Los Angeles *Free Press,* one of the few still in existence, made its mark when it printed the names of law-enforcement agents in California working on drug cases—the "narcs"—for which action the federal government took it into court (as it probably should have). A fat issue of Chicago's *Seed* once printed a multicolor cover of two joyful dancers, the caption saying, "We shall celebrate with such fierce dancing the Death of Your Institutions." The issue's thirty-two pages were filled with reports on revolutionary actions and "roving bands of pigs in squadrols" as well as with "Free City" directories of community services and groups ranging from "Spurgeon Jake Winters Free Peoples' Medical Clinic" (Black Panthers) to "People's Law Office" handling "criminal law cases free to members of revolutionary organizations" and "Problem Pregnancy Counselling." San Francisco's *Leviathan* proclaimed on a 1970 cover, "The Reactionaries are more and more alarmed:

They live in fear, seeing conspiracy everywhere, seeing subversion everywhere. And It's True, It's True!" Inside, the masthead announced that "subscriptions for political prisoners are free," and one of the main articles dealt with the origins of the League of Revolutionary Black Workers. Another *Leviathan* issue was devoted to "Cuba for Beginners," told in cartoons. The San Francisco *Good Times* published photographs of naked young men and women at the 1970 festival at Powder Ridge, Connecticut, and the customary column of practical advice "In Case of a Bust" by the police. Atlanta's *Great Speckled Bird* wrote in August 1970 of "arrests all weekend," named a police officer chosen to win any "Pig Popularity Poll," ran an article on abortion and an advertisement for "Guaranteed Organically Grown Fresh Cabbage —23 cents per pound." Its center spread celebrated Carl Hampton, a black militant "murdered by Houston Pigs." The Washington *Free Press* hailed "a group of heavy freaks" for fire-bombing four Latin American "pig embassies" and offered advice on how to write slogans on walls and not be caught ("Day-glo orange is very striking" and "dress right—sometimes you may want to look straight"). The New York *Rat,* published by a women's collective, hailed Angela Davis and the Palestinian woman guerrilla leader Leila Khaled, printed an article signed by "A Flaming Faggot" and another by "A Radicalesbian," and announced a "Fiesta to Open a People's Park" on the Lower East Side. The Santa Fe *Hips Voice* looked for organizers for a nonviolent "Hiroshima Day." Milwaukee's *Kaleidoscope* printed communiqués from terrorists. The Berkeley *Tribe* approvingly reported on a "rip-off" of ammunition at a National Guard armory in Massachusetts, published a woman's account of a summer in jail where homosexuality "was something that women got into to survive, something to build warmth and human closeness," and advertised hairpieces to "cover that groovy long hair but only to secure a job or for military service—Let it swing long again on weekends." Another *Tribe* issue commemorated the anniversary of the Cuban revolution and still another devoted its cover to cartoons illustrating how to "Build to Revolution": "Get It Together . . . Serve the People . . . Rip Off a Bank . . . Smoke Lotsa Dope!"

How and why narcotics entered the youth scene in America is something of a mystery. Suffice it to say that the use of marijuana spread like wildfire in America in the early 1960s. Nobody I know in the law-enforcement agencies has any idea how many young Americans have smoked a "joint" once or have made a habit of it. With adults joining in the use of marijuana because they felt it was sophisticated or "right on" (*always* the American youth cult), tens of millions of citizens in the United States must have tried it. Songs of the counterculture glorified drug use directly or indirectly.

Narcotics became part of revolutionary politics because, as many young people told me, it was part of being "turned on," "spaced out," and more "conscious" about what they were doing. Bernardine Dohrn's communiqué from the Weather Underground in 1970 bears witness to it. As a girl in Boulder, Colorado, told me one day, "Grass helps us to get it all together." A California student explained that smoking grass is "revolutionary" because it is illegal and for middle-class kids it thus represents a defiance of the Establishment.

Whether marijuana does or does not lead to harder and more pernicious drugs—heroin, cocaine, or LSD—and whether it is addictive remain matters of controversy even in the scientific community. But it is a statistical fact that the use of hard drugs in the United States skyrocketed. Among organized political militants, only blacks are dead-set against drug use, on the theory that "you don't win a revolution when you are stoned out of your mind," as a Panther leader once told me. George Jackson made the same point when I saw him in San Quentin. Because black militants also hold the theory that the white Establishment is deliberately condoning the use of hard drugs in order to keep the poor blacks in submission (they also see legalized abortion as "genocide" of blacks), they have been in the forefront of the battle against narcotics. I know from my own experience that no serious revolutionary movement—Castro's Cuba being a major case in point—tolerates drug addiction in its midst. And in countries like the United States, drug addiction dramatically increases juvenile delinquency because crime is the easiest way of supporting the habit.

The counterculture inevitably brought out the best as well as the worst in young Americans. The best, of course, was the dedication to causes, the notion that people should be kind to each other, the willingness to help and to share, tolerance, the deeprooted pacifism—in one word, the sense of caring. "Love" was the password.

This dimension of the counterculture led to attempts at creating alternative institutions to those already in existence: free medical clinics manned by volunteers in scores of American cities; "rap" centers where the lonely, the disturbed, the depressed, and the stoned could find someone to listen to them and guide them; "free churches" where enlightened (and not always young) ministers and priests made common cause with the freaks instead of ejecting them from the houses of God; phone "switchboards" providing round-the-clock information on where to get lodging, food, advice on drug addiction problems, legal aid in case of arrest; "crisis centers"; "free universities" where learning bizarre subjects was better than learning nothing at all; day-care centers.

In Berkeley, where in 1971 I spent many weeks looking at these alternative institutions, they became a vital part of life, even before the so-called radicals were elected to the full control of the

City Council. Elsewhere—in New York City, Washington, D.C., Cambridge, Boulder, Santa Fe, Palo Alto, San Francisco, or Iowa City—they were important in the nomadic life of the floating youth population. Around them formed communities that were open to all: revolutionaries, street people, marauding freaks, homosexual groups, women's liberation organizations, and everybody who wanted in and did "his thing." People tended to live together and to work together. "Collectives" of young men and women published underground newspapers, produced underground movies, put out publications concerned with Latin America, Africa, or Asia, operated free clinics and "revolutionary" nurseries, ran "food conspiracies" which purchased basic foods in bulk cheaply and resold them at no profit. They included married people without children and unmarried people with children. The talk was of abolishing once and for all the nuclear family as we know it, and replacing it with collective or communal living. Having been a guest at a number of such collectives, I almost invariably found warmth and hospitality—and a burning desire to explain the "whys" of the life style to a "straight" newspaper reporter.

Most Americans, I found, shy away from physically touching each other. A man casually or impulsively touching another man, or a woman touching another woman, is eyed suspiciously. Somehow it seems wrong sexually or emotionally to touch another person with whom one does not have a real intimacy. But young people broke through this barrier of personal coldness (men in Europe, Latin America, and Asia not only touch but kiss each other when the occasion requires it without damaging their masculinity), and they discovered that to touch a human being is a better way to communicate. And I saw in my peregrinations among the young that they treated one another with a thoughtful courtesy that I wished existed more often among their self-righteous elders.

But, as I said, the counterculture brought out the worst, too, in some participants. For many kids, the youth rebellion meant a "rip-off," meant living off the fat of the land, getting stoned, being unproductive, and generally not giving a damn. There certainly was a parasite and delinquent contingent in the Movement. More often than not, these street people—happily and sleepily homeless and indigent—lived on the periphery of the youth culture. The worst among them gave *all* the street people a bad name, although some street people were really good ones. The bad ones were available for riots and disturbances, but little else; when they could no longer extract money from their parents (they were, naturally, from affluent families), they demanded welfare payments and food stamps—and often obtained them from welfare offices too swamped to check out everybody's *bona fides*. Inasmuch as the only thing they absorbed from the politics around them was the notion that capitalist society must be destroyed, they felt it was morally justifiable to rip off. And ripping off was shoplifting, mugging, forging checks, stealing credit cards, inventing highly imaginative ways of making free long-distance telephone calls, and doing anything they could devise to get something for nothing. Tolerant as this society still remains —or because greed takes precedence over reason—book publishers issued best-selling texts on the techniques of ripping off. But the public sympathy that once existed for the Flower Children of Haight-Ashbury, a slummy district atop one of San Francisco's hills, became an angry reaction as the Flower Children turned into hopheads and rip-off artists. The last time I visited Haight-Ashbury, it had become a skid row of addicts and alcoholics.

We had a first-rate demonstration of the rip-off in operation when our daughter Nikki married a fellow radical at a ceremony at our Washington home late in 1970. In addition to both families, the young couple invited a few of their closest friends to the reception. But word spread quickly in the freak community that there would be free booze—and who knows what else?—at 4515 29th Street, Northwest. In short order, the reception was crashed by freaks of both sexes who guzzled our champagne, smoked grass in the garden, then proceeded to the serious part of the afternoon's activities. At one point, my son Tony spotted an uninvited guest making off to the back gate with a small carpet rolled up under his arm (we had spread carpets in the garden under the tent where the reception was held) and succeeded in tackling him. The next morning, we learned that two young women who had crashed the party had managed to steal all the credit cards from my sister-in-law's purse. (They were arrested a few weeks later in a New York department store after having charged hundreds of dollars on a Washington-to-Philadelphia-to-New York shopping spree.) From the pile of presents for the newlyweds in an upstairs bedroom, an expensive camera and I forget what else had disappeared. "My God," I said to my wife the following day, "would you believe freaks ripping off from their fellow freaks?" —Nikki and her husband liked to think of themselves in those days as freaks. We put the incidents down to experience. Now we laugh about it.

Because of its very spontaneity, the youth rebellion never could quite get it "all together" politically, which may be one reason why the antiwar movement finally ran out of steam and the "revolution" of the militants' dreams never seriously menaced the existing political system. Nevertheless, as subsequent events showed, the system did not remain unchanged. By 1972, even Republicans had discovered that the youth pressures, thoughts, and demands could not be ignored. Awkwardly, they tried to co-opt the kids.

Although the young activists have been called leftists, radicals, and revolutionaries by their nervous elders, they never had a discernible ideology or a reliable leadership. Some major issues they simply ignored. The deep-seated desire to avoid "elitism" and "power-tripping" did away with potential national leaders. SDS founders Tom Hayden and Mark Rudd fell by the wayside. Hayden, whom I last saw in Berkeley early in 1971, simply observing the doings of the town's political "freaks," was even read out of his own "Red Family" collective for "elitist tendencies." Presently, he married Jane Fonda. Rudd, as far as anybody knows, cast his lot with the underground Weathermen after the SDS split at the Ann Arbor convention in 1969. Abbie Hoffman, Jerry Rubin, and Rennie Davis never were political *leaders,* despite their roles in Chicago and their continued antiwar militancy.

In *The Greening of America,* Reich offers valuable insights into the counterculture's rejection of leadership. Discussing the new generation in terms of his Consciousness III concept, he remarks that it "postulates the absolute worth of every human being—every self. . . . Consciousness III does not believe in the antagonistic or competitive doctrine of life. . . . People are brothers, the world is ample for all. . . . Consciousness III rejects the whole concept of excellence and comparative merit. . . . [It] refuses to classify people, or analyze them. . . . Someone may be a brilliant thinker, but he is not 'better' at thinking than anyone else, he simply possesses his own excellence. . . . Because there are no governing standards, no one is rejected. Everyone is entitled to pride in himself, and no one should act in a way that is servile, or feel inferior, or allow himself to be treated as if he were inferior." Going straight to the heart of the matter, Reich writes that his ultimate consciousness "rejects relationships of authority and subservience. It will neither give commands nor follow them."

No doubt, this was a compelling set of relationships that Reich had described. But his was an ideal society: in the real world of the Movement the rejection of what would have amounted to leadership led to its ultimate decomposition, which is a pity.

In this ideological vacuum, the Socialist Youth Alliance—affiliated with the supposedly ex-Trotskyite Socialist Workers party —and the nonviolent Progressive Labor faction of the SDS actively concentrated their political action against the Vietnam war and racism. The Spartacist League, a group representing what it calls Revolutionary Marxism, denounced the Alliance and the antiwar Student Mobilization Committee for pushing "class collaboration." *The Sparticist,* a most articulate publication, accused the Progressive Labor group of taking a "rightward plunge," selling out to liberals, and shouting "Power to the People!" instead of "Power to the Workers!" The Revolutionary Marxists wanted a classical class struggle—in contrast to the racial battlefront decided on by the SDS leadership in 1971. To the horror of Spartacist purists, SDS's *New Left Notes,* once rather interesting ideologically, proclaimed in November 1971 that racism was "the main way people are oppressed today." Slowly the young New Left and the neo-New Left bogged down in theological debates, hurling around such esoteric epithets as "anarcho-freak," "underground-lumpen freak-yippy communes," and "anti-proto-fascist." But perhaps the failure of the New American Left to agree on a clear direction is more a basic commentary on the American Left as a whole and on the essentially nonideological nature of the American political animal.

College radicals contemptuously talked of workers as "lumpen" or "greasers." The class ideologues could not swallow black nationalism. In fact, the white and black rebellions ran on separate and seldom parallel tracks. Young white militants paid lip service to black leaders (Huey Newton, George Jackson, Bobby Seale, Eldridge Cleaver, and Angela Davis were their official heroes, but this was as far as it went) and carried anti-racism as their battle standard, but they could never find a common ground with the blacks. Divided or not, the blacks at least had identifiable leaders. But they had little use for white rhetoreticians and, in truth, distrusted them. "Guilt, that's what it was," a Yale-educated black militant lawyer in California told me contemptuously. "We owe them nothing."

Aside from political and street militancy, young blacks concentrated attention on improving their status in American universities. With 522,000 blacks enrolled in colleges and universities at the start of the 1970 academic year—about 7 per cent of the national enrollment but more than twice the number in 1964—the black view was that they were victims of discrimination, and the schools were rife with tension and frictions. Like white students, they demanded a voice with faculty and administrators in running the schools; also, more black admissions and the creation of black-studies programs. Their assertiveness led to confrontations not only with university authorities but with white students as well. When I visited Columbus in the summer of 1970, for example, I heard Dr. Charles Ross, a black professor, insist during a television interview that $40 million should be appropriated for black studies at Ohio State University. This amount represented 20 per cent of Ohio's annual higher-education budget for 1970–71, and Dr. Ross said this would be simply a fair allocation because 20 per cent of Ohio's total population is black. The university decided, however, that demographic yardsticks could not be applied in planning budgets. Similar controversies developed elsewhere. In July 1970, black-white tensions grew alarmingly at Douglass, a women's college that is part of the

New Jersey university system, at the time I was visiting a friend of mine, then the school's assistant dean. A special commission on "Ethnic and Race Relations," appointed to cope with the problem, reported early in 1972 that "the College buzzed with the general sense that black/white relations had reached dangerous levels of tension and that some major outbreak might be expected."

Because Douglass' problems reflected to a large extent those encountered in numerous other colleges, I think it might be useful to quote at some length from the report of the commission as well as from dissenting views of its black members. Besides, the Douglass people came up with some fresh ideas.

The commission found that "differences between blacks and whites centered around specific black demands, some of which were acknowledged as legitimate needs by the white community as it slowly came to consciousness of the extent to which Douglass manifested the same symptoms of institutional or traditional racism as has characterized American life since the beginning of this country. . . . While substantial progress was being made in meeting some needs, interpersonal relations between blacks and whites on campus showed clear signs of deterioration, and a general malaise and feeling of frustration about the future of black/white relations at the College began to manifest itself."

While all the incidents between blacks and whites do not "necessarily have their origins in racial perceptions, they have all developed racial overtones." And the "central" problem was that "whites and blacks often attribute different meanings to the same events." This, unquestionably, is the crux of racial relationships everywhere, and the Douglass commission stated it well: "The misperceptions, differing expectations and interpretations, and ambivalences in American racial relations are *not* symmetrical: blacks and whites are not mirror images of one another.

"Misperceptions are a dramatic cause of black/white difficulties. A black girl and a white girl have a run-in in the dining hall; the whole thing is trivial and it might be quickly forgotten but for the fact that others present perceive it as an 'incident,' exaggerate its importance, and increase everybody's sense of insecurity. The rumor mill does the rest. Misperceptions stem from crude generalizations on the basis of little evidence, from emotional tension which colors what one sees, and from ideologies which act as blinders to a more complex reality. Finally, the understandable sensitivity of minority group members to discrimination may sometimes bring them to perceive it where none exists.

"While blacks have long needed to have at least minimal understanding of white behavior in order to survive, whites are much newer at the business of trying to come to an understanding of blacks. Different modes of expression can be troublesome, since we are prone to interpret as threatening that which is unfamiliar. A black student may unknowingly frighten a white freshman when she only meant to tease her. The white student misreads the signals because they are unfamiliar. The public stance of some blacks, especially those that whites think of as 'militant,' tends to further aggravate fears, again frequently without cause: most whites are unaccustomed to the expressive rhetoric of black spokesmen."

The commission's report went on to observe that "whites regard blacks with a mixture of fear, guilt, and admiration. Blacks regard whites with a mixture of fear, resentment, and admiration. Thus we do not come innocently to our dealings with those of another race. Rather, we come with turbulent emotions and substantial prejudices that make it difficult to predict each other's behavior. Minor incidents become 'racial' ones because of this uncertainty.

"Blacks are more visible than whites, as are members of any

minority group—which is one reason whites perceive blacks as the troublemakers on campus. Another factor may be the differing lifestyle of blacks which troubles many whites. Many blacks, on the other hand, resent the pervasive lifestyle of white people, and some are openly contemptuous of it. Perhaps this uneasiness in the presence of differing clothes, language, music, play, etc. lies at the root of much of the tension in such places as the dining halls and residence halls."

The Douglass group went further in examining the racial relationships. "The way in which some whites and blacks who feel uneasy with each other respond is by being superficially 'nice' to each other. But obviously there are risks in situations where people relate to one another as if they were walking on eggs. When we are irrationally afraid of another person we dehumanize that person, and we should not be surprised if she ultimately strikes out at us (i.e., commits the very behavior she senses we are afraid of), because our irrational fear is highly insulting to her.

"Aggressive behavior by blacks could be interpreted as a negative way of drawing white attention to the immediacy with which black Americans are affected by the cruelties of American race relations. A basic difference between blacks and whites is that, for blacks, as the minority culture, black/white relations are an overwhelming, twenty-four-hour-a-day concern, while for whites, as the majority culture, black/white relations are a part-time concern. Whites can sometimes turn off the problem; blacks cannot. If, in an integrated system, tensions exist for whites, they exist far more so for blacks. This may be one of the reasons for the quite natural turn to separation by collegiate blacks precisely at a time when integration was becoming a conventional goal of American society. Integration is probably harder on blacks than on whites. Liberals who agonize over racial separatism fostered by blacks do not, therefore, help matters.

. . . The College need not feel at this particular point in history that some self-segregation in the residence halls, arrived at without pressure or intimidation of others, is anything but natural and, for some people, necessary."

By 1973, however, these antagonisms were replaced by a tacit agreement between the races to live separately, even under the same roof. This, I thought, was in its own way even more tragic than the enforced segregation of yore. Now it was voluntary.

This was strikingly like the situation at the Washington high school my son attended between 1972 and 1974. The school was fully integrated, though with a black majority, and it had a black principal. But, as my son told me, the whites and the blacks chose totally separate lives, to the extreme of using different doors to enter the building. In class, they sat in separate blocs. There was virtually no social contact outside the classroom. The whites tended to fear the blacks—and the blacks held the "honkies" in contempt.

The Douglass commission, again departing from conventional wisdoms, commented that "only in recent years have we begun to see that the melting pot thesis had within it the seeds of conformity, even repression. Indeed, it was black people who first dramatically argued, precisely at the point when American society seemed finally able and willing to offer them some acceptance, that 'joining' America implied giving up something precious, i.e., one's group identity. Other ethnic groups followed suit, so that the last few years in American domestic history have been characterized by nothing so much as the resurgence of ethnic identity and the destruction of the melting pot myth. In its place has come a new image of America as, if you will, a salad bowl. . . . An America based on the salad bowl concept as opposed to the melting pot concept will be a more interesting, exciting, and humane one. . . . We at Douglass must understand this if we are to understand race and ethnic relations at the College." This, of course, was what I had been finding all over the United States: the extraordinary rebirth of ethnic sentiment. But it was noteworthy that this process had been set in motion by the blacks, themselves a minority in the American ethnic community.

On another level, the commission found that "the repeated spectre of white students coming to Douglass with idealistic and liberal attitudes toward blacks and leaving as self-declared racists is an appalling reality with which the College must deal." It urged whites "to recognize their own fears of black people, which generations of conditioning have made almost endemic in white America." Then it told blacks that "giving the white person the benefit of the doubt is not weakness but strength. If blacks rebuff occasional white attempts to reach them, whites will have every reason to give up." Thereby, I thought, hangs the American racial tragedy.

A minority comment, written by two black commission members, found that black students arriving on campus "are, in fact, second class citizens." The new black students, it said, "are greeted with stares, avoidance, then hostility on the part of many whites. . . . From that point forth, blacks and whites begin to have particular kinds of negative relationships." Alluding to the socioeconomic condition of black students, the minority report said that "black students sit in the classroom all week and sit in the dormitories on weekends, for most cannot afford to go elsewhere. The tensions and frustrations which mount during the week continue to build and never find a constructive outlet."

In a way, it seemed to me, the Douglass commission report—a perceptive piece of work—provided many answers as to why young whites and blacks found it virtually impossible, and not even particularly desirable, to work together on behalf of the "new politics." I am reminded, for example, of a leading black educator in Washington, D.C., the holder of a Ph.D. in psychology from a northern university, telling me over drinks at my home one evening that the thing that had disturbed him the most since his arrival in our city was the refusal of blacks here to assert their identity. A Black Nationalist black-red-and-green flag emblem in his lapel, he asked: "Why, for God's sake, do they all want to be like the white man, make the mistakes of the white man, and even act as white men in treating their fellow blacks?" Then he answered his own question. "The traditional Washington blacks," he said, "have become a kept community. But our young people are quite different. You will see!" But only relatively few young whites understood this. Too much in their make-up was instinctual, romantic, starry-eyed—and, therefore, inconsiderate of all else.

Their absence of political acumen or coherence notwithstanding, young rebels never lacked in idealism and dedication. This was their principal strength, even if they were naive or downright misguided. And in this regard very advanced age, just as young age, may be a door to perception. This I learned on a morning early in May 1971 as I had coffee with the late Pablo Casals, the great cellist, and several music critics in the maestro's suite at a Washington hotel. It was the day before the "Mayday Tribe" was to attempt to "shut down" the government by blocking all accesses to the city, and thousands of antiwar militants were pouring into the capital. Police riot squads were downstairs, and the shrill sound of police sirens soared up from the avenue as we talked about music. Someone told Casals that young people were coming to town to try to stop the war. Casals, only a few months short of ninety-five, lunged out of his armchair. "Stop the war?" he asked. "Of course, stop the war!" He warmed up to the subject of young people protesting the war and kept coming back to it in between Schubert, Bach, and Mozart. "Teachers and parents know nothing. . . . There is a law to kill or be killed. This law, I don't respect. . . . The teachers and the fathers, they don't know anything about children. And the mothers? Why don't they protest the war? . . . They say, 'It is the law.' How ignorant, barbarian we are. . . . The law makes me kill or be killed? No! Do you understand? The essence of life is that we all are divine. . . . Music is proof of how divine we are. But we only want the material things? Ah, they're not the power. . . . For me, the secret how to stop wars is to have respect for life."

I pondered over Casals' words, his boundless admiration for the youthful protesters. But I also thought about the contradictions implicit in the determination of some young people to wage war on their own country—bombing, sniping, and killing if necessary—to stop *it* from waging war abroad. Talking with radical kids close to the Weather underground and reading interviews with the *guerrilleros,* one could not but ask, why do these young Americans seem to hate their own country so much? Most of the answers were rather banal: Amerikan imperialism (America was always spelled with a *k*, presumably to suggest a German Nazi connotation of what this country was thought to be) must be destroyed so that other peoples may live and be free, the end of "Amerikan economic colonial domination" of the "Third World," and so on. But, I thought, a better answer had been provided by Van Wyck Brooks when he observed that young Americans had the tendency of "attributing to one's own country the faults of human nature in general." In what a tragic context was this being applied in my day!

A standard justification for the proposed violence against the state was that peaceful antiwar protests and marches produced no results. And it is of course true that President Nixon ended the war only after carpet-bombing Hanoi and Haiphong and when he judged that his objective of "peace with honor" was met. The peaceful antiwar protests had little to do with it. As Kenneth L. Hurwitz, once a Harvard organizer of Boston and Washington peace demonstrations, concluded: "The simple fact of the matter was that the 'silent majority' Nixon referred to was an actuality. No matter how many millions we were able to draw to marches and rallies, the population of this country remained two hundred million, and the majority was his." But Hurwitz may have underestimated the seeds planted in the nation's conscience by the nonviolent antiwar movements.

Still, the hard-core proponents of armed action in the United States held fast to their views. I found them expressed in 1971 and even later in letters and interviews in the underground press as well as in conversations with young revolutionaries. When a young woman, Leslie Bacon, was arrested by the FBI in Washington in connection with the March 1971 bombing of the Capitol (she was later released after long months in jail), the Weather Underground wrote her mother claiming responsibility for the attack. The letter, published in the Berkeley *Tribe* and several other underground papers, said that "During the U.S. invasion of Laos, we attacked the very seat of U.S. white arrogance for several reasons: (1) to express our love and solidarity with the non-white people of the world who always happen to be the victims of 200 years of U.S. technological warfare; (2) to freak out the warmongers and remind them that they have created guerrillas here; and (3) to bring a smile and a wink to the kids and people here who hate this government. To spread joy."

The bomber groups called themselves, among other things, the "Proud Eagle Tribe," the "Smiling Fox Tribe," "Quarter Moon Tribe," "The Perfect Park Home Grown Garden Society" (which bombed a National Guard armory in Santa Barbara), "The Orange County International Communist Conspiracy" (which bombed the Stanford Research Institute), and the "Marion Delgado Collective," named after a mythical five-year-old "revolutionary boy" (which bombed the Army Mathematics Research Center at the University of Wisconsin, causing the death of a graduate student). Again, their communiqués were ripe with a

sense of romantic excitement. "Bring the War Home!," ex-
claimed the SDS *New Left Notes.*

Behind the communiqués were the terrorists themselves—a
typical cross section of the American middle class. In the Wisconsin bombings, one of the suspects was a twenty-two-year-old
Madison chemistry student who was a vegetarian and fluent
speaker of Spanish. His nineteen-year-old brother, also involved,
was a tenth-grade dropout who took organic-chemistry classes at
the University of Wisconsin Summer session. Another suspect
came from an affluent Pennsylvania home; he was a journalism
student, a sports writer for the University's *Daily Cardinal,* and
oar on the junior varsity crew. The fourth suspect was eighteen
years old and the graduate of a Delaware Quaker high school. At
the University of Wisconsin, he, too, was on the staff of the *Daily
Cardinal.*

In its 1971 issue on guerrilla war in the United States, *Scanlan's* magazine published a series of interviews with unnamed
revolutionaries which forcefully conveyed the sense of what
these young middle-class Americans were like. A young Washington woman said, "Basically, what I gained out of street actions
was a progressive feeling of coming together with my sisters and
brothers. We never did smash the state, but the streets laid the
foundations to make this possible. . . . We are moving on to urban
guerrilla warfare and a higher consciousness. . . . Our struggle is
one of armed love, and there's nothing contradictory about it.
. . . The culture I identify with comes out of LSD and the whole
hippie thing. Love, sharing. But the fact that most people are cold
and hungry, while a few buy new fur coats and cars, negates the
hippie as a stupid, selfish, bourgeois individual. So flower children carry guns instead of flowers because that's the only way
everybody's gonna eat."

A California youth told of bombing the Valley Junior College
in Los Angeles: "We decided to use Molotov cocktails to indis-

criminately bomb an office in the administration building so someone'd get the message that people are uptight on this campus. . . . Afterwards we realized we were all caught up in this romantic 'let's do it' type of thing. Our main reason for doing it was that if someone had the balls to do it here, people in other places would get the idea they could do it and get away with it."

A San Francisco man in his mid-twenties was described as a "Marxist bomber." This is what he had to say of his activities: "In the short run it's important to move in a revolutionary fashion against the oppressor, both from a position of self-defense and also in an offensive way against an enemy that is oppressing the people in a given situation. In the long run it's a matter of changing the whole system itself—changing capitalism and creating socialism. These various individual acts of revolutionary violence that we see now are only a prelude to what's going to happen. . . . I believe that at some stage a People's Liberation Army will be formed in America. Then it will become clear that it's one set of forces and political ideas versus another set of forces with another set of political ideas."

Being a parent myself, I cannot talk about the youth revolt without talking of parents and their roles in it. As in the case of children, generalizations about parents are misleading and pernicious, but I have listened to more parents than I care to remember over the past years and my principal conclusion is that both "generation gap" and "permissiveness" are, in their current usage, pure hokum.

The generation gap meant in its original sense that parents and children *belonged* to different generations and, therefore, had different interests, outlooks, viewpoints, and senses of values. This is hardly a mid-century American revelation. But the generation gap in the divisive and often hostile connotation used nowadays *is* an invention designed to cover up the misunderstanding between the two, for which the parents are probably more responsible than the kids. My feeling is that the so-called generation gap develops only when parents are unable or unwilling to make the required effort to understand their children's problems, anxieties, and individualities. There is no generation gap in the divisive sense when there is an attempt to understand and, therefore, to tolerate and to remain supportive at critical times. Mutual respect, born from mutual understanding, obviously does not require that the old and the young agree on everything. In fact, I can think of nothing more damaging than parents who pander intellectually or politically to their children, either to keep domestic peace or, even worse, to "get with it" and "stay young." To do so, in most cases, is instantly to lose the respect of children who know better.

This leads me to the myth of permissiveness. The classic complaint I have heard from distraught parents is that so many "other" parents are so "permissive" toward their children "that we can no longer hold the line at home. . . . The pressure is too great. . . . You know how these kids are." In my view, this is a cop-out, or an excuse for one's own inability to cope with children. And it has its own built-in backlash. Kids resent overpermissiveness as a sign of not caring, not being interested. One need not be a child psychologist to comprehend it. In the context of broad youth defiance, with political and cultural overtones, the kids tend to resent not only what they perceive as indifference to what they do, but, even more, to what they *think*. To them it is a form of subtle put-down. A State Department official once told me, "I don't care what my kids do or think so long as they don't get arrested for drugs, get killed, or embarrass us in any way." A long-haired young man said to me at the home of his upper-middle-class parents in a Philadelphia suburb that, "I wish Dad would just once, just once, sit down with me to talk about the things that are important to me. Like the war, you know, and the system. But all he does is hassle me about my hair and call me a 'nutty radical.' He always puts me down. I'm not a radical, I don't think, but *he's* going to make me one."

Men and women who have learned to reason together with other men and women should be able to apply the same patience and give-and-take at home. In our case, I think, and in other cases I know, young people have been known to listen if parents would listen to them. At twenty-four, my daughter is a pleasure to argue with. At seventeen, my son (long-haired and barefoot whenever possible) is a serious and delightfully refreshing questioner of the world around him.

Why, then, the obstacles, the breakdown in communications, the alienation in so many instances? The answers are many, but they include the parents' own sense of being threatened in their institutional and emotional security by the new life styles (always the hair!) and the (often superficial) incendiary talk, along with the young people's frequently irrational resentment of what the parents are, or stand for.

In this contemporary society of ours the parent class has "made it" (I am talking of the reasonably successful families which spawned the protesters) after coming out of the Great Depression and the Second World War. It is, therefore, a more security- and status-minded class than their children can possibly comprehend, and it shies away from experimentation—for itself as well as for its kids. The result, almost inevitably, is that the parents are determined to shelter the children from experiences of life, whatever they may be. Liberals are as guilty of this as conservatives. To the children, these attitudes are a denial of their individual right to inquire, experiment with ideas, dissent from conventional wisdom, and even seek redress for what they see as society's injustices and contradictions.

Then there are the parental hypocrisies. The classical question asked by kids is why it is acceptable for adults to indulge in alcohol but wrong for young people to smoke grass. I do not happen myself to be interested in marijuana, but there is something to be said for their argument. It is odd that parents will be understanding of a son coming home slightly or not so slightly intoxicated on beer or even booze—some parents will be benignly amused by it as a sign of growing up so long as there is no car crash connected with it—but will hit the roof if they smell a whiff of grass. Marijuana is an immensely complex legal, social, and medical issue. Many parents simply take the view that grass is illegal and therefore must not be smoked. But laws in most states are incredibly severe against the use and possession of marijuana, let alone its sale, and the horrors of legal punishment hover over the whole subject. To defy the marijuana laws becomes a "revolutionary act" against a system of which one does not approve.

Here I must come back to alcohol. Young people obviously know that there is no law against being drunk unless one is driving or making a public nuisance of oneself. Most of them have seen their parents, or a parent, in a state of drunkenness. Not, as we all remember, a particularly graceful spectacle. They also know that during Prohibition society regarded the violation of drinking laws with bemused acceptance, and the legal punishment for belting one down was virtually nonexistent. They have read the sagas of bathroom gin and the speakeasies. Why, then, they ask, the opprobrium of grass-smoking? Whereas it is a long-established fact that alcohol is addictive (and that alcoholism is one of the most serious social problems in the United States), most available medical studies suggest that marijuana is neither addictive nor physiologically conducive to hard drugs.

Then there is sex. The United States is undergoing a major

sexual revolution, a freeing of sex mores. But in the midst of this mid-century phenomenon, older people question the younger generation's participation in the sex awakening. Again, we deal with hypocrisies. Young people see the nation's streets filled with bars and restaurants openly advertising topless or nude waitresses and entertainers ("Businessmen's Lunch Specials"), "singles" bars as pick-up places, movie theaters offering sex movies and hard-core pornography, and "massage" parlors fronting for whorehouses. But they are condemned for skinny-dips, nudity in communes, and what they regard, not unreasonably, as free and sometimes beautiful lovemaking. They hear of their parents and parents' friends having lovers and mistresses, of their fathers furtively screwing secretaries and airline hostesses, but they are lectured on the sanctity of clean sex in wedlock.

Double standards practiced in our society on a larger and more public level are even more telling. First, there was the war. How was one to explain, in moral terms, the American involvement in Indochina and, especially, the "turn-them-back-to-the-Stone Age" bombings in 1971 and 1972? Wasn't America a basically decent society that abhors wanton killings? And if so, how could the air war be justified? And why should the kids accept their parents' standards of honesty when they read every day about tax loopholes, (even President Nixon's) tax cheating, and the free entrepreneur's pride in having gulled the public? We try to tell our children—we the tragic middle-class liberals—that we have the best political system in the world because it stands for freedom and equality. I still like to think that this is essentially true. But what, then, is the justification for the dirty political deals, the political espionage, lopsided taxation, the filthy game of campaign contributions, the high-level pay-offs, the sale of political jobs, the phony expense accounts, the accommodations, the compromises, the cheating of consumers, and all the other indecencies associated with our system? In my years in Washington as a newspaper correspondent, I navigated in a sea of secrecy, deceptions, outright lies, and unending political scandal. How was one to explain all these things and still argue for the validity of the system?

If parents could not be trusted, the young people inevitably had to turn to outside gurus. There was Benjamin Spock, the famous baby doctor, leading the antiwar protests. There were Herbert Marcuse, the revolutionary voyeur, and David Dellinger, the aging revolutionary. There were the SDS theoreticians, the black leaders, and the voices from afar: Castro, Ché Guevara, Frantz Fanon, Régis Debray, Ho Chi Minh. . . . Surrogate parents. Contemporaries.

I happen to hold the old-fashioned notion that parents should stand by their children under any and all circumstances—no matter what. Love must be total and not conditional. Loyalty goes all the way and is not negotiable. One of the tragedies of the American youth rebellion—and it was overwhelmingly the tragedy of the parents—was that too often the parents deserted their children in their hour of need—turned their backs when their understanding was vital to the emotional survival of their children, denounced their kids rather than be embarrassed by them, exacted a price for support begrudgingly given at times of trouble.

Among many examples, the one that struck me as the most chilling involved the nineteen-year-old son of New Hampshire's Republican Congressman, Louis Wyman. As I read it in a Washington newspaper, young Wyman was arrested in August 1970, on charges of possessing marijuana "with intent to distribute it," which is a felony. He was held on a $2500 bond at Maryland's Montgomery Detention Center. Congressman Wyman, who has sponsored anti-drug legislation, was at first inclined to let his son stay in jail. But after visiting him at the Detention Center and finding it "overcrowded," Wyman changed his mind and borrowed money from a bank to post bond. But, as he told the news-paper, he said to his son: "I'll give you one chance and give you written conditions. If you break them, I'll put you back in jail." Wyman's written conditions were for his son to "get his hair cut, and short, and now." The boy was ordered to keep himself shaved, see a professional barber every ten days, not wear "hip-pie clothes," go to school, avoid drugs, and stop living in a com-mune. My feeling was that a father had the option of helping his son or not—that was his affair—but he could not negotiate it. Congressman Wyman, however, took the view that since his son was "scared and remorseful," this "will be the turning point, I hope."

Congressman Wyman's preoccupation with long hair—and similar obsessions on the part of other parents—reminded me of a long dissenting opinion by Supreme Court Justice William O. Douglas in a decision against hearing the case of a public-school student who would not conform with regulations on haircuts. Justice Douglas, one of the last nonconformist and original voices on the Supreme Court, had this to say:

"It seems incredible that under our federation a state can deny a student education in its public school system unless his hair style comports with the standards of the school board. Some in-stitutions in Asia require their enrollees to shave their heads. Would we sustain that regulation if imposed by a public school? . . . Hair style is highly personal, an idiosyncracy which I had assumed was left to family or individual control and was of no legitimate concern to the state. It seems to me to be as much a purely private choice as was the family-student decision, sus-tained against a state's prohibition, to study the German lan-guage in school. . . . Opposed there—as in the present case—is the authoritarian philosophy favoring regimentation. . . . One's hair style, like one's taste for food, or one's liking for certain kinds of music, art, reading, recreation, is certainly fundamental in our constitutional scheme—a scheme designed to keep government off the backs of people. . . . I see no way of allowing a state to set hair styles for patrons of its schools, any more than it could establish a welfare system only for men with crew cuts and women with bobbed hair. Once these lines are drawn, a serious question of equal protection of the law is raised."

Justice Douglas then quoted from an earlier Court opinion: "Hairstyles have altered from time to time throughout the ages. Samson's locks symbolically signified his virility. Many of the Founding Fathers of this country wore wigs. President Lincoln grew a beard at the suggestion of a juvenile female admirer. Chief Justice Hughes' beard furnished the model for the frieze over the portico of the Supreme Court of the United States proclaiming 'equal justice under law.' Today many of both the younger and older generations have avoided the increased cost of barbering by allowing their locks or burnsides to grow to greater lengths than when a haircut cost a quarter of a dollar. Whether hair styles be regarded as evidence of conformity or of individuality, they are one of the most visible examples of personality. This is what every woman has always known. And so have many men, without the aid of an anthropologist, behavioral scientist, psychiatrist, or practitioner of any of the fine arts or black arts."

Had Justice Douglas waited long enough, he could have also noted that before he died former President Johnson let his white hair grow to shoulder length, like Buffalo Bill's.

SOCIETY IN AMERICA

Thomas Henry Huxley, the famous English biologist, visited the United States in the latter part of the nineteenth century. A humanist as well as a scientist, Huxley made this judgment of the country:

"There is something sublime in the future of America. Do not suppose that I am pandering to what is commonly understood by national pride. I cannot say that I am in the slightest degree impressed by your bigness, or your material resources, as such. Size is not grandeur, and territory does not make a nation. The great issue, about which hangs a true sublimity, and the terror of overhanging fate, is what are you going to do with all these things?"

A century later, the question of what America is going to do with her immense wealth and resources remains largely uncertain and unanswered. And as I traveled about, I found a sense of unease, malaise, disorientation, and alienation wherever I turned. To some, the American Dream was elusive or altogether lost. To others, it was turning into the American Nightmare. Need it be so? And, above all, why was it so?

A simple and superficial answer to this question might presumably be found in America's overwhelming "bigness," as Huxley put it, and the breathless pace of American growth. A society of more than 215 million people, unless it is entirely regimented from above, on the Chinese or even Soviet model, is bound to develop powerful inner tensions resulting from its own built-in contradictions, its social and economic dislocations and distortions. This is a danger if the nation does not come to terms with itself through self-correcting mechanisms and generally acceptable national policies. A related danger lies in self-imposed regimentation, rigidity, or societal conformity when this is a reaction against sometimes violent pressures for corrective change. Such reactions came from the defenders of the status quo. Watergate, and government strictures against the news media—parallel with a new conservatism in the administration and the Supreme Court—were part of this backlash. And, at the same time, young people were losing interest in causes.

In the 1970s, American society faced both these dangers. Old and new values had not yet been sorted out and, by and large, *all* the generations were caught in a social and political maelstrom. Enormous social and human inequities existed which no one knew how to handle. There were incredible political scandals and astonishing confrontations such as the prolonged and bloody siege at Wounded Knee. With the phony end of the Vietnam war and with the 1973 Mideast conflict, there was a sense that American power in the world was evanescent.

At the same time, America was beginning to discover herself and her root problems. Many of the new cultural patterns were part of a ceaseless American search for identity, self-discovery, and self-fulfillment.

In a very basic and important sense, the 1960s were ten years of extraordinary change in American history and psychology. Demographically, the nation grew by nearly 30 million people between 1960 and 1970, reaching over 208 million by the end of the decade and 216 million at the start of 1974, if the Census Bureau's latest estimated figures were correct. (Actually, the Bureau originally estimated the 1970 total at over 203 million, but later volunteered that it had "overlooked" more than five million Americans for reasons that in themselves told a great deal about the new society. Thus, the Bureau found "increased resistance to Census takers because of changing life styles and more alienation and distrust of authority"; "the existence of a number of organized attempts to protest the Census as an invasion of privacy"; and "the reluctance of some Census takers to work, especially at night, in some urban areas." The so-called undercount of blacks was 7.7 per cent, with wide and inexplicable undercounts of children under the age of ten, and of whites 1.9 per cent.) There were so many of us that a Census expert told me, "Oh, hell, give or take a million," when I pressed him for precise figures. The increase during the 1960s was roughly the same as the population growth in the preceding decade, but by the late years of the decade the nation was already instinctively aiming at a demographic "zero growth," in contrast with the record annual net gain of 3.1 million in 1956. In other words, in the relatively short span of twenty years the number of Americans had risen by well over 25 per cent. Put another way, the population had jumped by some 70 million between the time my daughter was born in 1950 and 1974, as this book was written. Put still another way, the American population doubled in the last fifty years.

Small wonder, then, that we felt cramped and crowded. In city after city I visited the sight was the same: ghastly traffic jams in the streets and on the freeways leading to the suburbs; overcrowded dwellings; packed stores and offices—in short, no elbow room. Basic services were breaking down, and the famous quality of the American product was rushing downhill. The mail service, so long the pride of America, was desperately malfunctioning; letters between, say, New York and Washington could take as long as three days to be delivered. Same-day Delivery was a forgotten legend. Computers could no longer cope with their load, and neither government nor private industry could therefore be quite sure what they were doing from day to day. Nobody seemed to have the time or desire to do anything well: assembly-line workers whose products had to be recalled by the million (eight million cars, three-quarters of all new American-made cars sold in 1972, were recalled because of mechanical defects); auto mechanics, split between incompetents and rip-off artists;

contractors overcharging for shoddy work; sloppy electricians, plumbers, and TV repairmen. Americans were victimizing themselves. And, to compound the demographic and service burdens, Americans by the millions were on the move as they had been since mid-century—from the countryside areas to the cities, from the cities to the suburbs, and from inland states to the East and West coasts.

Suddenly, too, the United States was short of fuel—oil, gasoline, and natural gas. Long years of government mismanagement of complex petroleum policies—a delicate balancing act between the regulation of imports from overseas sources and dependence on domestic production—combined with the greed of the oil companies to turn the United States, almost overnight, into a "helpless giant." The threat of shortages loomed for years, but only when Arab producers, using their oil as a "weapon" in the Mideast conflict late in 1973, embargoed most shipments to this country (because of our support of Israel) did we realize with bewilderment—and we panicked over it—that we were no longer self-sufficient. Never mind that this could have been avoided had the White House paid heed to warnings almost five years earlier that our energy needs exceeded domestic production, that we should have imported more oil regardless of the opposition of the oil-industry giants and forced the companies to build more refineries at home. With oil companies' profits soaring during 1973, the sudden shortages became an extraordinary illustration of corporate greed and short-sightedness—abetted by the Nixon White House. Even in the midst of the emergency, the White House successfully fought legislation imposing special taxes on the companies' "windfall" profits as prices began to skyrocket.

The energy crisis also served to demonstrate how much the American economy depends on oil, and how a permanent shortage might destabilize it and force a new life style on the nation. We took it for granted in this land of plenty that there would

always be enough of everything, so it never occurred to us to
what degree we were prisoners of petroleum. Because we had oil,
we kept building more and more superhighways for more and
more big cars burning more and more gasoline. We skimped on
mass transit and car pools—the guiding principle was "one man,
one car"—and allowed the destruction of our rail network. But,
by early 1974, shortages, and the fights at the pumps, and gasless
Sundays drastically cut down American car travel; airlines lost
a percentage of their fuel allocation, curtailing flights and laying
off personnel.

More than ten thousand gasoline stations went out of business
during 1973. Detroit laid off at least a hundred thousand workers,
as it reduced big-car production and began retooling for smaller
vehicles. Heating oil became scarce and industries across the
board started worrying about fuels they needed for full-fledged
operations. The stock market took its worst plunge in years. Government economists talked of depressionlike unemployment.
Resorts, hotels, motels, restaurants, and all roadside businesses
dependent on auto travel were deeply affected. Pharmaceutical,
petrochemical, and plastic industries (even toy makers) requiring petroleum by-products found themselves in trouble. And the
rising prices of imported crude—quadrupled during 1973—
raised the issue of whether the poor could afford to drive for
either work or pleasure. The era of cheap energy was over for
good, and the urgent question was how the nation would readjust
to the new situation. The cities, meanwhile, experienced electric
power and water shortages at peak-use periods. Meat was in
short supply, so were tomatoes and onions, newsprint and toilet
paper. The country also ran dangerously low on its blood-bank
reserves—voluntary donors seemed to vanish or could no longer
meet the demand. The price of blood went up in the blood market
(yes, there is such a ghoulish thing in America), but merchants
who advertised in newspapers for donors and bought it from the

needy at standard prices simply increased their profits. Donors were paid between $5 and $10 a pint of whole blood—the higher figure in the morning when hospital demand was at peak and the lower figure in the afternoon. In San Francisco's Mission district, poor people picketed a commercial blood bank, claiming that they were being exploited. A blood-smuggling business from Haiti, our hemisphere's poorest country, thrived for a while.

The essential dilemma in the 1970s was therefore how to provide for the population in general and how to absorb 70 million additional restless people since 1950, plus 20 million expected to be added to the rolls by the end of the decade. (The National Institute of Child Health and Human Development predicted that an upturn in the American fertility rate was likely to occur late in the 1970s. The Institute based this projection on the fact that the American woman of the 1970s seemed to prefer to wait longer than her mother to have children, a changed pattern made possible by modern contraception techniques. Thus fertility, according to the Institute, may rise again before the 1980s. If true, our demographic problem will soon become even worse.) People born in the early 1950s were entering the labor market. And proper care was needed for those born in the 1960s so that they could enter the 1980s, just around the corner, as reasonably well adjusted and prepared citizens.

Total annual production in the United States, an index of the overall wealth, was calculated in gross national product (GNP) at a record $1.2 trillion during 1973, nearly a 2 per cent jump in a year. The national budget stood in 1973 at an unprecedented $250 billion. The Dow-Jones industrial average, reflecting the value of shares on the stock market, broke once through the magic barrier of 1000 points before the 1973 cave-in. Because the personal incomes and purchasing power of many Americans were rising steadily, inflation notwithstanding, they were able to buy in 1973 about 12 million new cars, over 3 million new trucks, and untold millions of used cars. Consumers were in debt for over $158 billion on their installment purchases, exclusive of home mortgages. This meant that each of the 128 million Americans over the age of nineteen (one presumes that very few people under nineteen were able to buy things on time) was responsible for an average of $1230 in outstanding consumer credit. (This average figure is misleading, of course, because low-income groups are generally cut off from consumer credit. It is impossible to work out precisely the real average of consumer credit, but the per capita figure for middle- and upper-income groups would obviously be much higher than $1230. The citizen who bought, for example, a $4000 car and a $500 color TV set on credit, plus some other minor items, was burdened with some $5000 in installment debt. I know plenty of families whose credit indebtedness was even higher, which is presumably why so many Americans are broke despite relatively high revenues.) Americans held 70 million credit cards of every description—something of a status symbol. With home mortgages, the total debt of Americans in 1973 was around $725 billion. Overall consumer spending in 1972 had been $750 billion, although it slowed down in 1973. In a credit-oriented economy, this certainly looked like real prosperity.

Digging a bit deeper, however, American reality also turned out to be disturbingly lopsided in the distribution of income and wealth. The distortions rendered meaningless the old-fashioned yardstick of per capita GNP income ($14,500 annually) because most of the population did not participate to this high degree in the GNP formation. (By the same token, per capita GNP figures in, say, Saudi Arabia, Kuwait, or Venezuela mean absolutely nothing because the billions of dollars in oil revenue do not trickle down to the population at large.)

The 1970 survey of the Census Bureau drew this profile of the

American society: Out of nearly 52 million American families (a family is statistically composed of four persons), 3.5 million were in the median-income bracket of $9590 annually. Thus, half of all American families had an income above this amount and the other half below it—a more comprehensive way of reflecting real incomes than the GNP per capita calculation. The median figure rose to $11,120 in 1972, but, simultaneously, the poor got poorer.

This commendably high median level went far to explain why so many Americans appeared as comfortable home owners who could buy 12 million new cars in 1973 and go into debt for $158 billion. The appearance of prosperity was further reinforced by statistics that over eight million families took in $15,000–$25,000 in 1970 (the last year for which complete figures were available when I undertook my investigation), two million between $25,000 and $50,000, and 400,000 families showed incomes of $50,000 or more. Of course, there were several thousand millionaires, even a few black millionaires.

The income of top corporate executives was astronomic. The highest-paid man in the United States in 1972 was Henry Ford II, chairman of the Ford Motor Company, who received $264,567 in salary and $610,000 in bonuses for a total remuneration of $874,567. I would imagine he also had a decent expense account. Lee A. Iacocca, Ford's president, was a close second with $861,290 in salary and bonuses. Harold S. Geneen, chairman of the board of the International Telephone and Telegraph Company, was third with $813,311. In 1973, Richard C. Gerstenberg, chairman of the board of General Motors, jumped to the lead with $923,000. I have no idea how Messrs. Gerstenberg, Ford, Iacocca, and Geneen made out with their tax returns. But it is interesting that the nation paid the President of the United States only $200,000 annually (plus a $50,000 expense account), less than a quarter of what great corporations paid their top men. Of course, Mr. Nixon does not have to pay rent on the White House; travels free of charge aboard Air Force One, on military helicopters, and in presidential limousines; had $10 million's worth of improvements made on his private homes; and enjoys a representation allowance. Because of illegal deductions, however, the President paid less than $1000 in federal taxes in 1970 and 1971, roughly the amount paid by a $15,000 wage earner. Later, he was made to pay about $450,000 in back taxes.

But the obverse of this seemingly rosy state of affairs was that nearly 23 million families (about 100 million Americans) had incomes below the median line. And it was the breakdown of incomes in this group that revealed how much of the touted American prosperity was illusory. In the first place, 5.2 million families earned incomes below the official poverty line (raised in 1973 to $4137 annually), although welfare and social-security payments helped to raise their real revenues in many instances by a few thousand dollars. About 1.5 million (or almost a third) of them were black families, and almost 1.3 million of them earned *less than $1000 a year,* which is not quite $3 a day to cover housing, food, clothing, and everything else for four people.

To these totals of below-the-poverty-line families must be added over 12 million individuals usually living alone and statistically known as "unrelated." With these added, one arrives at the figure of 25.6 million Americans under the poverty levels in 1973, taking into consideration the fact that a certain percentage of individuals lived some of the time as members of families. And we should remember that in 1973 the minimum legal hourly wage was only $1.60.

What does all this mean in terms of basic expenditures and daily necessities? As far back as 1967, when life was considerably cheaper, the Bureau of Labor Statistics set $6000 as the "minimum urban-family budget." And early in 1973, the Community Council of Greater New York estimated that a family of four needed $11,880 "to live at a moderate level." (The Agriculture

Department estimated that a family of 3.2 persons needed $1458 annually *for food alone.*) This was before the annual inflation rate hit 8 per cent. At that point, the average earnings of a New York City factory worker were $8320.

There are, obviously, many ways of looking at the additional statistics which reveal the relative impoverishment of minority groups. Such analysts as Ben Wattenberg and Richard Scammon chose to emphasize the positive by noting that between 1960 and 1970 incomes for black families virtually doubled—which is accurate statistically—while white families' incomes rose by almost 70 per cent, and stressing that nearly one-third of all black families earned over $10,000. From this they concluded that more than half of black America had entered the middle class. But aside from the difficulty of defining just where poverty ends and middle-class status begins, this type of analysis overlooks the fact that the number of blacks on welfare has almost quadrupled in the last decade and that most of them remain at society's lowest levels. It is still premature to talk of "revolutionary" social breakthroughs for this racial group.

A special report issued by the Census Bureau late in 1973 demonstrated how the poor are getting poorer despite the overall statistical increase in living standards suggested by the higher median incomes. Notwithstanding earlier optimistic data interpretations by Wattenberg and Scammon, the Bureau concluded that the number of poor black families and poor families headed by women had gone up between 1971 and 1972. Poverty families headed by women were the worst off: the Bureau said that their proportion in the poor population rose from 23 per cent in 1959 to 43 per cent in 1972.

In general, the distribution of wealth in the United States was even more imbalanced than the distribution of incomes—in a way, the result of a geometric progression over time in the inequality of income. Edwin Kuh, a professor of economics at the Massachusetts Institute of Technology, has written, "The richest ten per cent of the population receive 29 per cent of personal income but *own* 56 per cent of the national wealth, while the poorest ten per cent receive one per cent of the income and are in debt to boot." Professor Kuh claims that "at the top of the wealth distribution, one per cent of the wealth-holders own 25 per cent of physical and financial wealth. Among those with incomes in excess of $100,000, inherited wealth amounts to 57 per cent of total assets."

And this enormous disparity in wealth distribution—with the rich becoming richer and the poor becoming more and more numerous—was aggravated by glaring inequities in the tax system. The burden of paying income taxes fell on the poor and the middle class, while Americans with high revenues were increasingly protected from the tax collector. Former Treasury Assistant Secretary for Tax Policy Stanley S. Surrey has estimated that the actual tax rate for individuals with incomes above $100,000 annually was between 29 and 33 per cent although it should have been 45 per cent under the existing federal income-tax schedule. He also found that some Americans with incomes over $200,000 paid no personal tax at all (this was true of 276 individuals in 1972) and others only around 10 per cent. Senator Edward M. Kennedy has calculated that the 3000 American families with annual incomes over $1 million pay less than 30 per cent in taxes. In other words, those who had capital to invest in tax-shelter ventures—or claimed Nixon-type deductions—received tax breaks bringing their taxes to a bare minimum, while those who earned just enough to keep body and soul together had to pay the full-schedule rate. Plain tax evasions were rampant among the very rich. So the poor, in effect, paid for their poverty and subsidized the rich. The Treasury estimated that tax shelters deprived it of $1 billion annually in income taxes. In general terms, half of 1972 tax collections came from the poor and the other half from the rich.

The example of this sort of inequity I know best from personal experience concerns tax deduction on mortgage interest because I own my house in Washington (in partnership with my bank, which collects the mortgage and the interest) and have benefited from it. The national median monthly apartment rent in the United States in 1970 was $108 (for a two- or three-room apartment), while my monthly mortgage payment for a twelve-room house with a finished basement, two kitchens, four bathrooms, a large garden in the back, and a lawn and driveway in front was only $339, including interest. Had I been renting it, the price would have easily been $600. Dwellers in America's 15 million rental households received no tax deduction on their rents, but I, like millions of other home owners, both acquired equity in my house from monthly payments and received a tax credit for the interest portion. This provision was written in the law many years ago to encourage home owning, a commendable idea, but like so many other things in this vast country it soon became socially damaging. Current estimates are that the tax credit on mortgage-interest payments is depriving the government of $7 billion annually in potential tax. It is beyond calculation how much developers, builders, and contractors have made over the years from the tax-subsidized building boom, but it certainly was a bonanza. And they too had tax advantages resulting from "shelters" available in the construction industry. There were shelters in gas and oil and stock-breeding, too. In the absence of an equitable tax reform, it appeared odd that President Nixon took the view in 1973 that taxes would have to be raised for the average American if the nation wanted to maintain social programs for the poor.

Another example of wealth disparity was the situation in American universities. In 1973, it cost nearly $6000 annually to send a child to Harvard or Yale—this was tuition, room, board, books, and extras. Parents with two or three children of college age thus hardly could afford it even if they earned $30,000, although this would make them ineligible for financial aid. So the middle class was being pushed out of the colleges. William W. Jellema, an official of the Association of American Colleges, warned that the way things were going, American colleges would soon be split into two elites: the very rich, who could afford the ever-rising costs, and the very poor, who got scholarships and other forms of assistance.

This grotesque disparity of incomes and its consequences provided an ironic touch to the dispute that raged in 1973 over the ethics of welfare programs for the poor.

Much of the public argument, both before and after Congress rejected in 1972 President Nixon's Family Assistance Plan (FAP), was over the welfare aspects of poverty. FAP might have put some order in the "welfare mess," which was quite real, but complex Washington politics succeeded in killing it. In 1973, Nixon dismantled much of the welfare bureaucratic apparatus on grounds that under his "New Federalism" public assistance would be better administered by local governments through revenue sharing and the direct injections of federal funds. This quickly became a mere invitation to local politicians, instead of the federal bureaucracy, to play the tragic welfare game with vastly reduced funds. Regrettably, it left unresolved the basic question of whether poor people really stop being poor when welfare in its many forms affords them the magic "guaranteed income" of around $6000 a year. (This total supposedly should represent earned income plus the welfare supplements.) And the philosophical battle continued over the degree to which this supplement may or may not discourage poor people from seeking work, or extra work, inasmuch as, in the words of rigid conservatives, "it's easier to be supported than to work." Few social scientists familiar with patterns of poverty accepted this facile claim, stressing that welfare had built-in limits and that if reasonably well paying jobs were available, most of the poor would reach out for them in hopes of doing better than the $6000 ceiling.

I thought it was absurd to argue, as many people began doing after the 1970 Census data was published, that too many Americans had been listed as being under the poverty line. (This argument ran that by adding such welfare benefits as food stamps, social security, Medicaid, and Medicare to a family's earned cash income, millions of them would be raised *above* the poverty line.) Such a bookkeeping switch would make the administration, and American society in general, look better. It would also tend to sweep the poverty problem under the carpet, as the new statistics would show a generally prosperous America. (In fact, the Nixon administration ordered the Census Bureau in 1973 to drop the word poverty in favor of the euphemism "low-income level.") Mollie Orshansky, a leading government expert on poverty statistics, evidently had some skepticism over this proposed reshuffling of the figures when she commented, "The inclusion of all the free medical care and the food stamps received by the poor and of all the benefits that go to the middle class, including health insurance benefits, expense accounts, vacations, free tuition, and commodity discounts, would hardly change the result; now money income, like income tax benefits, would go mainly to the nonpoor. The full effect of incorporating these benefits into the income distribution, if we were honest, might be to skew it even more than now, and since poverty is relative, the poverty line would have to be moved up."

This was another way of saying that if statisticians were to remain honest, they would have to upgrade the incomes of the middle class as well. The obvious result would be that all income levels would have to be jacked up and in the end would become meaningless—except that the statistics would make American society *appear* richer. Other experts made the point that the reduction of the number of Americans under the poverty line from 40 million in 1960 to some 24 million in 1968 (before it soared again to 25.6 million in 1973) was also essentially a matter of manipulating arbitrary statistics—the usual government shell game. Inflation, too, had to be considered to make the dollar figures meaningful in purchasing power. In 1973, inflation was running at an unprecedented 15-per-cent annual rate.

Clearly, the poor will not cease being poor simply by being reclassified in the statistical tables. I cannot quite conceive a situation in which, say, a San Antonio or South Bronx slum dweller is cavalierly informed that as far as the government is concerned he is no longer poor. What is he supposed to answer? Whatever the arguments over the precise meaning of the poverty line, human misery in America remains a reality.

The worst poverty was in the South, despite its rapid modernization. Black families' median income in the South was $4936 in 1969, while white families had $8721—Mississippi and Arkansas were in the forefront here. Almost exactly half of all American families below the poverty line inhabited the sixteen southern states and the District of Columbia, and nearly half of the families with incomes of less than $1000. The bulk of the southern poor, of course, were black. Most of them festered away in the new southern urban slums: New Orleans, Memphis, Little Rock, Atlanta, Baltimore, Washington, Jacksonville, and so on.

There has been no visible change in the poverty status of these families since the Census Bureau took its decennial look at America in 1970. Given the social immobility of poverty families —the closed circuit of the poverty culture—there was no reason to hope seriously that the new poor Americans born in the 1960s and 1970s would break out of the poverty pattern in a meaningful way. The American economy is so structured that, in relative terms, high-wage jobs are unlikely to become more plentiful and poverty wages to start vanishing. This has been the track record for decades, especially for blacks. In the words of a Washington sociologist, children of the poor "are in a chronic, static condition of dependency from generation to generation." Thus the accretion in population is bound to increase the absolute number of the poor. And the new unemployment resulting from the energy crisis will be an aggravating factor.

Housing offers a particularly striking point in talking about the demographic explosion and poverty. Although birth rates have been diminishing since the mid-1960s, the high fertility of the late 1940s and the 1950s planted a time bomb ready to explode in the 1970s. This time bomb is called "household formation," which happens when individuals reach maturity and form families, thus requiring additional housing. Specialists have estimated that while the annual rate of household formations in the early 1960s was only 890,000 (birth rates were low in the late 1930s and during the war), it was soaring to 1,340,000 in the early 1970s with the arrival on the housing scene of those born twenty-odd years earlier. This is why, when the Housing and Urban Development Act was passed by Congress in 1968, government planners were projecting the need to build or rehabilitate 26 million dwelling units between 1969 and 1978, 20 million of them through private industry. Of this total, 13.5 million units were to serve net household formation. Five years later, it was obvious that this objective could not possibly be reached—particularly in low-cost housing. The Nixon administration's freeze in 1973 on federal housing funds and the parallel disappearance of mortgage money from the market made the outlook even bleaker.

Traveling around the country, I saw over the years the fantastic construction boom in suburbia and the impressive renovation of downtown business districts. Tens of thousands of new homes were rising around the cities from coast to coast to accommodate well-off Americans. Manhattan's great avenues—Park, Madison, Third, Fifth, and Sixth (which is officially known as the Avenue of the Americas)—were beautified with gleaming new edifices. Other cities were expensively renovating their downtown districts with skyscrapers and pedestrian malls. But where were inexpensive houses for the low-income families? Private builders were not interested in this sort of investment. Existing housing was decaying at an alarming rate—around ten million units were considered dilapidated or deteriorating.

A recent study by the Joint Center for Urban Studies of the Massachusetts Institute of Technology and Harvard University noted that only 20 per cent of urban housing is of "pleasantly good" status or better; less than half of the so-called working-class population (earning $7800–$11,900 per household) can afford "standard-comfortable" housing; the others must settle for "standard-marginal" homes. "To be less well-housed, and to be of an age and family stage at which one has children in school, is to risk being identified as below working-class average in community standing. . . . To be no better housed than in a 'standard-marginal unit' almost always leaves a working-class family vaguely dissatisfied." Only a very small portion of Americans with middle-class incomes have homes identified as "very good" in the upper-middle-class sense—and less than 13 per cent of us are classified by the Center as "upper middle class." To sum up: "The dynamics of our stratified society are such that increasing affluence leads people to raise their standards about what they expect from housing. Each class moves a bit higher in its aspirations, retaining its edge over the group beneath. The lower class remains at the bottom, although raising its sights a bit too."

President Johnson's War on Poverty addressed itself to the stark issue of being poor by trying to upgrade government programs in housing, welfare, and ancillary fields, as well as by making efforts to eradicate the causes of poverty through training, retraining, and job-placement programs. It put a lot of money into education and quite a bit into public housing. But this war of the "Great Society" was not won, and even its advances were limited. In the 1970s, then, poverty (and its dreadful social consequences) continued to hover over the United States like a menacing dark cloud. Yet the earlier recognition that poverty *did* exist in the United States (I remember President Kennedy's understatement in 1960 that every night seven million Americans went to bed hungry) had been a psychological watershed, and, subtly, it resulted in a new sense of class consciousness—even planting the seeds of class conflict—for the first time since the Great Depression.

It became plain that the cherished notion that America was an infinitely rich land of infinite opportunity was rapidly evaporating. As I traveled around the country, the young people I met— high-school or college graduates or dropouts—no longer had the high hopes and expectations of earlier American generations. Rich or poor, they were on the whole cynical and prematurely disenchanted about life. I was struck by how many students simply had no notion of what they proposed to do with themselves after graduation, if they stayed around long enough to graduate. At a graduate school near Boston, students at a seminar just shrugged their shoulders when I asked them what plans they had for the future. "I think I'll travel for a year, or something," was the stock answer. Interestingly, the only one out of a group of twenty men and women in this particular seminar who knew precisely what he wanted was a black candidate for a master's degree. Three months before graduation, he had already secured a job as a television newsman, a career in which he had an abiding interest.

American attitudes change faster than one can record them, and I tend to be skeptical about surveys, especially when they cover a period already belonging to the past. Nevertheless, I was interested in a study by the American Council on Education issued early in 1973 and addressing itself to student attitudes as they changed from 1967 to 1971. The Council researchers, who first interviewed the students when they entered college and then again when they graduated, concluded that during the four years in school the most notable change in their outlook was that they lost to an important extent their earlier interest in succeeding financially and in business. Of the 1967 freshmen, 43.5 per cent emphasized the importance of financial success, but only 29.8 per cent of the 1971 seniors thought so; on succeeding in business, the drop was from 46.4 per cent to 29.4 per cent. These data, however, need the qualification that 1967–71 was the high point of the youth rebellion when material values were being loudly rejected. I would be curious to know what seniors in 1974 had to say about it.

Although the quality of life of the middle class (these students' parents) remained ostensibly high in the 1970s—it went on buying, usually on time payments, record numbers of homes, cars, color television and stereo sets, and just about everything industry turned out, as well as spending heavily on recreation—the inflation and the brutal jump in food prices began to push middle-income families against the financial wall. A hostile sense of class consciousness thus expanded from the bottom level of American society to the middle sector. Driving one rainy spring day through the lovely Chestnut Hill section of Philadelphia, a cab driver said angrily to me: "This is where the rich people live. I live on the edge of the slum." He spat out of the car window. In Chicago, a middle-aged office worker told me with great bitterness about "all these bastards who can afford to live on Lake Shore." And this attitude coexisted with a continuing American Dream of making money and joining the leisured classes. During the 1972 election campaign, a friend of mine running for reelection to Congress told me of a conversation with an elderly woman in a blue-collar district.

"I won't vote for you if you support George McGovern," the woman said. My friend asked her why. "Well," she answered, "you've gotta look at me. I am a widow and I've worked for years down on my knees scrubbing floors so that my boy could go to college. I won't leave him anything when I die. But if Pete, that's my boy, gets a good job and makes money, I want him to be able to leave something for his children so that they can have an easier time than he did. Now this fellow McGovern wants to pass laws against inheriting money. He is against the American Dream!"

After I recounted this story to a sociologist of my acquaintance, he nodded knowingly. "This is an extraordinary country," he said. "No matter how much Americans complain about their lot —and with more and more reason—they still aspire to rise from rags to riches themselves or, at least, their children. But it's each man for himself. I know this sounds corny, but Horatio Alger is still America's greatest hero. Christ, what does this mentality do to the society as a whole? How do we give *everybody* a decent break instead of just making room for the Horatio Algers?"

During the Republican National Convention in 1972, my wife and I watched television shots of private jets and yachts bringing millionaire supporters of the President to Miami Beach. I made a comment to the effect that this display of riches was certain to antagonize lots of poor people in this country and even those who barely make ends meet. My wife, a child of the Great Depression, shook her head. "No," she said, "you're wrong. It's much more complicated. In a way, people do resent this sort of thing, but, on the other hand, they admire it and identify with it, and hope for the same things for themselves, even if it is a dream they know will never come true. That may be a contradiction, but it's the way people are."

A black educator I know in San Francisco made a roughly similar point talking about the ghettos. Deploring "black movies" because some of them tend to glorify easy money and illegal ways of making it, he went on to say, "But you must look at it as a cultural phenomenon. The people in the ghettos are miserably poor, destitute, but whom do they admire and try to imitate? The cool cat who made it somehow—and you can be sure it was not from the sweat of his brow—and now he drives his new Cadillac and flashes his mod clothes and rings. He may be a narcotics peddler or he may run a numbers racket, but this is no stigma in the ghetto culture and you have no idea how many kids want to be just like him."

I spent a long evening discussing poverty and non-affluence with a sociologist who had just completed an in-depth study of the American labor force. His meticulous research brought him into contact with poor whites and blacks as well as with equally discontented white- and blue-collar workers.

"One myth we can lay to rest right away," he said, "is that the only overwhelming American social problem is racial. Sure, racial problems exist. It's probably getting even worse because society hasn't caught up with the new aspirations and improved education of the minorities. So we have something of a revolution of rising expectations.

"But the class problem is infinitely more serious. It affects all races. It is the result of deepening economic and social inequality —you know, the disparity between the blue-collar worker who may be lucky enough to take home $150 or a little more a week and the folks in the suburbs who live in $50,000 or $75,000 houses and have all these fantastic expense accounts and tax breaks we read about. Then, there is the hostility toward the huge corporation which has us at its mercy—it may lay you off any time—and, on top of that, flaunts in your face its cozy tax havens, executive jets, and plush offices. These days, you must remember, the guy in the South Bronx or Gary, Indiana, or Oakland, California, whether he reads about all this, sees it in the movies and on television. Naturally, he gets bitter about the corporation and its bosses when he compares it to his own reality of the tight budget and installment-plan payments on his car or TV set.

"Among ourselves," the sociologist said, "we have coined the expression that the problem we really face is 'the collar, not the color,' or, if you prefer, 'the color of the collar.' This is because the disparity in incomes affects the poor whites just as badly as the poor blacks. Statistically, we find that there are more white than black 'working poor.' And you have the battered middle class, whose aspirations exceed their means. So what happens is the beginning of class resentment, if not yet conflict. And, in part, this is why you have so much work absenteeism, alcoholism, drug abuse, and industrial sabotage. It's the pent-up anger."

My sociologist friend remarked that after publishing a report which made all these points, he had been accused in print of "Marxist tendencies" because of his emphasis on the renascent class conflict. "That's nonsense," he said angrily. "I was not engaging in Marxist analysis or dialectics—I'm not even ideologically motivated—but in analyzing present-day American realities. I think this country will be in bad trouble if people refuse to face these realities and, instead, try to dispose of them by tarring with a Marxist or communist brush anyone who calls attention to the very serious problems in our society. It makes me really mad!"

When the energy crisis erupted late in 1973, the potentials for heightened class conflict were quickly discernible. Thousands of truckers, angered by fuel shortages and the sudden rise in prices, blocked the country's main highways, defying the police and the National Guard. This time, we saw helmeted lawmen facing the burly truckers as, not so long ago, we had seen them facing the rebel youth. It was a technological version of a classical bread riot and, interestingly, quite a few drivers were mustached young men who, generationally, belonged to the fighting breed of the late 1960s. These truckers' episodes, it seemed to me, made the fundamental point, not yet fully perceived in American politics, that class self-interest automatically overrides more abstract allegiances. Studs Terkel put his finger on it in a recent article when he wrote of the truckers, "They're conservative. They were heavily in favor of Nixon and law and order and especially keeping the blacks in their place. I'd say they voted for Nixon 90 per cent and now they see the thing has come back to haunt them. They see the Administration they voted in has betrayed them. They see they voted against their own interests. They see that this thing boomeranged. It didn't only hurt the blacks and the so-called guy who didn't want to work—the welfare cheat and the hippie university student—it hurt *them.*"

The same syndrome of class resentment appeared in a special survey published in December 1973 by pollster Louis Harris, who found that "for the first time in nearly a decade . . . a new majority of disaffected Americans exists in this country." Harris' poll, conducted for the Senate Committee on Governmental Operations, said that 55 per cent of the public are disenchanted with the way things are in America as compared with 29 per cent in 1966. Even more to the point, Harris reported that in 1973, 76 per cent felt that the "rich get richer and poor get poorer," 74 per cent thought that "the tax laws are written to help the rich, not the average man," 74 per cent believed that "special interests get more from the government than the people do," and 55 per cent said that "people running the country don't really care what happens to you."

The pattern of wildcat strikes all over the country in the 1970s suggested a new labor militancy along class lines. AFL-CIO, which is Establishment, no longer held absolute control of organized labor. And predictions of class strife came from the Right and the Left. James A. Michener, the author, said in a recent interview that he found hostility to the "elite" is a "very strong attitude" and will grow among urban ethnics. He also expressed concern "about the possible consequences of class cleavage as a result of Vietnam." Robert Cherry, a young Marxist economist, wrote in *The Review of Radical Political Economics* that in the context of the re-emerging class struggle in America, "industrial workers—by witholding their labor power, they can withhold profits from the capitalists—are in a strategic position."

Class cleavage, of course, has a long and rich tradition in the United States, something that is often forgotten in our affluent society. It goes back to the bloody labor militancy straddling the latter part of the nineteenth century and the opening decades of this century. There is the history of the anarchist movement, the Wobblies, and the labor radicalization of the Great Depression. I found it interesting that at labor meetings there is increased talk of such legendary figures as Joe Hill, Tom Mooney, and Sacco and Vanzetti. So the new militancy feeds on old traditions. The feared recession of the mid-1970s may turn into a major test of renascent class conflict.

In March 1973 the Supreme Court rendered a decision affirming the constitutionality of the states' financing public schools in part from local property taxes. This was a landmark decision because, whether the Court intended it or not, the ruling had the effect of institutionalizing the American division between affluence and poverty. Thus it also carried seeds of class antagonisms. In practice, the decision meant that poor neighborhoods, where real-estate taxes are low, cannot expect to share in the school-tax money provided by wealthier districts and therefore must be satisfied with inferior educational facilities. (The suit which resulted in the Court's opinion was brought, not surprisingly, by a group of Mexican-American families in the Chicano slum district of Edgewood in San Antonio, Texas, where the median family income in 1969 was under $3500, below the poverty level, as compared with the $8490 median family income for the whole state of Texas. Edgewood could raise only $21 per pupil from its property taxes whereas Alamo Heights, a wealthy nearby district, could raise $307.) The decision, rendered by the Court's conservative majority, represented as much of a pronouncement on social philosophy as on constitutional law. It perpetuated the ghetto culture of poverty, that awesome vicious circle affecting the trapped American poor, and effectively denied the Edgewood children (and children of the poor everywhere in America) the equality of opportunity which is supposed to be the hallmark of the American Dream.

In a dissenting opinion, Justice Thurgood Marshall, supported by Justice William O. Douglas, made this crucial point, when he wrote that the existing system upheld by the Court is a "scheme which arbitrarily channels educational resources in accordance with the fortuity of the amount of taxable wealth within each district." He went on: "The right of every American to an equal start in life, so far as the provision of a state service as important as education is concerned, is far too vital to permit state discrimination. . . . Nor can I accept the notion that it is sufficient to remit these appellees to the vagaries of the political process which, contrary to the majority's suggestion, has proven singularly unsuited to the task of providing a remedy for this discrimination. I, for one, am unsatisfied with the hope of an ultimate 'political' solution sometime in the indefinite future while, in the meantime, countless children unjustifiably receive inferior educations that 'may affect their hearts and minds in a way unlikely ever to be undone.' "

The public high school which my son Tony attended in Washington could afford to pay teachers around $12,000 a year and to provide adequate classroom and other facilities because our district is relatively affluent. But in Edgewood and in other thousands of America's 93,000 elementary and high schools, teachers were woefully underpaid, and, as I saw in city after city, basic facilities simply nonexistent. Inevitably, schools in poor districts could afford fewer teachers than they needed—yet the country has a surplus of 75,000 teachers—and those they had were often inferior. (This, incidentally, was one of the major complaints of the Edgewood parents who brought the suit: they were alarmed by the low caliber of those who taught their children.) The Nixon administration's cuts in federal aid to education—one of the manifestations of its social philosophy—forced the dismissal of thousands of highly qualified teachers and teacher-substitutes. (A case in point I know personally was the firing of my sister-in-law, a teacher of advanced English with a master's degree in education, from a high school in Croton-on-Hudson, a fairly affluent village in New York's Westchester County, ranked in 1970 as the nation's seventh-richest county. She was fired along with several other teachers after federal funds dried up; keen to work, as so many suburban wives are nowadays, she wasted for a while her educational talents in the employ of a big corporation.)

The Nixon cutback in school funds also meant that fewer books can be purchased for the students. A New York publisher of juvenile books told me early in 1973 that the fund freeze was reducing sales to schools somewhere between 20 and 40 per cent. And, as I discovered earlier, the richer the school districts, the less willing are the parents to approve public-education bonds to get better schools and teachers and more books. This was brought home to me forcefully not long ago when I visited several public schools around fashionable McLean, Virginia, a Washington suburb, and found them without heat or usable bathrooms. Fairfax County was the county that refused to approve school bonds in 1970, but finally changed its mind three years later.

The irony of all this is, of course, that poor parents are always eager to provide for schooling because the traditional American ethic proclaims that education is the way to lift oneself out of poverty. This is supposedly how the immigrants did it, and it is part of the Horatio Alger legend. But the deplorable quality of education in ghetto schools negates this principle. Modern researchers question at this stage whether American schools truly aid upward social mobility and whether, as matters now stand, there is any relationship at all between formal education and higher earnings in the labor marketplace. One social scientist I know believes that American schools simply serve the purpose of creating an "internal social structure of discipline habits." Creativity is thus suppressed, and the United States regresses to eighteenth- and nineteenth-century concepts where manufacturers desired the "structure of discipline habits" the better to control the labor force. In this age, it would appear, the corporations evince the same desires.

And indeed, corporations have again become the target of resentment on the part of the American "common man" as they often were in the past, since the days of the "robber barons," the great railroads and oil monopolies. Their immense power and faceless anonymity are the *bête noire* of the worker and the consumer alike. When I traveled in Pennsylvania—a good cross section of American industrial society, what with its steel mills, decaying coal mines, and blighted towns—during the 1972 presidential primaries, I was astonished over the extent of smoldering resentment against American corporate power. This came out in all sorts of different ways—casual conversations over beers in taverns in a working-class district in Pittsburgh across the black waters of the Monongahela River from the new skyscrapers housing the corporate headquarters—United States Steel, Gulf Oil, and so on—and in more formal discussions with newspaper editors and politicians. Some of the talk sounded like dialogue from a John O'Hara novel. And I heard more of the same in factory and mining towns of Indiana, Ohio, and West Virginia—wherever the big corporations owned much of the town and its people.

Over lunch in Philadelphia, a young ward politician from an ethnic district asked rhetorically: "Why do you suppose so many of our people are voting for George Wallace—here and in Michigan and in Wisconsin? Because Wallace is, or people think he is, for the screwed-up little man. They think that all the Democrats and Republicans are plugged into the corporate establishment, and they don't want any part of it. They don't trust the corporation."

There seemed ample reason not to. In April 1973, corporation after corporation reported record profits for the first quarter of the year, just as inflation was running at an equally record rate of 6 per cent before hitting 8 per cent in the autumn. Profit *increases* over the previous year ranged around 15 per cent in all the major business categories, presumably at the consumer's expense. It was a bonanza for shareholders—dividends were growing and growing—but pay increases for workers were artificially held down by government controls, on the theory that higher wages meant more of the inflationary spiral. And, in relative terms, taxation was borne by the salaried American because corporations benefited from every imaginable type of tax favoritism.

To make Americans buy their products, corporations were spending close to $25 billion annually on advertising, mainly on television. Procter & Gamble, which leads the field with $275 million spent annually on advertising, reported that its sales for the first quarter in 1973 had exceeded $1 billion for the first time in 136 years; net profits for the quarter (after taxes, advertising, and everything else) were over $86 million. Scores of corporations had similar success stories to tell their stockholders. I raised the question of corporate profits versus the shrinking purchasing power of the consumer as I chatted one evening with a top business executive. Wasn't there a bit of a distortion in this state of affairs, I asked him. The executive shrugged his shoulders: "Sure, we urge people to buy, but we can't force them to buy," he said. "So they shouldn't bitch over our profits."

Still, stockholders' annual meetings increasingly brought to the fore the mounting concern about industrial pollution, employment of minorities, social aspects of big business, and corporations' international policies. Minority stockholders—led in numerous instances by clergymen—challenged corporations over their involvement in the production of weapons for use in Indochina and elsewhere. The challenges, not surprisingly, were easily beaten down by the corporations. Executives would not answer questions about ecology or employment practices. But, obviously, a new mood was developing toward corporations even if Americans kept filling their coffers.

When I visited Chicago and Pittsburgh, I listened to corporate managers complaining bitterly about "negative attitudes" shown about their work by younger people. Citing the "good money" they were paying the workers, the fringe benefits, and so on, they wondered why the worker was so sullen and hostile. President Nixon, of course, publicly deplored what he believed to be the erosion of the traditional "work ethic" in the United States and the reliance on welfare rather than "workfare." This "workfare" is one of those virtually meaningless terms or slogans so easily spouted by Washington speechwriters; in practice, "workfare" programs turned out to be a total fiasco because no jobs can be found for the overwhelming majority of welfare recipients who register for work. But neither the corporate managers nor the President have adequately addressed themselves to the immense national malaise stemming from unrewarding jobs in which millions of workers find themselves trapped, and from the parallel phenomenon of recirculation of low-paying and insecure jobs among the "working poor."

There are other dimensions in the great American social misunderstanding. One of them is the confusion between employment and underemployment. Official statistics, tending to create a false sense of societal security, tell us that in the early 1970s around 95 per cent of the labor force was employed (the mini-recession of 1970 brought it down temporarily by one percentage point). But these statistics fail to distinguish between full em-ployment and part-time or temporary work. In other words, the basic American problem is not of employment as such but of the income level it provides on a full- or part-time basis. Underem-ployment is the province of the "working poor." The extent of this state of affairs was brutally illustrated in the 1970 Census. Thus, more than 17 million males over the age of sixteen— roughly a third of all males in the labor force—worked less than six months during 1969. Nine million of them were between the ages of twenty-five and sixty-four, normally the most productive period of a man's life. Among females, over 20 million, which was about 60 per cent of all females in the labor force, worked less than six months in 1969. This meant that close to 40 per cent of all Americans were underemployed at the turn of the decade. Actual numbers were probably higher when one considers that the Census missed over five million Americans.*

To say, as some have said, that the poor prefer welfare to work strikes me as arrant nonsense when one looks at this dismal subemployment situation, affecting millions of Americans, and the government's inability to find jobs for those on welfare regis-tered for work.

*Figures for the late 1960s showed the wide disparity between unemploy-ment and subemployment in the American urban ghettos. In New York's East Harlem, for example, official unemployment was 9.1 per cent but subemployment stood at 33.1 per cent. In North Philadelphia, it was 9.1 per cent and 34.2 per cent; on the North Side of Saint Louis, Missouri, 12.5 per cent and 38.9 per cent; in the slums of San Antonio, Texas, subem-ployment was 47.4 per cent. Among those employed full-time, 4.7 million males and 6.6 million females earned in 1970 less than the minimum wage of $1.60 an hour.

What does the subemployed American do to make both ends meet? Welfare payments as supplementary income to bring him *up* to the poverty level are only one source. Another source is, in ghetto parlance, the "hustle," which ranges from organized prostitution and numbers rackets to grand theft and narcotics peddling. Sociologists say that about a quarter of all adults in Harlem lived entirely from the "hustle"; in Washington, D.C., it provided some 15 per cent of ghetto incomes. But the recourse to this "irregular economy" creates a vicious circle of its own. As Stanley Friedlander, a student of ghetto problems, has written, "The larger the source of illegal income, the fewer people in the slums who persist in looking for legitimate jobs."

A black community leader in Chicago, who deplores the "hustle," remarked, "It's very easy to blame these people for illegal activities. . . . But, man, you've got to understand them. Why should a man want to work his ass off in an underpaid menial job when he can score in the hustle?" Social economists of the new generation recognized that the "hustle" was almost entirely the province of blacks because of their exclusion from the mainstream of American economic life.

Back-to-back with subemployed Americans are the increasingly discontented blue-collar workers. Robert Schranck, who has examined "blue-collar blues" in depth, wrote that worker discontent results "from rising expectations of status and mobility and the apparent inability of the system to deliver." The HEW report *Work in America* warned in 1973 that "great care must be taken to interpret wisely the signs of discontent among workers. Increased industrial sabotage and sudden wild-cat strikes portend something more fundamental than the desire for more money. Allegiance to extremist political movements may mean something other than hatred of those another color." In other words, worker unrest went far beyond mere fears that black mobility may threaten some of the good white jobs. Thus, in 1973, the United Auto Workers fought against mandatory overtime in automotive assembly-line plants on the grounds that it exhausted the men beyond a reasonable limit. (Management, on the other hand, had found it cheaper to pay overtime than to hire extra workers.) Overtime was good money, but the point had come where the American worker wanted more out of life than just money. Demands for short work weeks and retirement with full benefits after thirty years on the job have acquired the force of a major new social movement. A man could stand only so much.

But the HEW report went even further. "The dissatisfaction of the assembly-line and the blue-collar worker is mirrored in white-collar and even managerial positions. . . . Secretaries, clerks, and bureaucrats were once grateful for having been spared the dehumanization of the factory. . . . But today the clerk, and not the operative on the assembly-line, is the typical American worker,* and such positions offer little in the way of prestige. Furthermore, the size of the organizations that employ the bulk of office workers has grown, imparting to the clerical worker the same impersonality that the blue-collar worker experiences in the factory." (The searing unhappiness among factory workers, clerks, and managers may help to explain why nearly 80 million Americans, teen-age and adult, find it necessary to experiment with alcohol. There is no real difference between the tension-ridden executive who puts away three martinis over lunch and three highballs before dinner and the worker who pops into the nearest liquor store morning and afternoon to pick up a pint of gin or whiskey or a jug of cheap wine.)

*In 1970, white-collar workers accounted for almost half (48.2 per cent) of the American labor force and the blue collars for only 36 per cent. (The balance were so-called service workers—ranging from restaurant waiters to gas-station attendants—and farm workers [a tiny 3.1 per cent]).

Other contradictions developed in the fabric of American working life. On the one hand, there is the worker who holds a steady job in a big company. His chances to advance or attain a more creative or responsible position are limited by the prevailing system—at best he may rise from laborer to foreman or from filing clerk to superclerk—but he dares not quit, despite the stupefying monotony of his work, because he has invested years in a retirement plan and in seniority. Talking to a social researcher at a steel plant in Gary, Indiana, a young operating engineer put it this way: ". . . like you gotta go to the same parking lot for forty years and park your car . . . go in and see the same people. . . . I just couldn't handle that. The longer you're there, the harder it is to quit. Seniority is really good, you know." On the other hand, there is the unskilled worker whose peripheral employer requires only routine tasks of him. Because the employer has no investment in his worker—and usually can hire him for substandard wages—he does not try to keep him. In time the worker develops a virtually pathological inability to hold a job for any decent length of time. The turnover in unskilled jobs is so high that in 1968, for example, over 3 million Americans had two or more "spells" of employment during the year. One can well imagine how this perennial job instability damages the individual, the family, and the society. As Barry F. Bluestone, a labor specialist, bitterly summed it up, "The economy creates good jobs and bad ones and then parcels them out on the basis of race, sex and luck."

Finally, we had the problem of the Vietnam war veterans—some 2.5 million of them—who found themselves largely rejected by the nation that had sent them to Indochina. While sufficient data were not available immediately, the Bureau of Labor Statistics estimated that 308,000 Vietnam veterans could find no work in 1972. (In New York City alone 15 per cent of its 250,000 veterans had no jobs early in 1973.) Another 300,000 were disabled, making it even harder for them to obtain work. Since many veterans had been drafted in the first place because they were poor and uneducated (they were the ones ineligible for college draft deferments), they lacked the skills needed to get decent jobs, so they, too, joined the poverty pool. Service in Vietnam had left them two years behind their peer group in work advancement, and, as an unemployed veteran told a TV interviewer, "What is the use, in terms of getting a job, that the army taught me how to handle a flame thrower?"

In violent contrast with the red-carpet treatment accorded the returning prisoners of war, mostly officers—and even in contrast to the veteran of 1945—the new veterans enjoyed no priorities. In fact, employers tended to be wary of them: many had grown long hair and beards—this often was enough to deny them work—and many employers who should have known better quickly convinced themselves that every Vietnam veteran was probably a drug addict. (Between 60,000 and 400,000 veterans were believed to have actually smoked pot or tried heroin—100,000 may be the best figure—but was this a reason for society to turn its back on them? A study by the Defense Department said that only around 4000 veterans who served in Vietnam in a three-year period were heroin addicts on their return home.) I have seen in many cities long queues of young veterans, looking aged and dispirited, waiting for interviews at dreary employment offices, not quite understanding why they were being treated like second-class citizens. Monotonously, newspapers carried reports about veterans who survived the war but could not hold their own at home, ending up as suicides or psychological wrecks. This was "the terror of overhanging fate," in the precise sense of Huxley's observation.

There was more than a touch of irony in the fact that the new, all-volunteer U.S. Army was turning into a major employer of poor young men. Under the draft, the army had fairly represented a cross section of America (though college deferments had tipped the balance toward the less educated), but when the army turned professional in 1972, it became clear that it would mirror the civilian poverty society and, consequently, that acceptance standards would have to be lowered. To be sure, poor young people were eager to volunteer for military careers—the army offered guaranteed employment, unaffected by economic cycles, immeasurably higher living standards, medical fringe benefits, early retirement with pensions and, above all, education. When I asked a young man why he had come down to volunteer at a Washington recruiting office, he looked at me with astonishment. "Man," he said, "this beats washing dishes or hustling or being on welfare or getting laid off from a job." Another man in line nodded approvingly. "It's status," he said.

In any case, during the first year some 150,000 men enlisted in the army. A Pentagon manpower expert told me that the new recruits were in large proportion black, southern, high-school dropouts, and very young (about 70 per cent were under nineteen; though the pattern was not yet entirely clear, enlistment rates showed that over half were dropouts and a quarter were black).

Manpower experts claimed they were not particularly concerned about this: they had fully expected it. The view, I was told, was that even if the army had to compromise on admission standards, "the boys can be educated and made into good soldiers." The Pentagon experts with whom I talked took an enthusiastic view of their new professional army. (Its authorized peacetime strength stood at 850,000 men.) They thought it would in the long run form a first-rate professional fighting force and they spoke volubly of the pleasant life in the new army: college-type bedrooms, on-base entertainment, freedom to drink beer in the men's quarters, and so on. The recruits responded to the appeal of army life, though the enlistment rate reached its target only with the 1973 recession. It seemed to be a perfect arrangement—except, I thought, was it right to have the option of joining the army be virtually the only positive option open to the poor? Eventually, the Pentagon began to realize that its voluntary army could well turn into a disaster.

The gathering American malaise, I thought, was infinitely more dangerous and unsettling than the youth rebellion of earlier years. It lacked, for one thing, the optimistic forward thrust of the young people's revolt. Instead, it had the grim inexorability of a storm. Between the discontent of those who worked and those who could not find decent jobs or any jobs at all, it was hard to accept the complacent judgment that all was well—provided that we maintained the good old work ethic. The ethic was there, all right, but the same could not be said of work, particularly decent work. The erosion of Nixon's Presidency (not to mention Spiro Agnew's Vice Presidency) obviously undermined national trust in government ethics. And, yet, I felt, this was a basically decent society, willing to question old ideas and accept new ones. So, instinctive optimism about America was pitted against pessimism.

I have frequently mentioned the fantastic shift in population patterns, literally transforming the nation, that occurred during the 1960s and 1970s, particularly in the years 1965–68: from the rural areas to the cities, from the cities to the suburbs, and from the hinterland to the two oceanic coasts.

This vast inner migration created new cultures and subcultures and destroyed the accustomed ones. Poverty at home—or hope for better opportunities elsewhere—sent millions of Americans scurrying from farms and rural regions to already overcrowded cities. The big-city bus terminal became the Ellis Island of the 1970s, a port of entry for rural Americans into modern urban society. But the combination of this influx of the poor into the cities and the physical deterioration of the latter shot out the middle-class city dweller into the ever-sprawling suburbs. Population shifts, then, occurred along economic and racial lines.

But they were uneven shifts. Almost as a general rule, the farm was the first to suffer. By the late 1960s it had simply become uneconomic to be a small landowner or farmer, to say nothing of being a sharecropper or farm tenant, especially in the South. Extensive mechanization and government agricultural policies favored big farms and farming corporations—agribusiness—which could turn a better profit with a minimum of manpower. In thirty years, between 1940 and 1970, the number of farmers in the United States dropped from 30 million to 10 million. In 1940, farmers were 25 per cent of the total population; in 1973, they were less than 5 per cent. In the 1940s, the exodus from the farm had been generally regarded as a positive social trend; thirty years later it was seen principally as an urban tragedy.

But not *all* farmers and farm hands fled to the cities. Those who chose the urban road were chiefly either southern blacks or hillbillies from Appalachia; their poverty was so appalling that nothing, even conditions in the cities, could be worse. The white population in many rural areas remained fairly stable, however, even growing somewhat around new industries and services. I noticed a certain prosperity—neat white frame houses and cottages, cars in a few driveways, and well-dressed people—when I drove around Charlottesville in central Virginia, sections of Missouri, the prairie states from Illinois to Nebraska, the Sierra foothills in northern California. But the remaining rural blacks hardly shared in it.

A second demographic distortion was that the big cities actually lost population. Thirteen out of America's twenty-five largest cities—New York, Chicago, Detroit, Boston, Cleveland, Saint Louis, Pittsburgh, Philadelphia, San Francisco, New Orleans, Baltimore, Milwaukee, and Seattle—had a net drop in inhabitants between 1960 and 1970. Washington, D.C., lost inhabitants between 1970 and 1973. There were several explanations for these losses. One was the massive and continuing flight to the suburbs. Then there was a shift of city dwellers to other American towns where decay seemed less menacing and life more promising. Those who left the cities were often employers, including corporations, and those who streamed into the urban centers were a mass of cheap labor in search of work, and as opportunities shifted away from the central cities, urban jobs began to vanish; New York City lost a quarter million jobs between 1969 and 1973, and this trend was observable elsewhere. The cities, of course, were still bursting at the seams, but more and more of the people in them were unemployed or subemployed, and the long-range outlook was for further deterioration.

Meanwhile, the number of Americans living in the "urban fringe"—the statistician's name for suburbs—rose by 44 per cent, to 55 million people, which is about a fourth of the total population of the United States. And although thirteen major cities lost inhabitants (as did smaller impoverished ones like Newark, Bayonne, and Camden, New Jersey; Johnstown, Pennsylvania; Charlestown, West Virginia; Abilene; Duluth; Augusta, Georgia; and Fall River, Massachusetts), quite a number of others experienced considerable growth. Among them were Los Angeles, San Diego, San Jose, and Santa Barbara in California, Phoenix in Arizona, Dallas and Houston in Texas, and Miami, Jacksonville, and West Palm Beach in Florida. Climate and more pleasant and presumably profitable conditions evidently accounted for this—with retiring people swelling the numbers. (Surprisingly, Indianapolis also grew appreciably, probably from the absorption of neighboring farm populations.) Moreover, medium-size cities could suffer an overall population drop while gaining an impressive daytime-commuter influx from their own suburbs. Newark, for instance, claims that its permanent population of 400,000 is doubled by commuters on every working day. But the cruel irony of it is that unemployment is extremely high in the permanent population, whose percentage of blacks and Puerto Ricans keeps rising, and the city's bid for business—advertising its harbor and airline facilities and erecting modern office buildings downtown—has not solved this problem. Gary, Indiana, is another example of a blighted city whose permanent population is becoming increasingly black and unemployed while its best jobs, even in the steel mills, are reserved for the commuting whites.

Because cities and their suburbs virtually merge in this new socioeconomic pattern (many cities and towns began annexing surrounding townships, villages, and unincorporated areas), the concept of the Standard Metropolitan Statistical Areas, the SMSA, has evolved for the classification of urban populations. Using this new statistical yardstick, the Census Bureau could report that in 1970, some 150 million Americans—three-quarters of the population—lived in the 230 SMSAs. On behalf of phonetics and aesthetics, I tend to cringe when demographic experts tell me I live in a SMSA. I like to think I live in a city. But the next logical step along these lines is the concept of the megalopolis— connected urban and suburban areas stretching for hundreds of miles. City planners talk seriously of the BosWash Megalopolis, the Atlantic coastal strip running from Boston to Washington, D.C., with New York City and its environs as its focal point. High-speed trains could serve this megalopolis, supplementing the incredible intensity of air-shuttle traffic already filling the East Coast corridor. The San Francisco Bay Area—San Francisco itself, Oakland, Berkeley, and a whole string of communities stretching past San Jose—is another major megalopolis. No matter where one drives in the Bay Area, one never has the sensation of having left the *urbs*. Looking down from the elevated freeways, one sees a continuing city, though local names and jurisdictions keep changing. This is also true of Los Angeles and Chicago.

One can no longer tell, then, where one city, suburb, or township ends and the next one begins. They merge with each other. If a traveler paid no attention to signs announcing the name of the town—*Welcome to Jonesville, Pop. 11,225*—he would not know where he was. This kept happening to me all during my trip when I stayed off the freeways and beltways. Sheepishly, I would ask a gas-station attendant for the name of the town—but I never got a dirty look; local civic pride seems to have been lost in the resigned acceptance that one's town looks just like the one two or three blocks away, past the arbitrary administrative dividing line.

Driving along the coastal highway in Florida, say from South Miami to Palm Beach, I never had the sensation of advancing from one place to another, though I crossed three counties. It was one continuous, homogenized, semi-urban landscape. All the motels and seaside cottages looked alike as did the gas stations, used-car lots, restaurants, ice-cream and hamburger stands, and bars. The deeply tanned empty-eyed retired men and women dressed and acted the same all over Florida—usually sitting or strolling in the sun. The younger housewives were in shorts and halters. The men wore the same colorful sports shirt. Youngsters drove convertibles. Only the profusion of signs in Spanish and the sound of this language in stores and cafeterias—the overwhelming Cuban presence in the state—made these Florida urban strips in the sun different from similar strips in the Southern California megalopolis. But Florida evidently never ceased to attract: its population rose 13 per cent between 1970 and 1973.

In the bedroom communities of northern Virginia and southern Maryland, where we often drove to visit suburban Washington friends, it was impossible to tell which county one was in. I
developed the habit of identifying localities by the sprawling
shopping centers sitting astride the main highway intersections.
"Aha," I would say to my wife, "so-and-so lives somewhere
around Tysons' Corner" (or Bailey's Crossing or what-have-you).
It all just went on and on. To cross from Washington to Montgomery or Fairfax county, one only had to walk to the other side of
a street. And a drive from New York City to a Westchester town
or village over secondary roads is a similar experience. Where
does the Bronx or Bronxville end to make room for Yonkers or
White Plains or Tarrytown? In New Jersey there is no way a
stranger can differentiate in the drab industrial and slum
monotony of Newark, Elizabeth, or Jersey City. It was one vast
grim blob, punctuated here and there by modern office buildings.

In this slow and featureless exurban sprawl, one must not overlook the fantastic growth of certain unified metropolitan areas
(yes, SMSAs) and certain older (and attractive) cities, towns, and
resorts—the result of selective migrations and the annexations of
nearby territory. And brand-new towns also sprouted, literally
custom-built for the waiting public. Finally, America turned to
mobile-home communities—a further escalation of the suburban life style. This most unattractive contribution to the suburban scenery affords relatively cheap (no land purchase is
necessary) and functional housing, while offering a strange
sense of togetherness that a great many people seem to welcome.
The most extreme example of an urban population explosion is
Virginia Beach, Virginia, whose population rose between 1960
and 1970 by *2027 per cent* to 172,000 inhabitants. How could *any*
city have grown so much so quickly? The short answer is that
Virginia Beach, already fueled financially by surrounding navy
installations, turned into a year-round retirement haven for senior military officers, as well as a fashionable resort for Washing-

ton-based diplomats and their coteries. It also attracted families of naval personnel, who preferred the Beach to nearby Norfolk, and it was favored by tourists by the bushel from as far away as Canada. Virginia Beach swallowed a whole adjoining county to achieve its demographic eminence, and it became the real-estate operator's paradise. (I shall return later to the astonishing story of Virginia Beach.)

Other metropolises-in-the-sun and consolidated areas did remarkably well, perhaps too well. Huntington Beach, California, grew by 909 per cent to 116,000 inhabitants; Scottsdale, Arizona, by 576 per cent; El Monte, California, by 430 per cent; Lakewood, Colorado, by 379 per cent; Bellevue, Washington, by 377 per cent; Overland Park, Kansas, by 263 per cent; Hollywood, Florida, by 203 per cent; Orange, California, by 192 per cent; Aurora-Elgin, Illinois, by 172 per cent; Tempe, Arizona, by 152 per cent (it is a new college town); Fremont, California, by 130 per cent; Las Vegas, Nevada, by 115 per cent. Between 1970 and 1973, Arizona's population rose 16 per cent—the highest rate of growth in the nation.

The new towns—the "planned communities" started from scratch for the benefit of commuters, retired people, and others —were the futuristic, if not always altogether successful, dream of urban planners and architects apparently come true. Planned along community lines (and meant, of course, for the fairly affluent) the new towns, from Columbia and Saint Charles in Maryland and Reston in Virginia to Southbury, Connecticut, Arcosanti, Arizona, and similar projects in California, were the latest fad in modern living. But a host of problems arose almost immediately. I visited several of the new towns and I shall return to this subject, too.

All this gigantic ebb-and-flow of people could not fail to affect the population levels of individual states. The basic pattern in this redistribution of the population was that states offering good climates and work opportunities or convenient suburban clusters grew, while the poorer states shrank. California, which outdistanced New York as the most populous state in the Union, Florida, Texas, Arizona, Colorado, and New Hampshire benefited from the syndrome of good climate–new work opportunities. Among dozens of examples that come to mind, there was a Washington lawyer of my acquaintance who one day bid farewell to his suburban Virginia home and daily commuting and moved his family to a small Colorado town. Occasional dispatches from him suggest that he is doing as well financially as he did in Washington, and that he feels ten years younger and healthier. I know the son of a New York socialite who began practicing law in a county seat in the Texas Panhandle rather than fight it out in the big city. In Florida and Texas, however, the tendency was for the new influx to concentrate in the metropolitan areas. Whereas in 1950 the cities housed half of their respective populations, this proportion had risen to two-thirds in 1970.

New Jersey, Connecticut, and upstate New York, on the other hand, were favored by the flight from New York City to suburbs and beyond. People in rural areas past Bear Mountain and West Point were alarmed over invasions from New York City, nearly a hundred miles away. The corporate exodus from the city was felt all over upstate New York, as it was in Connecticut and New Jersey. When a top executive was asked why his company's headquarters were moving to New Jersey, his terse answer was, "Why stay in New York?" Illinois experienced an overall population rise because of the heavy influx from midwestern farms and the South and Appalachia, while Chicago lost inhabitants to such commuter areas as Aurora-Elgin. Losses predictably hit Mississippi, West Virginia, and the farming and ranching states of South and North Dakota and Wyoming, where young people simply could not conceive a plausible future for themselves.

When I visited Wyoming, which is so beautiful that it is hard
to leave it, I had occasion to chat with a part-time waitress in a
Cheyenne restaurant who was studying interior decorating at
the state university. "As soon as I graduate, I'm getting out of
Wyoming," she announced firmly. "I don't see much future in
being an interior decorator in Cheyenne." She pointed across the
room to the big-hatted mountain ranchers, in town for the annual rodeo weekend, as they ate their steaks, drank their whiskey, laughed over off-color stories, and talked cattle, feed, and
water. "They don't need the likes of me in Wyoming," she said.

In the Dakotas, the collapse of the small-farm economy was
closing down not only farms but also one town after another. I
vividly remember the photograph in a local paper of the totally
deserted main street of a nearby township, the wooden buildings
boarded up, a pile of threshed grain blown about by the wind.
"There just is no incentive to hang around," said an embittered
farmer from near Fargo. "Let's give it back to the Indians," a
South Dakota rancher told me on another occasion, oblivious to
the concurrence of his view with the Oglala Indians' own attitude.

In West Virginia, where I used to go often when I was part-
owner of a racing horse at one of its small tracks (it was not a
very good horse though a linear descendant of Man o' War),
poverty so extreme reigned over the hills and in the shanties of
Wheeling that any young person with the slightest hope for the
future simply packed up and left as soon as possible. Things were
not much better in sections of Arkansas, Tennessee, and Kentucky. In town after town, little seemed to have changed since the
Civil War: old men sat on courthouse steps staring vacantly into
the distance, chewing and spitting tobacco. Even the innumerable Baptist, Pentecostal, and other Fundamentalist churches
were empty (I counted twenty-three separate churches in just
one Arkansas town that could not have had more than ten thou-

sand inhabitants), although it was explained to me that the folk, especially womanfolk, crowded into them on Sundays and sometimes evenings. Perhaps religion was the only thing that kept people going. But the youngsters went on emigrating to the cities in search of jobs, taking along their fiddle music and Fundamentalism. (A keen-eyed reporter in Detroit discovered five bars named after Li'l Abner.)

These massive internal migrations reached a new peak in 1965–68. During those years, over 61 million Americans moved into the houses or apartments they occupied by the 1970 Census. In 1969–70, the number was 48 million. We were, indeed, a mobile and nervous society. But in 1949, only 15.6 million had moved to new residences. When the 1970 Census was taken, it turned out that no more than 12.3 million Americans had always lived in the same house. Percentally, the greatest shifts occurred throughout the South because of regional migrations. But California and New York, the most populous states, were the ones with the highest number of Americans who had changed residences in the 1960s. Nothing in America was more dated than last year's telephone directory. And, to be sure, Americans were increasingly strangers to one another. Unlike twenty years earlier, people no longer asked new acquaintances, "Where are you from?" The new questions were: "What do you do? Where do you live?"

Because of the huge shift to the suburbs, some 14 million Americans were daily commuters across county lines. Forty per cent of working Virginians were in this category, chiefly because northern Virginia is one vast bedroom for people who work in Washington. One out of every ten persons holding a job in the largely rural Fauquier County in Virginia, stretching to the Blue Ridge Mountains, commuted sixty miles (spending at least three hours a day in the car) to Washington. For similar reasons, 37 per cent of the Maryland labor force were cross-county commuters.

In New York State, the figure was 32 per cent, and in New Jersey, 33. But in California, so much of which has acquired quasi-megalopolis characteristics, people tended to work within their counties of residence.*

Since mass transit was inadequate in most American metropolitan areas, commuting usually had to be done by car. Despite warnings by environment specialists about growing air pollution and despite gasoline shortages and threatened rationing, it seemed that the use of the automobile would keep increasing in the years to come. Yet, by early 1974, fuel shortages were already affecting commuting patterns and life styles. Not only was the fantastic number of 12 million new cars sold in 1973, but Congress again refused to allocate an adequate part of the three-year $20 billion Highway Trust Fund for urban mass transit. This meant a halt in the planning for many new railroad commuter lines and new subway, bus, and monorail systems—a victory for the highway lobbies that threatened to produce further absurdities in our social system along the lines of what happened in the Watts ghetto. There, a major job-training and placement program was set in motion after the riots of the 1960s, but it quickly became obvious that absence of a good mass-transit system virtually prevented the new workers from commuting between Watts and jobs elsewhere in the sprawling city. Most of the Watts people remained trapped, still jobless or underemployed.

Using their own resources, cities and states are doing what

*The *Wall Street Journal,* which became fascinated with the problem of "long-distance commuters," reported not long ago that several hundred thousand Americans traveled more than 100 miles to and from work. Its reporters discovered a woman in Illinois who drives 160 miles a day (four hours), a Pennsylvania dentist who lives 100 miles away from his New York office and commutes twice a week, and a Dallas fireman who flies his own plane every day between work and his home on Possum Kingdom Lake, 125 miles away.

they can to create mass-transit systems. Washington, D.C., and Atlanta are building subways, New York City is adding a new line, the San Francisco Bay Area now operates a rapid-transit system, Boston has banned new urban freeways, Miami is thinking of a rapid rail system from Coral Gables to Miami Beach, and so on. The energy crisis came as something of a blessing for mass transit. Yet millions of Americans still had something akin to a love affair with freeways and superhighways. I dimly remember a song in the 1950s about being "In Love with the New Jersey Turnpike." I suppose that the first reason for this attitude is primarily functional: it is obviously easier to use a freeway, rather than clogged streets or ill-paved secondary roads, to get from one point to another. But there are other reasons, too.

There is for a start the American's deeply engrained love of the automobile. Tradition has it that young boys start tinkering with cars in their early teens and cannot wait for the chance to drive. My son, Tony, applied for a learner's permit the day he turned sixteen, and Nikki has crossed the United States from coast to coast at least a half-dozen times behind the wheel of her car. I do think there is something to be said for the heady freedom of the superhighway ("Speed Limit: 80") in a crowded and congested society; when I had my old convertible, I loved to go out speeding in the sun and the wind. All this was before the new speed limits imposed by the fuel shortage. But television advertising portraying beautiful girls and handsome men in romantic situations, always in superb cars with names like Jaguar or Cougar, has left a deeper imprint on us than we are probably willing to admit. A friend of mine, a woman activist, wrote in an article some years ago that the desire for an impressive car on the part of the American male relates directly to his sexual appetites; the rationale, she wrote, was, the better the car "the better I can get laid." This is not peculiar to Americans and I certainly do not dispute her observation, but it seems to work both ways. A more recent magazine article by a male reporter describing the California freeway culture reported interviews with women who confided that they occasionally take to the road in their own cars to be picked up by men driving "exciting" sports cars—and to wind up in bed with them.

In any event, by early 1970, some 51 million Americans, including myself, drove to work in their own cars carrying along nine million more commuters as passengers. Nobody seems to know how many housewives get behind the wheel to shop, ferry their children, and do other errands. But they must be in the millions. Only a half-million commuted by train, what with the progressive elimination of passenger railroad service. But I was impressed to find out that nearly six million Americans *walked* to and from work every day; they may well be the healthiest of us all. Bicycles, too, have been rediscovered to the point where they had to be imported from Poland and South Korea.

Parking, naturally, has become a nerve-wracking American obsession. Someone has calculated that Americans spend $750 million annually on parking, though I would have thought the figure was higher. Cities are disfigured by ugly parking lots and garages, while suburban shopping centers from coast to coast are surrounded by enormous parking lots that from the air make one think of automotive plants where new vehicles await shipment to customers. At the College Park campus of the University of Maryland, near Washington, 27,000 of its 35,000 students drove to class, but the campus had only 15,349 spaces in its fifty-seven parking lots. Parking becomes so important that, for example, I had serious difficulties in selling a house in an otherwise desirable section of Washington because it had no off-street parking. Nobody wants to buy a daily parking ticket or live in expectation of having the car towed away.

Despite so many shared or similar problems, the great American cities have exquisitely different personalities. Cosmopolitan

New York is completely distinct from provincial Washington. Hilly, misty San Francisco bears no resemblance to Los Angeles. Boston and Philadelphia share a certain historical charm, but neither has anything in common with Chicago or Detroit. Quasi-tropical Miami and tough-minded Dallas and Houston are worlds apart. American cities must not be compared any more than Paris should be likened to Prague or London to Athens.

Yet there are common denominators. They all fascinate and attract. They stupefy and repulse, probably are ungovernable in the long run yet go on existing despite rather than because of their administrators. Pessimistic social scientists tell us that the American city is doomed. Optimists are equally hopeful that the American *urbs* will survive and emerge the better for its crises —these are the Americans who refuse to throw in the towel and flee to the suburbs (others, of course, stay or keep coming because they have no options). But a 1973 survey showed that only 13 per cent of urban dwellers actually *wanted* to live in their cities.

There is no dispute, however, that the crisis of the American city was very real indeed, President Nixon's disclaimers notwithstanding. In the simplest terms, the main ingredients were poverty, shortage of good jobs, frightful overcrowding in the inner city, dilapidated housing, racial tension, worsening public education, pollution, and a generalized breakdown in public services. Each factor weighed differently in the total urban equation (and varied in intensity from city to city) but the problems were closely linked.

In earlier years, Americans tried to cope with the urban crisis through remedial actions aimed to cure the symptoms, particularly when the riots of the 1960s—in Detroit, Los Angeles, Newark, Washington—shocked so many Americans into awareness of the urban plight. There was a great deal of soul-searching, breast-beating, and hand-wringing. Books were written. Presidential commissions were appointed. Recommendations flooded the White House, the state capitals, and the city halls. Some were heeded, others quickly forgotten. But in any case the structural problems, deeply embedded as they were, though fairly well recognized and identified, were left untended and free to perpetuate.

Lyndon Johnson's War on Poverty was principally a war against the symptoms of urban disease, and as I have said, even this failed to a large degree. At the other end of the spectrum, law enforcement was tightened in response to the worst symptoms of the crisis: crime and drugs. Criminal laws were reinforced through such procedures as the "no-knock" provision in the District of Columbia crime law, allowing the police freely to enter homes on suspicion of illegal activities. Police forces throughout the country were beefed up and equipped with everything from helicopters and communication and crime-detection devices to specially trained dogs. (Federal funds for this purpose were channeled through a special agency to local police departments.) Programs to break heroin addiction were organized everywhere. Cities installed high-intensity vapor street lighting to discourage common crime. But whether or not all this helped to reduce crime is a matter of how statistics are interpreted. In fact, serious doubts arose over official claims that crime was decreasing: it seemed that statistics were doctored. Prisons were as full as ever, judges across the land despaired of keeping up with their case loads, and it took suspects longer and longer to stand trial. The accent continued to be principally on law enforcement instead of crime prevention. Congress still would not approve gun-control legislation although by 1973, Americans were being killed by firearms, mainly in the cities, at the *weekly* rate of 350 as compared with 206 in 1969.

If the vicious circle of poverty is the root cause of the urban crisis, the immediate question is whether we have the resources, let alone the will, to destroy that circle. The liberal view is that, yes, solutions are possible within the existing structure if every American bends his shoulder to the wheel and a wise government properly directs the great enterprise. I tend to have rather serious reservations whether this is possible, short of drastic changes in the organization of society and in human attitudes. For this reason, I was struck by the brutally honest comments by Elliot L. Richardson when he left his post as secretary of Health, Education, and Welfare early in 1973: "The cost of extending the present range of HEW services equitably—to all those who are similarly situated in need—is estimated to be approximately one quarter of a *trillion* dollars. That is, the additional cost would be roughly equivalent to the entire federal budget!" Obviously only a small percentage of Americans eligible for some form of assistance were receiving it. A pragmatic man, Richardson went on to remark, "We must first level with each other about present approaches to social problem solving. We must acknowledge that passing narrow categorical legislation does not in any way ensure the intended remediation of problems; that, indeed, it may be counterproductive; it may further squander limited resources by spreading them too thinly or by allocating them to areas for which the state of the art is inadequately developed; and it may further complicate a service delivery system already paralyzed by ill-organized complexity. We must recognize, as we have with both foreign affairs and natural resources, that resources we once thought boundless—human, financial and intellectual resources—are indeed severely limited."

Whatever one may think of the Nixon administration's bizarre philosophy of reducing or eliminating federal poverty programs, I, for one, could not disagree with Richardson that the previous system could not cope. Evidence stretched from one rotten urban core to another that people as well as the physical facilities were being destroyed. Richardson put it this way: "As an administrative matter, the system is, at best, inefficient. As a creative matter, it is stifling. As an intellectual matter, it is almost incomprehensible. And as a human matter, it is downright cruel."

All this, then, takes us back to the first causes of the urban crisis. The racial ingredient is enormously relevant when one bears in mind that America's black, Spanish-speaking, and Indian minorities added up to 35 million people, well over half of them living in cities. The contemporary American central city was increasingly black, but coexistence within city walls has not brought real integration. Instead, it has produced almost total *de facto* social segregation and much new hostility. Whites who have remained in the cities form bigger or smaller islands among the blacks and Hispanics, with a minimum of intercommunication and plenty of ugly antagonism. Blacks and other ghetto dwellers were isolated from each other, usually by choice; the cultural and social gulf between them was even greater than between whites and blacks.

In New York City, blacks and Puerto Ricans accounted for about a third of the population by 1973, and current projections were that by 1985, the city would be only half white. In some areas of the city, whites were already a minority. South Bronx, the most blighted of all New York neighborhoods, was entirely inhabited by 400,000 blacks and Puerto Ricans. Elsewhere, whites fought to stem the tide: a famous case in point was the battle waged in the borough of Queens by Jewish families against the construction of a public housing project out of fear that too many blacks would move into the neighborhood. I stopped by Forest Hills one afternoon to watch the confrontation between the two groups at the excavation for the project: it was quite a study in hatred.

In Newark, where 72 per cent of the population is black and Puerto Rican, tensions were formidable. For nearly a year, ethnic Italian groups kept up the picketing of a site in the North Ward where an association of black nationalists planned to erect an apartment building to be known as Kawaida Towers. Jersey City was a frequent scene of racial riots. Gary, Indiana, was 75 per cent black and the white exodus gained momentum.

The racial tension was infinitely worse in the North than in the South, as southerners for years had said it would be. Washington, D.C., which has 71 per cent blacks and some 9 per cent Hispanics, has been relatively peaceful over the years (except for the savage 1968 riots after Martin Luther King was murdered), but the whites in Washington's residential districts were isolated: we had no truly integrated neighborhoods. In Atlanta, which is 50 per cent black, Maynard Jackson became late in 1973 the first black mayor of a large southern city, a notion that would have been unthinkable five years earlier. In the West and Southwest, the greatest friction was between whites and Chicanos, frequently erupting into violent physical confrontations, but the black ghettos in Los Angeles were not without nightmarish tensions.

Racial strife is fueled by poverty and lack of jobs; since work is a central fact in human life for every conceivable reason, but especially in its relation to income and well-being, the question of work in American cities is the most significant element requiring examination. It is the backbone of the life of the individual, the family, and therefore the community as a whole. Now, by and large, decent work is not within the reach of minorities living in our cities. "Minority workers and their families are serious casualties of the work system in our society," said HEW's report *Work in America.* "One out of three minority workers is unemployed, irregularly employed, or has given up looking for a job. Another third of minority workers do have jobs—full time, year 'round jobs, but these are mainly laboring jobs and jobs in the service trades which often pay less than a living wage. . . . Many look for jobs—the only ones they are likely to get—that they know before-hand they will hate. In effect, minority workers are the unwilling monopolists of the worst jobs that our society has to offer. Yet, even these jobs are not so much despised because the worker can't take satisfaction from the work itself, but because he can't earn a minimally decent living by doing them."

Once more, statistics help to convey the economic meaning of this human condition. (Because the Census Bureau does not in every instance count Spanish-descended Americans separately from whites, the available figures are for blacks alone. But, as a practical matter, Puerto Ricans and Chicanos are roughly in the same bracket and somewhat worse off.)

Whereas 9.8 per cent of all American males and 33.6 per cent of females in cities had no income in 1970, comparative figures for blacks were 17.1 and 30.5 per cent. (The statistical fact that a higher percentage of white than black females lacked any income at all is interesting: the percentage of white American women over the age of sixteen in the overall labor force was only 40.6 as compared with 47.5 per cent of black women, this being due to the fact that in poor black families women had to work more than their white sisters to supplement the household in-come and that in cities black women accounted for 80 per cent of all American female family heads below the poverty line.) While the largest single group of males in urban areas—17.6 per cent—had annual incomes in the $10,000–$15,000 range, the larg-est group of black urban males—13.4 per cent—had incomes be-tween $1 (yes, one dollar) and $999, and 6.3 per cent of black males were in the $10,000–$15,000 bracket. The HEW report also showed the median income of all adult males as $6429; the figure for minority males was $3991. (For women, the comparable in-comes were $2132 and $1084.) Of course, "Not all poor people

. . . are black, Chicano, Puerto Rican or Indian, nor are all minority persons poor. . . . The point here is that minority workers are, to a striking degree, disproportionately unemployed or working at bad jobs," and "this disproportion reflects the persistent, systematic discrimination and closed-off opportunities that racial minority persons experience in work, education, and other major institutions in our society."

Unquestionably, American minorities and blacks in particular have won important advances since mid-century. A stranger walking through the business district of many an American city may even conclude that America has achieved reasonable racial equality. Like so many white Americans, I have black friends and acquaintances who "made it": men and women in high government jobs (we even have a sprinkling of black and Spanish-descended ambassadors representing the United States abroad); mayors of cities, congressmen, military officers, scientists, professors, educators, journalists, doctors, and lawyers. A friend with whom I share my active interest in horses is the co-discoverer of a vaccine against rubella. But, regrettably, these are exceptions that prove the rule. The rule—and the reality—is that the minorities remain trapped at the bottom of our social system. Continued discrimination prevents them from attaining the cultural and educational standards that would emancipate them.

The problem of minorities—and especially of blacks—has always been "An American Dilemma," to borrow the title of Gunnar Myrdal's monumental work. Writing in 1942, the Swedish sociologist gave his study the subtitle "The Negro Problem and the American Democracy," and said, "To the great majority of white Americans, the Negro problem has distinctly negative connotations. It suggests something difficult to settle and equally difficult to leave alone. It is embarrassing. It makes for moral uneasiness. The very presence of the Negro in America . . . in fact his entire biological, historical and social existence as a participant American represent to the ordinary white man in the North as well as in the South an anomaly in the very structure of American society. To many, this takes on the proportion of a menace—biological, economic, social, cultural, and, at times, political. This anxiety may be mingled with a feeling of individual and collective guilt."

I made a point of going through Myrdal's two volumes when I embarked on my American travels in 1970 because I was curious to what extent the situation might have changed in the thirty years since he undertook his research and whether his basic observations remained valid. I also read a "postscript" to Myrdal's book written in 1962 by Arnold Rose, his original research assistant. Dr. Rose seemed encouraged by the positive changes that had occurred in the previous two decades ("prejudice as an attitude was still common, but racism as a comprehensive ideology was maintained by only a few"), yet he was not complacent. "Negroes *still* experience discrimination, insult, segregation, and the threat of violence, and in a sense have become more sensitive and less 'adjusted' to these things. To them the current problems and current conflicts have much more significance than those of ten or twenty years ago."

Thirty years after the original Myrdal study and ten years after the Rose "updating" appreciation, my own impression was that the United States had entered into another phase in dealing with racial problems. American blacks had become, as Dr. Rose put it, "more sensitive and less 'adjusted' " to discrimination. Precisely because advances were made and because blacks had developed an intense sense of identity and self-assertion, new conflicts came to the fore. Because, in terms of education, jobs, housing, and everything else, the blacks and the other minorities had not yet achieved a real breakthrough, black militancy quickened—though it, too, operated in a much more sophisticated and politicized fashion in the 1970s than before—and what Myrdal called our "moral uneasiness" increased. (This uneasiness, of course, goes far back into history. I happened to be reading recently a collection of Joseph Conrad's letters and was amused to see that in 1897 he changed the original title of his novel *The Nigger of the "Narcissus"* to *The Children of the Sea* for the American edition, "in deference to American prejudices." I take it that by "prejudices" Conrad meant sensitivity.)

Another important change since Myrdal's study is that in absolute terms our black population has almost doubled, although the percentage increase has been negligible. (In 1940, there were nearly 13 million blacks in the United States, just under 10 per cent of the population; in 1973, there were 25 million, or just under 13 per cent. The white-black ratio stabilized after the massive European migrations earlier in the century, but it is worth noting that in 1790, when the first census count was taken, blacks were nearly 20 per cent of the continental population, due to the heavy slave trade.) In the 1970s, however, black births again began to exceed white and Census Bureau projections were for a steady black population increase in coming decades.

Until roughly 1940, some four out of five of all American blacks lived in the South; by 1970, this proportion was reduced to only half, as blacks moved north and west in response to an increased demand for industrial manpower. One conclusion traditionally drawn from this migratory pattern was that southern blacks were largely responsible for the northern cities' welfare problem —President Nixon, for example, suggested in 1969 that the migrations resulted in part from the fact that northern states offered higher welfare payments than were available in the South. This remained conventional wisdom until 1973, when, Census demographers said, new evidence indicated that the black migrants who had gone north between 1950 and 1965 were less likely to be poor and go on welfare than the poor natives of those northern urban centers, since they were relatively successful economically and better qualified to compete for jobs. But the Bureau also discovered with some perplexity that blacks coming north *after* 1965 were the most likely welfare candidates of all; a tentative explanation for this shift was that blacks' economic conditions in the South had deteriorated during the 1960s, or that a different type of migrant—possibly from rural areas rather than southern cities—had begun to appear.

In the 1970s, there was still the matter of Spanish-speaking persons. There was no precise figure for them, partly because many of them do not choose to identify themselves in this manner and partly because of the large number of illegal Latin American immigrants from Mexico and farther south. But 9 million was an educated guess with Chicanos accounting for over 5 million, Puerto Ricans for about 1.5 million, and "others" for 2.5 million (Mexicans and Latin Americans living here legally or otherwise, including Cuban refugees).

As late as April 1971, I listened to George Jackson, a man of great brilliance and intelligence, telling me in the tiny visiting room at San Quentin Prison that revolutionary destruction of the existing American system was the only solution to racism and oppression. But by 1973, the violence of black protest in the 1960s was already history, already documented and chronicled, just as was the rebellion of the white Establishment youth. George Jackson in his prison-cell isolation may not have fully perceived the speed of the American historical process. And with his death, and the death or decline of other black revolutionaries, a new black leadership emerged, practiced in the pragmatism of American politics and resolved to use the white man's tactics to break down the barriers of discrimination and poverty.

Writing in *What Black Politicians Are Saying,* a collection of political essays, Julian Bond, a militant and sophisticated black politician, argued: "Black politicians and political activists, as the only representatives of black people selected in a democratic fashion from a base in the mass of the black community across the country, had better begin as soon as possible to pull together a coherent strategy for 1972 and beyond." But he addressed himself as much to the young white rebels who had so suddenly vanished as to his fellow blacks: "It can be done, but it never will be done by people who think they can smoke America to her knees. It will not be done by a people whose major concern is macrobiotic diets, or music, or drugs, or the relative revisionism of the late Ho Chi Minh, or the romantic rhetoric of revolution, or the ennobling sacrifice of self-induced poverty, or if you enjoy Woodstock while you tolerate Watts, or if Boone's Farm or bid whist is your major preoccupation, or if shouting 'Off the pig' replaces the hard and dirty work of organizing the dispossessed into an effective force for change."

When I was in Oakland in 1971, Huey Newton returned home from three years in prison, for the courts had finally decided he was not guilty of manslaughter charges. I tried to see him, but he had gone into seclusion in a well-guarded penthouse apartment to write his autobiography, *The Revolutionary Suicide:* "Our grievous error had been that for a time we, too, had joined the suicidal dance around the golden calf . . . the American Revolution had only reached the end of the beginning, not the beginning of the end."

Bobby Seale, chairman of the Black Panther party, released from prison shortly after Newton and likewise cleared of most charges (as were defendants in other Panther trials), came close to being elected mayor of Oakland in April 1973. Eldridge Cleaver, denounced by Newton as an irresponsible revolutionary, vanished from sight in his Algerian exile. What had happened? I would have been intrigued by whatever new analysis George Jackson might have offered of the new times. Out of prison, I thought, he might have seen life through a different prism, for he was a man of intelligence.

In Washington, power is beginning to be exercised by black

politicians whose overriding concern is the solution of black problems and poverty problems. In a turn of events that would have been impossible in the previous decade, black power in the most literal political sense emerged in 1973 in the capital as it did throughout the nation. Thus Michigan's Representative Charles C. Diggs, Jr., was elected chairman of the House committee that runs the affairs of the District of Columbia (notwithstanding the grant of home rule, a limited form of autonomy, to the District by Congress late in 1973) after an old-time southern politician was defeated in his own district. The fifteen-member Black Caucus in Congress acquired a considerable importance as a solid voting bloc. Walter Fauntroy, a minister turned politician and the District's elected (though nonvoting) delegate in the House, quietly became a local power. Walter Washington has served as appointed mayor for a decade.

In Chicago, fourteen out of fifty aldermen were black. In California, blacks held key positions in the state senate and assembly and the superintendent of public instruction was black. Alabama, with a 27 per cent black population, had 110 black elected officials; blacks won control of Greene County and a black was sheriff of Lowndes County. A dozen important cities had black mayors since the early 1970s—among them Cleveland, Newark, and Gary, Indiana—and during 1973, Tom Bradley was elected in Los Angeles, Maynard Jackson in Atlanta, and Coleman Young in Detroit in a series of political surprises. Whether or not self-imposed social segregation between the races remained a reality, the fact was that enough whites in these cities were willing to give highly qualified blacks a chance to move to city hall to deal with urban crises of which blacks themselves were the principal victims. In racial terms, then, coexistence seemed possible at least on the political level. Countrywide, some 2991 blacks served in 1974 as congressmen, mayors, state legislature members, and aldermen—up from 475 in 1967.

From these positions power could be and was being exercised. As Julian Bond, a member of the Georgia state legislature, put it: "It is politics that decides that black people live in a permanent depression. And it is politics that can put money into our pockets and give us jobs and a livable—not laughable—income right now. . . . It is politics that will enable us to take over the cities where we live and turn them into the kind of places where everyone wants to live and raise their children. . . . Our politics ought to be the art of saying who gets how much of what from whom. And quite naturally we are the 'who' who have not got anything of anything from 'you-know-who.' . . . The solution is that we learn to play this new kind of politics for our own benefit. . . . The time ought to be here in America for politics that would mean we can vote without voting for our own enslavement, that we can cast a vote that would bring us jobs, income, freedom and food and real power in this country's decision-making process."

Chicanos and Puerto Ricans have been learning the same lessons. Reies López Tijerina's dramatic raid on the Tierra Amarilla, New Mexico, courthouse in 1967, to assert Chicano rights, now belongs to history. Instead, La Raza Unida, the Chicano political party, has begun to make its weight felt in the West and Southwest. New York's Puerto Ricans have an influential congressman in Washington in Herman Badillo, a man with further political future. Puerto Rico's resident commissioner in Washington, Jaime Benítez, has been sitting on congressional committees concerned with labor, education, and the fate of the cities. Benítez, long the president of the University of Puerto Rico, has been an increasingly important figure in the drafting of legislation.

For the blacks, Chicanos, and Puerto Ricans, the new strategy for improving the lot of their people has thus become the exercise of traditional political power, backed by constituents who work politically at precinct level, register voters, vote themselves, and make sure that elections are not stolen from them. To use a phrase often used by minority leaders, the primary task is to "raise the consciousness of our people."

American Indians are the most recent minority to assert themselves. Countless books have been written about the white man's destruction of Indian populations in the nineteenth century and his subsequent practice of exploiting the survivors and breaking treaties signed with them. Every American knows about the "Trail of Tears." The guilt thus has been firmly established, although only in the late 1960s and the early 1970s did the government begin to face up seriously to the Indian problem.

Numerous factors contributed to this. Young Americans discovered the Indian as the pure American, and turned to his traditions for their own life styles and sartorial characteristics. Indian jewelry and adornments were "in" everywhere. More important, younger Indians themselves engaged in a major cultural revival. As I traveled through Nebraska, Wyoming, Colorado, New Mexico, and Oklahoma I found signs of this rebirth everywhere. Young whites went to work on Indian reservations—which display some of the worst American rural squalor—as teachers and social workers, while editorialists busied themselves with the issues of Indian land ownership, or with the attempts by mining corporations to extract cheap leases from the tribes and by utilities to take away Indian water for power production. Then, when militant Indians finally resorted to violent action, the federal government reacted with astonishing mildness and restraint. An Indian group was left undisturbed for a long while after capturing Alcatraz island, in San Francisco Bay. Another group established itself in an abandoned Coast Guard station on a Minnesota lake. Just before the 1972 elections, Indian militants took over the Bureau of Indian Affairs building in Washington, and the police, usually quite firm with demonstrators, refrained from a frontal attack on them. Early in 1973,

Indian militants captured the tiny village of Wounded Knee on the Pine Ridge Reservation in South Dakota. They held it for two months, alternating negotiations with federal officials with almost daily shoot-outs with federal marshals and FBI agents. The government brought armored vehicles on the scene, but no attempt was made to dislodge the Indians.

The HEW report I quoted earlier was primarily concerned with the quality of work in America in general, but it offered a number of observations touching on the point of minority consciousness. "The most dissatisfied group of American workers . . . is [that of] young blacks in white-collar jobs. . . . They feel that they have been denied full and equal participation in American society. . . . They have had little control over the institutions that affect their lives—community, political, educational, or economic." Noting that more than a third of blacks under the age of twenty covered by a recent survey "express negative attitudes about their jobs," the report went on to say that "through age 44, blacks are about twice as likely as whites to be dissatisfied with their current work." Then it made what I thought to be an important observation: "Older blacks are twice as dissatisfied with their lives in general as they are with their jobs (most other groups are about as satisfied with one as they are with the other). This suggests that older black people—who often have experienced years of employment discrimination—are unique in that they view the issue of job satisfaction primarily in terms of employment versus no employment—a sad commentary on the long-range effects of racial injustice."

Another section of the HEW study demonstrated how the poor in general and poor minorities in particular are forced to pay an extra price for being poor and black. Blacks with incomes below $10,000 "apparently feel that small increments in income do not offer them sufficiently greater ability to consume" since "the minority dollar at that level of income does not buy the same amount of housing, education or consumer goods that the dollars of whites and wealthy minority group members buy." And indeed, it is a gruesome truth that a "black dollar" (or a Puerto Rican or Chicano or even poor white dollar) is worth considerably less than the usual white dollar. The cost of *everything* is higher in poor city areas than in affluent ones—whether we are talking about food, medicine, and clothing or a car or a television set. I was appalled by the difference in price for the same cut of meat between the supermarket where my wife shops in our white neighborhood and the food stores in black areas of central Washington—it was easily in the 10 per cent range. A spot check by a Washington radio station came up with the fact that drug stores in the all-black northeast section of the city often charge twice as much for medicine or even vitamins as pharmacists in white residential or downtown districts. Sales practices, particularly when credit is granted, are deceptive.

This massive rip-off is practiced by white, black, and Spanish-speaking merchants alike. There is no noticeable sense of solidarity between the black grocery owner and his black customer. The *bodega* owner does not bleed for a fellow Chicano or Puerto Rican. Life in the ghettos is governed by such economic realities as extremely high insurance rates (resulting from damage caused by past riots, vandalism, pilferage, and shoplifting) and the generally high cost of doing business at all. Minority businessmen are usually charged higher interest rates by banks and finance companies than merchants in nonpoverty areas. Social and therefore economic risks are greater. Substandard merchandise is palmed off on the poor because either they do not know any better than to buy what is on the shelf, or because for a variety of reasons (such as lack of transportation) they keep shopping in their own neighborhoods. A ghetto businessman told me, "If I have to pay more to stay in business, I have to pass it on to my customers." Another one, a shop owner on Washington's Seventh Street, said: "If I get ripped off by some dude, everybody else who buys from me has to make up for it, man. I just charge more."

As for the rat- and vermin-infested slum housing, landlords both white and black charge what the traffic will bear. A recent study has shown that renters paid about 8 per cent less and home owners 5 per cent less in all-white areas than in all-black areas. (Blacks pay between 2 and 5 per cent more than whites for *any* kind of housing.) Fortunes are thus often made at the expense of the poorest of all Americans.

Likewise, credit on legal terms is virtually unavailable because the poor are considered poor risks. Their options therefore range from borrowing cash at fantastic prepaid interest from loan sharks to paying of finance charges as high as 36 per cent a year for time purchase of goods. In the ghetto, protective legislation like the Truth-in-Lending Act is not worth the paper it is written on. And of course the merchant enjoys the enormously profitable opportunities of repossessing cars, TV sets, and whatnot when the buyer is in default on his time payments. An unusually candid businessman told me one day, "My daily prayer is for nonpayment, so that I can repossess."

Knowing how the urban poor pay for the sin of being poor, one realizes that income statistics and comparisons become meaningless. A family income of $5000 is in real-life terms considerably less than half of a $10,000 income outside the ghettos. The "poor dollar" just does not stretch as far as the "rich dollar." The food stamps buy proportionally less. It is social distortion to the nth degree.

Still, the poverty culture produces what seem to be extraordinary contradictions. When a nationwide meat boycott was launched by consumer groups in April 1973 to protest the skyrocketing prices of beef, pork, and lamb, the movement was totally ineffective in poor neighborhoods all over America. While middle- and upper-income groups faithfully boycotted the meat counters, the poor (white and the minorities) went on buying meat as before. I am not sure I can explain this behavioral disparity. Some people contend that black communities ignored the boycott because "they are used to being ripped off." A black psychologist friend of mine remarked, "When you're on welfare or living below the poverty line, it just doesn't matter if the goddam pork chop costs you another dime or quarter. Prices are just a blur to those people; they're so desperately poor anyway." Another explanation, which I think requires more thoughtful analysis, was that blacks considered the meat boycott like everything else "a white man's problem" and refused to be involved. An analogy offered in support of this viewpoint is that blacks likewise stayed away from the antiwar movement, although a large proportion of troops in Vietnam were blacks. But of course this does not explain why poor whites did not boycott the meat counters.

Most young sociologists and social economists believe that it is a basic structure fault of the American economy that keeps the poor trapped in poverty-level jobs. I have discussed this problem at length with a number of younger specialists—those who reject the traditional notion that in American society upward social mobility is truly possible—and I have read many of their studies. What follows is a rough summation of their analyses and conclusions.

The first conclusion was that income level, rather than any statistical fact of employment, forms the central American problem when one makes any attempt to do away with the social nightmare of poverty. The second was that the American economy is divided into primary and secondary labor markets. (This has become known as the theory of the "dual economy.")

The primary labor market is offered by the great industrial and trade corporations. There, the employer operates with high-quality capital equipment and has a major investment in the worker, who has been taught necessary and complex skills. He therefore has a vested social interest in the worker and in maintaining as limited a labor turnover as possible. He makes the decision when a worker is laid off for whatever recessional reasons and when he is hired or rehired. Because of this importance of the worker—as well as because of the pressure of well-organized labor unions—the primary employer is agreeable to paying decent wages. Increases in pay and other production costs are passed on to the consumer to avoid profit erosion. This sector of the economy, "blue-collar blues" notwithstanding, is quite stable although the corporations must increasingly address themselves to the mounting problem of the well-paid but morally discontented worker.

The worker I am describing here is the regularly employed family head who takes home close to $10,000 annually (and often more), drives his own car, is probably a home owner (with the bank holding the mortgage), and is very much part of consumer society, though mostly on credit. In all probability he is a high-school graduate and participates in societal life by voting in elections, becoming involved in parent-teacher associations, and so on. His discontent, such as it is, stems from the boredom of his job—usually in an industrial plant—rather than his economic status. He also knows that he is probably fixed forever at the level of his present job because he has no other real options; also, he has an investment in both seniority and (if there is one) his retirement plan.

The secondary labor market—some specialists call it the economic periphery—lacks all the advantages of the primary market. It begins with the employer who is usually engaged in a form of commerce or service activity. He exercises no market control, works on a small profit margin within the framework of a narrow operation, and has no interest either in modernizing his antiquated capital equipment, if any, or in his worker. He requires no special skills of and demands only routine tasks from his worker. Job stability from his viewpoint is irrelevant; in fact, he often benefits from instability and quick turnover because he will not then be forced to increase wages. Almost as a rule, his workers are not unionized. He draws his labor force from the vast pool of the unemployed and subemployed; he has no interest in the worker's education; he pays poverty-level wages.

The worker caught in the secondary market is for the most part a city dweller, often but not always black, Puerto Rican, or Chicano, though America's countryside, too, has its share of the secondary market. He is the expendable American. Chances are that he or she lives in a tenement and is partially on welfare. One sees these workers in every American city—as dishwashers, delivery boys, stockroom employees, or handymen. (To be a truck or bus driver, elevator operator, or garbageman represents a certain stability and status since most of them are unionized.)

Somewhere between the two markets are skilled workers with seasonal jobs. A bricklayer in Akron, Ohio, for example, earns ten dollars an hour when he gets work. In Washington, D.C., some sheet-metal workers make as much as $339 a week, and the predominantly white unions are gradually accepting black journeymen.

But given the very real racial discrimination in employment (which, more or less subtly, ignores equal-opportunity legislation), the black and Hispanic workers are the principal victims of the secondary labor market. For them, even just a high-school education will not necessarily be a bridge to better work opportunities. Although the Census Bureau found that whites and blacks under the age of thirty-four have attended school for roughly the same median number of years (the whites are ahead by decimal percentage points), they are faced with sharp wage differentials in the labor market. So social scientists increasingly question the validity of the traditional theory that formal education is relevant to the quality of the job one eventually works at. They reject the cherished old American notion that "poverty is a function of inadequate human capital" (human capital being defined as the combination of skill and knowledge). Instead, the younger social researchers say, what is relevant is the real "institutional racism" of the American economy. They have documented the "racial division of labor" in the United States, and they propound a so-called crowding hypothesis according to which some jobs simply are not open to blacks (and Hispanic Americans). When jobs do open up, the wage differential between whites and minorities is "crucial," as one study put it. There also exists "class discrimination" against poor whites in America's central cities. (For reasons mentioned earlier, Vietnam war veterans are among this class of poor whites.) The unstable white laborer in a central city has a hard time finding a good job because the employer frequently shies away from the cultural characteristics of the poor white out of fear that his and his firm's respectability will suffer.

Assuming as they do that no major changes in the American social or economic structure are likely to occur, most of these young sociologists agree that high-wage jobs in America will not increase in the predictable future and that poverty jobs will not be reduced. At best, labor experts say, there will be "some substitution." Social economists have calculated that even if racial discrimination disappeared altogether, the resulting reduction of no more than 6–9 per cent in the incomes of white men with no high-school diplomas will benefit minorities only on the lowest poverty level. But low-income whites in the cities, particularly the ethnic groups, are obviously aware that they will suffer with the advent of true racial equality in employment, and they find it in their interest to advocate continued discrimination.

To digress for a moment, this so-called ethnic question is enormously complicated in part because of the impossibility of defining clearly who the ethnics are and how many of them there are. Let us say here simply that ethnics are clearly identifiable and closely knit groups of descendants of European immigrants who have maintained and even accentuated their special cultural and religious characteristics. For reasons of history, culture, and religion, Jews of Eastern or Central European extraction do not consider themselves as ethnics in the usual sense; a Pole, a Czech, or Ukrainian of Roman Catholic or Orthodox faith is an ethnic (as are Italians and Irishmen), but a Polish, Russian, or Rumanian Jew is not. A further complication, sociological as well as statistical, arises when one has to decide where to draw the ethnic line: at the first, second, third, or fourth generation after immigration?

One way of resolving these difficulties is simply to allow that an ethnic is an ethnic if he says he is one. In this sense, there were a lot more of them in 1970 than there had been in 1950 or 1960. The Census Bureau, as perplexed as everybody else, came to the conclusion that, in 1970, 82.1 per cent of white Americans could be classified as "native of native parentage" (as compared with 61.3 per cent in 1900) and 13 per cent as "natives of foreign or mixed parentage." This last category comprised 3.2 million Italian-Americans of foreign or mixed parentage, 2.8 million Germans, 1.8 million English, 1.2 million Irish, 1.8 million Poles, 1.5 million Russians, and 5.5 million described as "other Europe." But this stringent definition according to parentage was offensive to many ethnic organizations, which protested indignantly that the yardstick was unfair and that their second- or third-generation people had been undercounted. A Polish-American leader, for example, informed me that there were between five and ten million ethnic Poles in the country.

Most social scientists and observers agree nowadays that the old "melting pot" concept has vanished—it is debatable whether in fact it ever really operated in practice—to be replaced by the "salad bowl" idea, and this reveals an interesting transformation in attitudes. Since the nineteenth century, children of European immigrants had a strong urge to achieve the quickest and most complete identification possible with American society. Names were changed and origins often denied. American literature of the 1920s and 1930s is full of tales of immigrant children ashamed of parents who had not mastered the English language and who clung to "old country" customs. This was certainly true as late as 1947, when I first came to live in America. Traditions were kept alive by small nuclei of people, with churches and social and fraternal groups playing a central role in their maintenance.

Still, attitudes were ambivalent, and people almost lived double lives. Most of the time they acted as Americans, which, of course, they were. But at the same time they clustered together in their own little cities-within-cities, and until the 1960s, they formed clearly defined political voting blocs, almost always supporting the Democratic party. In those days, of course, *all* minority votes were for the Democrats: ethnics, Catholics, Jews, and blacks.

But the white ethnics' renewed assertion of *their* heritages was more than a mere cultural response to the black cultural revolution. It was a defensive social and economic move. Most of the ethnics, particularly the East Europeans, were blue-collar workers who experienced a very slow rate of upward social mobility in terms of education, jobs, and incomes. In a relative sense, their upward mobility was even less than that of blacks when the latter finally began climbing the social ladder. So a great deal of the white "backlash" against the civil-rights movement came from East Europeans, who in all matters of job, status, and even neighborhoods were more discriminatory against blacks than the long-maligned WASPs. From this, as commentators have begun to note, it is only a step toward class strife against the "elites."

My first exposure to this phenomenon came during the 1964 presidential campaign when, given my own Polish background, I was assigned by my newspaper to travel to upstate New York to look for the "backlash" in Polish-populated areas. I found it even stronger in 1972 when I toured industrial centers in Pennsylvania and New York where there are large concentrations of Polish-descended workers. In 1964, the ethnics had gone along with Lyndon Johnson—the black revolution was only just beginning—but in 1972 they deserted the Democratic party for Nixon's Republicans or went to George Wallace. (Had Senator Muskie been the Democratic candidate, he would have probably carried the Polish vote; as the editor of a Polish-language newspaper in Scranton remarked to me, "How often do we get a chance to elect a Pole to the White House?") My interviews left no doubt in my mind that the ethnic swing to the Republican Right was principally motivated by anti-black economic and social considerations, although the ethnics were never liberals. In the past they had voted for Democrats because men like Franklin Roosevelt gave them the socioeconomic advantages they sought. But in 1972, they saw George McGovern as a threat to the positions they had achieved in preceding decades. Nobody made any bones about these sentiments. In Pittsburgh, I discovered, most of the key Muskie organizers in Polish communities were registered Republicans.

Thus in 1972 the revival of ethnic identities and heritage might be seen to be the cultural component of the rallying against nonwhite minorities. Membership in Polish, Czech, and other East European clubs was growing; fourth-generation Poles were suddenly learning Polish and were irked by "Polack" jokes. A Philadelphia frozen-food millionaire of Polish descent (he does not speak Polish) launched a remarkable nationwide campaign through huge newspaper advertisements to convince Americans that Poland had made a rich contribution to Western civilization. He was the moving spirit behind the anniversary celebrations in 1973 of Copernicus' birth, which reached their climax at a black-tie inauguration of a Copernicus exhibit at the Smithsonian Institution in Washington. Television produced a Polish-named detective—in the somewhat-less-than-successful "Banacek" series. And so on. Italian and Irish organizations, traditionally powerful, gained still further strength from this ethnic cultural revolution. For all the wrong reasons, presumably books and movies like *The Godfather* put an Italian imprint on the American consciousness, but Italian groups prevailed on television and movie executives to cease identifying the Mafia with Italians.

In any case, to return to the labor situation in the inner cities, welfare became a public subsidy for low-wage employers in the secondary labor markets. These employers knew that the black and ethnic workers they depended on would survive despite the impossible level of wages because of welfare benefits paid out by the state to families with dependent children, food stamps, public-housing allowances, Medicaid, etc. They also knew about the ghetto "hustle." So they felt no pressure to improve wages or working conditions. For the workers, what has developed under this system is a vicious circle of poverty where they are caught between the employers and the welfare bureaucracy. Even government job-placement programs do no more than recirculate the few inadequate jobs available and function, in the view of one scientist I know, as "a passive accessory to discrimination." Much has been made by welfare critics of the welfare recipients' alleged refusal to work, and a law now requires recipients to register for work. But the results were not at all what had been expected, as a HEW report published in April 1973 made clear.

In the first place, out of 15 million Americans receiving some form of welfare, 11 million were getting full-fledged benefits. But 8 million of them were children, and out of the balance of 3 million, only a million have registered for jobs under the Nixon "workfare" program since July 1, 1972. The other 2 million may be mothers with small children, elderly or ill people, and, presumably, those who really prefer welfare to work—nobody knows the breakdown. But the real story is that of the million who did register for jobs; only a little more than a quarter were certified as being *able* to work. Out of this small number, the government, incredibly, was able to find work for *only* 82,075 persons. This should dispose of the facile notion that the welfare poor should go out and get to work. Work *where?*

A growing body of opinion, proceeding from the premise held by many social economists that "the majority of the poor in America work for their poverty," holds that society's principal objective should be to create good jobs and not to "train people for non-existent jobs," in the words of one student of the problem. For nearly a decade we have been doing the latter. Since the early 1960s, billions of dollars have been spent on training and retraining programs for young and poor, on the theory that once a person is taught a skill, he or she will quickly find a decent job. Even an economist of the stature of John Kenneth Galbraith believed that "the effect of education and related investment in individuals is to enable them either to contend more effectively with their environment or to escape it and take up life elsewhere on more or less equal terms with others." The result of this kind of well-meaning argument was an extraordinary proliferation of training programs.

But there were no jobs awaiting the trainees. The planners of the 1960s overlooked the fundamental reality of racial discrimination against minorities and class discrimination against poor whites, and were oblivious to the truth that with the American

economy weighed down with discrimination and secondary labor markets, it simply made no sense to train people. As the track
record shows, all the programs did virtually nothing to alleviate
American poverty. The General Accounting Office daily commented, "No one knows how many people are being trained, for
what occupations they are being trained, or the impact of the
training on the demand for skilled workers."

It is not just a failure in the job-training programs. The new
generation of social scientists question as well the value of the
American public school, which theoretically offers the same
education to rich and poor, to whites and minorities. Here criticism centers on the argument that American public education is
too theoretical—aside from the basic "three Rs"—and fails to
prepare the student for the cruel realities of the post-graduation
world, while at the same time unfairly raising the expectations
of the poor. To use Theodore Roszak's expression, we are faced
by "iatrogenic" social problems, that is to say, problems induced
by "doctors" seeking to cure the society. In his book *Inequality,*
Harvard professor Christopher Jencks persuasively advocates a
rethinking of our whole approach to education in the light of
social and job opportunities. The unresolved question is, of
course, whether schools should prepare people merely for careers or for life as well.

In a recent study devoted to jobs and education, the point was
made that "increased educational investment may only increase
the effective supply of secondary labor, driving black wages even
further down." By "educational investment," of course, the study
meant traditional schooling. "Conventional education in the
ghetto" "prepares [the student] to accept uncreative, routine, unskilled jobs after 'graduation.' . . . [It] frustrates the development
of aspirations which might be socially destabilizing."

This, of course, brings us back to the nineteenth-century concept that education should discipline the worker for the benefit

of the employer. But we do not live in the nineteenth century, and blacks educated in this conventional way also come under powerful outside influences, such as the new black pride and black nationalism. The preservation of the existing educational system only seems like an invitation to young blacks to strengthen their militancy. A black educator in California summed up the whole problem when he spoke of how American society must find some way of relating education to work. "Otherwise," he said, "there is bound to be an explosion. If there is no explosion, you'll have the next worst thing: a decision by blacks to separate themselves altogether from white society."

But, in the meantime, and bearing in mind the failures of school and government programs to open up the labor situation for the minorities, what type of employment *did* they hold in 1970 as compared with whites?

The Census tells us that minorities accounted for 30 per cent of nonfarm laborers (twice their representation in the whole population), 7 per cent of what the Census Bureau calls "craftsmen and kindred workers" (less than half of their percentage in the population). There were as many minority as white private household workers—cooks, butlers, chauffeurs, and cleaning women—and in the case of more than half a million black women thus employed, the overwhelming majority were welfare mothers. Minorities held just over 3 per cent of all urban posts as managers and administrators (one-fifth of their percentage in the population), and out of a total of more than 30 million blacks and Hispanics, there were in 1970 only 25,892 physicians, dentists, and other medical practitioners, most of them in cities. The 538,746 white physicians, dentists, etc., accounted for more than 96 per cent of the national total. Only with teachers was the racial balance in proportion to the overall population balance.

For the urban poor, the best opportunity for decent employment was provided in public service, that is, in jobs on the federal, state, or local government payroll. In the words of a social scientist, "The public service job is the port of entry for the 'underclass.' " This was especially true of blacks, who could compete for government jobs on the basis of qualification and without fear of racial discrimination, since government agencies obviously had to enforce the laws on equal opportunity. I must say it strikes me as immensely ironic that in a capitalist society, ostensibly devoted to the principles of free enterprise, the state provides the bulk of decent jobs to underprivileged and minorities. It would appear that free enterprise has little respect for the laws of the land, or even for simple human decency.

Government is, of course, a primary labor market on all levels. Federal employment offers such inducements as retirement and health plans as well as civil-service job protection; many state administrations do likewise. So public jobs provide considerable stability which in turn affects social and family stability. (For example, 77 per cent of all Americans employed full-time in public administration worked year-round in 1969. In the urban private sector, the figure was only 58 per cent.) Criticism of "big government" has always been heard from America's conservatives, and it is entirely possible that government, particularly in Washington, is, indeed, too big. There are about 2.5 million federal workers. But given the attitudes prevailing in the private sector, government has been the savior of America's central cities.

Between 1960 and 1970, jobs in state and local governments rose by 63 per cent while employment in the private sector went up by only 20 per cent. (Because purchases of goods and services by state and local governments from the private sector jumped from $58 billion in 1962 to $121 billion in 1970, new private employment resulting from it rose by 50 per cent in the cities.) President Nixon has, however, steadily reduced the ranks of federal employees. It is obviously unpredictable what will happen in the central cities if the Nixon budget reductions cut too deeply into black employment at a time when welfare programs are being slashed as well. But this is what I found a few years ago in three major cities with a high racial explosive potential. In Detroit, 60 per cent of the blacks held government jobs while 14.8 per cent were in private-sector employment. In Philadelphia, government jobs were held by 55.7 per cent of the blacks while only 12.2 per cent of them are privately employed. And in Memphis, 66 per cent of them held public jobs and 26 per cent private jobs.

Public jobs held by blacks in American cities range from mayoralties to garbage men. Incomes vary, of course, but, by and large, the jobs are stable. In my own contacts with black officials and workers, I discovered in them a fine sense of pride and dignity. They considered themselves finally out of the ghetto poverty culture—they had gone through the "port of entry" into the American society—and as the backbone of the emerging black middle class. They had high hopes for their children and, as other Americans, they were beginning to move into the suburbs. "Yes, man, I can hold my head high," a black city official in Philadelphia said. "I'm like everybody else in America. I have a steady job and I have respect from people. From the whites and from the blacks. That's the way it should be."

Washington, D.C., where I live, is a special case. What keeps Washington from all-out racial struggle is the existence of a black middle class based on government jobs and, indeed, on the tradition of having them. Black families in the capital have an average annual income of $9600, just under the national median. In the last decade, the number of black families earning more than $14,000 rose to almost 30 per cent, while those with incomes under $4000 dropped to 17 per cent. (Still, 119,000 Washingtonians—more than a seventh of the capital's population—were on welfare in mid-1973, with the case load rising for the first time in five years.) Washington's stable black population of "cliff dwellers" coexists quite peaceably with the city's white "cliff dweller" class, both going back several generations, but they live in nearly total separation. The black community—whether in the affluent northeast section, with its neat and fairly expensive homes, or in the slums of the northwest inner city and Anacostia southeast—has a strong social fabric. Sure, there is crime and drug addiction—what city doesn't have these scourges in this day and age?—but the community polices itself quite effectively, with the churches and community organizations, especially women's groups, playing an important role. (In fact, most of Washington's active politicians have church backgrounds.)

During April 1973 it was my lot to serve briefly on a jury in the D.C. Superior Court. I spent a week, from 9:00 a.m. to 5:00 p.m., in the crowded jury lounge awaiting a call to come down to one of the courtrooms to sit on a case. But there were 499 of us in the April jury pool, and most of my time was spent just sitting around and chatting with the others. Perhaps four out of five of us were black men and women, and they represented a perfect cross section of Washington's black middle class. All of the well-dressed black jurors were remarkably relaxed and at ease in the court surroundings, even though they knew that almost in every instance they would be sitting in judgment on fellow blacks. I found them to be of unfailing courtesy and dignity.

Jobs, I have argued, are obviously key to every other aspect of urban life. But a related issue is the quantity and quality of housing, for it, too, defines other social attitudes. Housing means home, and home is where people ideally spend most of their nonworking time. When homes are unlivable, people, especially young people, move to the streets—and this can mean crime, prostitution, drug addiction. Children become "street-wise."

A city is, of course, more than the sum total of its buildings, houses, and streets, and the people who inhabit it. But it is axiomatic that cities as we now know them will survive only if conditions are created for the inhabitants to exist in a modicum of decency. If the people are neglected—and this is where we are thrown back to the question of proper employment—the cities will inevitably decay. The cancer presently eating away at the inner core of America's cities will surely spread. People and jobs will continue to disappear.

The more American cities I have seen, the more I have become convinced that they are caught in the throes of terrible social misunderstandings and self-defeating contradictions. After my last extensive tour of the country, I happened to read a housing study written by Henry J. Aaron, a Senior Fellow at the Brookings Institution in Washington, and I think he hit the nail on the head: "Governments tend to treat the problems of decaying neighborhoods—the dilapidated structures, poor schools, inadequate transportation, high crime rate—with programs aimed principally at physical renewal or reconstruction. That tendency may reflect a recognition that it is easier to renew structures than to deal with other problems; it may also reflect the confusion of the physical, social, and economic problems of decaying neighborhoods with the 'housing problem.' "

For my part, the main confusion lay in the willingness of governments and private industry to engage in extraordinary investments to modernize and beautify the downtown business districts while virtually ignoring the real housing needs of most of the urban population. What was the purpose of grandiose monuments that were completely irrelevant to the human requirements of the city's inhabitants? If anything, these amazing efforts appeared to be aimed at the pleasure and convenience of out-of-town commuters whom the cities did not want to lose, or at satisfying misguided civic pride. A city government is presumably remembered for what it built for posterity, but I hate to think of it as an attempt to create modern Romes and Athenses whose spectacular ruins a future civilization may admire. Our civilization can already admire the ruins of present-day inner cities. I must agree with Aaron that the whole approach to the cities is based on the fact that it is easier to erect a building than to face a human problem.

As matters have developed, many American cities have acquired a certain architectural beauty (or, at least, ostentation) thanks to policies jointly devised by local governments and private enterprise. These policies have achieved everything except a social purpose, but there has been no stimulus to do otherwise.

Let me start at home—in Washington. It has always been a lovely city, ever since Major Charles Pierre L'Enfant designed it under George Washington's and Thomas Jefferson's supervision. It has wide tree-shaded avenues (although many now have lost both their trees and their charm to become slum thoroughfares), the still-unspoiled Rock Creek Park (where I ride my saddle horse over some thirty miles of wooded trails and my dog, Jason, hurls himself after squirrels and ducks), a half-dozen other smaller parks, the spectacular Mall and Reflecting Pool, surrounded much of the year by banks of flowers, the imposing Lincoln and Washington Memorials, the classic architecture of the White House, Capitol, and Supreme Court, hundreds of old mansions and Georgian and Federal houses, and the lazy sweep of the Potomac (too polluted for swimming, but beautiful) with its wooded Virginia bank. It is a city where one hears birds singing every morning. I always experience a sense of intense pleasure and relief when my plane, bringing me from some less-fortunate city, glides down over the river for the landing in Washington.

Beginning in the late 1950s, however, Washington decided to modernize itself, partly because of a growing population and the gradual shift of corporate and financial power here. Besides, a lot of the city was beginning to decay. Shedding its provincialism, Washington built the Federal Triangle downtown, the Kennedy Center and the Watergate complex on the Potomac, the monstrously modern Sam Rayburn House of Representatives Office Building, and the relatively graceful L'Enfant Plaza and Mall in the southwest section of the city. L'Enfant Plaza and its new office buildings was part of a larger urban-renewal project which cleared away the old slums for poor blacks between the Capitol and the river, replacing them with elegant townhouses selling for anywhere between $40,000 and $120,000, high-rise apartment buildings with swimming pools, and a luxury hotel.

Midtown Washington, too, underwent a remarkable transformation. The steady movement of business headquarters and offices from New York and elsewhere to Washington—because of the combination of the city's relatively easy, pleasant way of life and the government's growing centralized power—created a huge demand for office space. The expanding downtown area became filled with luxury office buildings, some of them quite remarkable architecturally. (The District authorities had the good sense to ban skyscrapers that would have destroyed Washington's fairly harmonious ensemble. In contrast, tall office buildings rise in an absurd modernistic cluster in Rosslyn, Virginia, across the river from Georgetown.) Concurrently, the city was forced (and pleased) to provide services ranging from brokerage offices to restaurants. New French restaurants have been opening in Washington as quickly as others have closed down in New York. Culture—in the form of the Kennedy Center, the suburban Virginia warm-weather performing center at Wolf Trap, and a half-dozen new theaters—has caught up with other aspects of the city's growth. In recent years, I have had as many opportunities to hear Rubinstein, Richter, Oistrakh, or Menuhin in Washington as I would have in New York. More and more major Broadway plays now open at the Kennedy Center's Eisenhower Theater.

Washington has ambitious plans for downtown malls for pe-
destrians (automobile traffic will be banned there) and a general
prettying up of the shopping district. Excellent housing is available for those who can afford the new apartment buildings, the
southwest townhouses, and the comfortable homes in the northwest with their azalea gardens. But—especially since the Nixon
administration froze federal housing funding in 1973 in favor of
vague revenue-sharing plans—there is neither money nor serious official desire to improve housing conditions for low-income
groups. The District's Redevelopment Land Agency, which has
become something of a slum landlord in Washington, may get as
much (or as little) as $50 million to rebuild the "riot corridors,"
the inner-city areas burned out in the 1968 riots. But this leaves
nothing for the rest of the city and its less-privileged inhabitants.
Among other programs reduced or terminated by the freeze was
Washington's Model Inner City Community Organization
(MICCO) serving the Shaw ghetto area north of downtown which
comprises about 40,000 inhabitants. MICCO was an experiment
in citizen control of urban renewal. The notion behind it was that
blacks should no longer be simply removed against their will
from an area to make room for urban redevelopment for the
affluent. Created in 1966 as the first such national experimentation community control, MICCO was to be the recipient of federal funds for low-income housing for the community itself.

The MICCO story as it actually developed is instructive in what
it tells about the realities of inner-city life. Although MICCO
received around $50 million in six years, it immediately ran into
what is everywhere the growing nightmare of well-intentioned
neighborhood developers. The quandary for MICCO was
whether to spend its money on moderate-income housing, which
would improve the quality of the local urban environment, or try
to go for the familiar low-income public high-rises which, experience has taught everyone, breed crime and so forth. In the end,
MICCO built four comparatively small projects for families with

$6000–$13,000 incomes, but the rub was that less than half of Shaw's population could afford this type of housing.

Whether or not MICCO was wise or responsive to community needs became irrelevant when the administration ruled in 1972 that rental income in publicly funded low-income housing had to cover 115 per cent of operating costs. *The Washington Post* calculated that in the case of single-family houses (preferred to the high-rises), the home owner "would have to earn enough to cover 10 per cent above monthly charges without exceeding 25 per cent of his income." This was out of the reach of the Shaw poor who were otherwise eligible for public housing because MICCO, no more than the home owner, could not handle such a financial burden. Seven years after it was created, MICCO thus had little to show for its activities except the ownership of condemned slum property. To compound the misery, two corporations linked to MICCO used their funds to buy two fully occupied apartment buildings outside the Shaw area. By 1973, MICCO funds were cut further, forcing it to abandon a whole series of social projects such as adult education, senior-citizen centers, and store-front libraries.

New York City, which saw billions of dollars invested in spectacular office buildings from the twin towers of the World Trade Center to offices in the Bronx, could find no solution for the housing of its poor. The housing deficit was estimated in 1973 at 800,000 units (approximately the needs of some three million people), but the Nixon administration froze work on fifty-two housing projects. Simultaneously, 38,000 apartments were being abandoned every year as unlivable. In a series of articles on the South Bronx, *The New York Times* described the area as a "necropolis." An expert put it succinctly when he said that welfare families had become "refugees"—from their homes and environment, squatters in abandoned buildings or "welfare hotels."

The tragedy is, of course, that nobody except the poor wants low-cost housing around. The popular image, not always a wrong one, presents low-cost housing projects as centers of crime and other social problems. Even if the local administration wants federally subsidized housing, neighborhoods often oppose it on the grounds that the resulting influx of the poor, especially non-white, will force property values to drop, disturb racial balance in the schools, etc. At this point the federal government often has to act to prevent discrimination. In Hamtramck, a largely Polish city near Detroit, a federal judge ordered that new housing be built for four thousand black residents forced out of their homes by urban-renewal programs. In Parma, a pleasant suburb of Cleveland, the Department of Justice charged that local officials were denying housing opportunities to blacks by blocking construction of a federally aided housing project. In Saint Louis (where the Pruitt-Igoe housing project was dynamited after its inhabitants abandoned it), the federal government has challenged the right of the Black Jack suburb to use its zoning laws to exclude federally financed low-cost housing, mostly designed for blacks. In Chicago, a judge ordered in 1965 the building of public housing in white neighborhoods—yet nothing was done because contractors wanted no part of it.

Despite such occasional interventions under the Open Housing Act, the federal government has made no concerted effort to enforce housing equality. The United States Commission on Civil Rights said in a report in 1973 that housing segregation "is the result of past discriminatory practices in which the private housing industry and federal, state and local governments have been active participants." Now the Commission, whose members are appointed by the President of the United States, is a totally independent body whose responsibility is to act as something of a national conscience concerning the rights of citizens. It has been one of those refreshing and courageous voices speaking out in the stifled atmosphere of our society, where so often nobody is willing to be blamed for anything, and it has long been at odds with the Nixon administration. In any case, it charged that in practice the government is a "key participant" in decisions by private parties as to where housing will go: "The housing industry, aided and abetted by the Government, must bear the primary responsibility for the legacy of segregated housing. . . . Residential segregation is so deeply ingrained in American life that the job of assuring equal housing opportunity to minority groups means not only eliminating present discriminatory practices but correcting the mistakes of the past as well."

As of June 1970, more than 2.5 million Americans lived in federally supported housing units. In 1968, the Housing and Urban Development Act had committed the United States to build or rehabilitate 26 million housing units by 1978 (the idea was that the government would be responsible for 6 million units and private enterprise for 20 million), but it is obvious that neither the government nor private builders will attain this objective. For one thing, incredible abuses by private contractors and speculators have demoralized the programs. And the Nixon freeze has virtually eliminated any serious hope that the poor will be assisted. New York City, for example, needed about $1 billion a year to solve its housing problem; this was ten times what it received from Washington in the "best year" of 1968. Baltimore concluded that ten thousand eligible poor would have to wait indefinitely for new housing because of the moratorium.

Private industry has turned its back on public housing because it ceased to be profitable, despite a 1969 tax provision intended to encourage investments in the slums. Private builders now concentrate only on the most expensive areas, where cooperative or condominium buyers or renters can pay any price. The administration's attitude on this point is best expressed in a speech given in March 1973 by Robert M. McGlotten, a special assistant to Labor Secretary Peter J. Brennan. McGlotten, who is himself black, told the National Association of Minority Contractors to forget ghetto building and turn to profitable industrial and commercial work. "You and I," he said, "know there's going to be some construction in the ghetto, but that ain't where the money is." McGlotten mentioned white contractors' projects and advised his audience, "If you want to make some money, you'd better get next to them and find out what they're doing." His comments, it seemed to me, went quite a distance to confirm what the Civil Rights Commission had to say.

Notwithstanding all the problems associated with low-cost public projects, hundreds of thousands of families are on waiting lists to be assigned space in them, since they offer the only alternative to slum dwellings of the worst type. Who should be eligible for the little there is around? I have talked with housing administrators and social workers in half a dozen cities to find something approximating an answer, but I found no agreement. Each expert had his own view. In his book *Shelter and Subsidies,* Henry Aaron stated the dilemma in this way: "The uneven political fortune of public housing expresses a continuing lack of consensus about its objectives. Which poor people should get housing assistance when there isn't enough to go around? The poorest, who can pay little for their own housing, or the not-quite-so-poor, who can pay more rent and get along with smaller subsidies? The mostly white aged who might otherwise be a burden on their probably middle-class children? Fatherless, frequently black, families with many dependent children? Intact families with heads unable to earn an adequate income? The one alternative clearly eliminated by the modest size of the program is that all poor people should be eligible." I remember meeting a welfare mother in East Harlem who asked, after having her application turned down for the third time for a public-housing apartment, "Why not *me?* . . . Why can't I get a home? . . . What's wrong with me and my kids?" There was no answer to her question.

This housing crisis continues, as I have said, alongside major downtown renewal plans—a strangely imbalanced arrangement that can be found across the country. Detroit, with miles and miles of slums, the scene of ugly racial riots in 1967, has launched a $30 million project to develop thirty-two acres of land on the banks of Detroit River not far from City Hall. Plans are for a seventy-story hotel, several office buildings, shopping arcades, and riverfront luxury apartments. But the city can no longer build low-cost housing, and uses its meager funds to demolish abandoned buildings where crime thrives. Cleveland has been erecting a downtown complex of high-price apartment buildings known as the Park Center. Cincinnati has designed a modernistic plaza around its Fountain landmark, rebuilt the old waterfront, and erected a new Riverfront Stadium for its baseball and football teams. Indianapolis, still a growing city, has invested in a huge sports arena, as well as Market Square and Lincoln Square projects to include hotels, offices, and apartments.

In the Southwest, oil-rich Oklahoma City has come up with the Myriad, a $25 million convention and sports center that the traveler can see from the elevated freeway crossing the city. (He can also see the oil wells within city limits that make it all possible.) Another $17 million is earmarked for Myriad Gardens, intended to be one of America's greatest parks. Inevitably, new office skyscrapers complete the Oklahoma City landscape. Dallas built an attractive hotel-and-office complex in the early 1960s, with the slums just a short walk away. Denver, an integral part of the fabulous growth of the state of Colorado, is spending $40 million on a downtown development which includes luxury offices and apartments as well as low-income housing structures and a pedestrian mall. An $80 million bond issue will finance a performing arts center.

In the East, it is Albany, capital of the state of New York, that may vie for the honor of having one of the most ostentatious downtown areas. Along the great Albany Mall, estimated to cost

$1.5 billion, five out of the planned eleven marble towers have been built, to serve as offices for state employees and private businesses. (In the center, ninety-eight acres of concrete parking spaces hide under the mall.) A critic has compared the project to something that might have been produced by a Stalin, Hitler, or Mussolini. But its sponsor, former Governor Nelson Rockefeller, has described it as "one of the marvels of the world." White Plains, no longer a New York suburb but a city in its own right, has spent millions of dollars on new downtown facilities serving its own suburbs.

In the South, Atlanta, the "Cinderella City" of America, has made a major effort to attract business and industry—thus creating jobs—and to beautify itself by erecting shopping and entertainment malls over its railroad tracks. Less ambitiously but just as fervently, Winston-Salem, North Carolina, has redesigned its downtown area to build a shoppers' mall ($20 million) around old Trade Street. Last time I visited, it was coming along almost on schedule, but the tobacco factories' workers still lived in their old slums.

In Miami, which is now a megalopolis on the verge of suffocation, the accent is on more and more luxury apartment buildings, condominiums, and hotels; there is no particularly rational plan to any of this. The once tranquil islands in the bay and inland waters have been turned into "instant cities." Because demand was skyrocketing and private money was available—Dade County is a boom region—41,000 new luxury apartment units were authorized in 1972 alone.

At the same time that all this is going on, local officials across the United States have been worrying about the steady abandonment of substandard buildings. This happens—and I have seen it in a half-dozen cities—when the landlord reaches the point where the meager rents he can collect (even if they are not meager by the tenants' standards) can no longer cover his taxes and his repairs, much less provide a profit. So he simply flees, and the building quickly becomes no longer habitable. Heat and running water cease. Broken windows are replaced with newspaper and rags. Garbage is not collected. The tenants leave, and the empty structures turn into "dope houses" where addicts shoot up and homeless squatters hide for the night. And abandonment is contagious. When one building goes, a whole area may follow. Touring such a place is like being in a town or village where the bubonic plague has struck. And, since no money is available for renewal programs, the best the cities can do is to demolish the abandoned houses. Nobody has any idea what to do with the people—other than to watch them being demolished too. Is this the proper approach to solving the great American urban crisis?

The new America of the second half of the twentieth century is the huge suburban fringe. The suburban phenomenon offers extraordinary concentrations of wealth and power, as well as a wholly new culture, a new mercantilism and life style. The irony is, however, that in their haste to flee the crowded cities the suburbanites have created perhaps insurmountable problems of excessive growth. Unless ways are devised to control this savage growth, the suburbs will turn into a parody of the old cities from which their founders ran away. The first signs are already clear.

By mid-1974, 60 million Americans lived in the suburbs, satellite urban areas, and the new planned communities near the cities. (The Census figure for 1970 was 55 million, but steady migrations and the population growth in suburbia have added at least 5 million in less than three years.) Statistically, most of these Americans were inhabitants of those Standard Metropolitan Statistical Areas (SMSA) I talked about earlier, but this arbitrary concept became even more meaningless as suburban counties, towns, and villages developed lives and identities of their own. "We're not New Yorkers any more," a friend told me shortly after he moved his family from Manhattan to a village on the Hudson some forty miles away. "As far as I'm concerned, we belong to our village and our county: this is where we live, where we play, where we pay taxes, send our kids to school, vote, shop, eat out—and die. It's completely immaterial whether I earn my living in New York City. It's just an economic and geographic accident. I couldn't care less about New York's problems: they're no longer mine. I get there in the morning, do my job, and get the hell out as soon as I can in the afternoon." Another friend, this one in Berkeley, lived pleasantly in a split-level house in the hills and went to San Francisco as rarely as possible. His interest in the affairs of San Francisco or Oakland (which is separated by a street from Berkeley) bordered on zero. That Berkeley and Oakland are statistically part of the San Francisco SMSA was completely uninteresting to him. The same was true of many of my friends in Virginia and Maryland. Most of them worked in the District of Columbia (and commuted there for social occasions, to catch a good concert at the Kennedy Center, or to spend fifty dollars for dinner in a posh French restaurant) but were entirely uninterested in Washington's problems.

Where, then, does a city begin and where does it end? We need to know not only for our sense of identity but even in an aesthetic sense. A new definition has become known among architects and urban planners as the "city edge," and, in 1973, the federal government earmarked over $1 million for conceptual studies on how best the city edge could be marked. In an odd way, this was the return to the medieval practice of building walls around cities so that it would be absolutely clear what and who was inside or outside the walls. The new walls were not meant for physical protection from an invader; instead, they were intended in whatever form (they could even be parks or landscaped areas) to protect the inhabitants' sense of identity.

When I say that American suburbs contain an extraordinary concentration of affluence, even wealth, then I am pointing to one of the reasons why the centers of political power in the United States are gradually shifting away from the big cities to their surrounding counties—something that national and state candidates for elective office have come to realize for more than a decade. The suburbs are where money for campaigns is more and more likely to be found, along with votes cast by the best-educated and therefore theoretically the most politically conscious citizens. In the old days, the candidate who carried New York City carried the state, but this, as Democrats have discovered, is no longer necessarily true. And the same goes for Chicago and Illinois, Pittsburgh and Pennsylvania.

Suburban affluence is best measured by median family incomes, and the best way to measure these incomes is by counties. The 1970 Census tells us that only three out of the nation's fifty richest counties with a population of 50,000 or more incorporate major cities. That New York City's Kings (which is Brooklyn), Bronx, and Queens counties, Los Angeles County, Cook County (Chicago), or Dade County (Miami) do not make the top fifty is telling. The forty-seven wealthiest counties in America are suburban. And suffice it to say that the fifty richest counties all showed median family incomes above the $9590 countrywide figure.

The greatest concentration of wealth was to be found in the suburbs around Washington and New York. The first two counties on the list were Montgomery County, Maryland, with a 1970 median family income of $16,710, and Fairfax County, Virginia (where the "new city" of Reston is located), with $15,707. Arlington, Virginia, with $13,743, was ninth; Howard, Maryland (which has the "new city" of Columbia), was twelfth with $13,472; and Prince Georges County, Maryland, was twenty-sixth with $12,450.

The evolution during the last ten years of suburbia has made these richest counties less and less directly dependent on their original function as bedroom towns, and increasingly self-sufficient in jobs and services. Businesses and industries have moved into these counties whose residents now earn money and spend it at home in an ever-growing volume. Montgomery County has two full-fledged towns—Bethesda and Silver Spring —within its confines, along with classical suburban neighborhoods. One still tends to think of them as part of Washington for they are an integral part of the metropolis, but they are quickly acquiring their own identities. The Pentagon and the Central Intelligence Agency are located in Arlington and Fairfax Counties respectively, providing tens of thousands of high-paying jobs. Howard County, Maryland, has been in a class by itself since the town of Columbia was built there as a planned community. In the New York cluster, the richest county is Nassau, in the central section of Long Island—it also is the third-richest county in the country, with a $14,632 median income. (It was number six in 1960.) Westchester was seventh in 1970 with $13,784; chances are that it will grow even more affluent as new industry and corporate headquarters keep moving in, making White Plains a city in its own right. Its airport is now the home of one of the nation's largest fleets of corporate aircraft and the scheduled stop for a number of commercial airlines. Then come Rockland, New York, eighth on the national list; Bergen, Somerset, and Morris counties in New Jersey; and Connecticut's Fairfield County, which, surprisingly, given its reputation for great wealth, is only eighteenth in the country.

To be sure, American cities always had suburbs and Americans always lived in them. But until the 1950s, the suburbs were by and large for lower-middle-class families who could not afford decent homes in the cities or for the affluent or slightly eccentric who did not want to live and bring up their children in the urban centers. For the lower middle class, suburbs meant small brick or clapboard houses, appendices to the cities that somehow carried a social stigma. The suburbs were just not "in." For the rich and the eccentric (often artists in the second instance), it was "living out of town," and it had its special amenities and exclusiveness. The life style was built around the country club, something along the lines of Marquand's *Life at Happy Knoll* or even earlier John O'Hara stories.

But around the mid-1950s suburban migrations began in earnest. Quickly, the social stigma vanished—chiefly because suburbanites found strength in numbers, and, perhaps more to the point, more and more families realized that only the very rich or the very poor could plausibly go on living in the city. Not only did the dollar stretch further in the new suburbs—an hour, say, from the city—but the quality of life was better, what with fresh air, green spaces, trees, and freedom from noise.

I remember my own reaction—it was a touch of alarm, I guess —when my brother-in-law bade farewell to the apartment in Greenwich Village (not only livable but downright pleasant in those days) and moved his wife and son to what was the first of the houses he was to own in Croton-on-Hudson, a quiet community with a lovely view across the river and all the peace in the world. For some undocumented reason, Croton then had the reputation of being a community inhabited by communists, radicals, or at least liberals. This made my brother-in-law, a real-estate executive in New York, something of a pioneer; it was like putting the family in a covered wagon and striking out West among the Indians. Living in Manhattan and enjoying it, I thought he had made a slightly demented move and I would shake my head in pity over his plans to commute two hours a day by train between home and office. How could he turn his back on New York's theaters, movies, and restaurants for the questionable pleasures of semi-isolation on the banks of the Hudson? But I suppose I underestimated not only my brother-in-law's determination, but also the thrust of a great migratory trend.

Soon afterward I left New York on my first newspaper foreign assignment, and I gave no further thought to the problems of American suburbia until I returned to the United States in 1961, this time making my home in Washington. For the next four years I was vaguely aware that people were moving in growing numbers to the suburbs, and that places like Croton-on-Hudson were attracting more and more New York City executives and developing their own services and facilities. My sister-in-law, for one, no longer needed to go shopping in New York because the department stores had followed her to the suburbs. But only on my final return late in 1969, again to Washington, did I realize the extraordinary magnitude of the suburban trend. And this was before I read the mind-bending Census reports on where all the Americans had gone.

Since then, I have become a dedicated student of the subject. I still live in Washington proper, but ours is a peculiar city with comfortable residential neighborhoods and houses with gardens fifteen minutes away from midtown so, in a sense, I am *almost* in the country. Rock Creek Park is just behind my house and we are visited by squirrels and occasional raccoons, baby foxes, and other small animals that drive Jason, my golden retriever, to anguished distraction. I imagine this is the best of both worlds, something that I always bear in mind when we go off visiting suburban friends or when I plunge into suburbia in other parts of the country.

Suburban culture can be summed up, I suppose, by such notions as informal life style, self-containment, selfishness, exclusivism (where it can still be exercised), neo-conservatism, and, therefore, a noninvolvement with anything that does not directly affect one's own suburb.

The motive force behind the suburban migration is an understandable desire to escape the enormous pressures and tensions of city life. That enough Americans are now rich enough to afford this escape is a plus for the society, but those who have made it to the suburbs—they are overwhelmingly white—have to an important extent withdrawn from larger responsibilities toward society in order to protect their hideouts.

I said that much of the American political power base has shifted to the suburbs, but I must also report the apparently contradictory findings that suburbanites tend to stay away from participation in local self-government. A five-year National Public Opinion Survey, begun in 1967, concluded that "upper-status people . . . always vote at a higher rate and take part in campaigns no matter where they live. But the high-status citizen is less active in suburbia than his counterpart living in a small city or town miles from any big metropolitan area. He is even less active than his counterpart living in the supposedly stagnant central cities." Sidney Verba, a Harvard professor specializing in political participation, offered this explanation for the noninvolvement of suburbanites: "The thing that really depressed the level of activity is the fact that many of the suburbs don't have very clear social and political boundaries. People may live in a particular place but they don't work there. People . . . lose their sense of focus and they don't participate as they would if they lived in a small city."

When the suburban migration began in the 1950s, many observers were convinced that America stood on the threshold of a new era of local self-government and would see a revival of the town-hall traditions of yore. But this is not the way it happened: things became politically distorted, to the point where many experts now fear that the whole political system is threatened. In the words of Robert C. Wood, president of the University of Massachusetts, the suburbs are "a source of institutional weakness in our urban society" inasmuch as they "insulate a minority in a position of privilege in the metropolitan region [and] promote conflict in areas such as housing and education, rather than facilitating solutions."

David S. Broder, political commentator for *The Washington Post*, wrote recently that the suburban communities "will grow even more selfishly independent and less willing to shoulder a portion of the responsibility for those left behind in the older cities." There is a difference, he observed, between broad-gauged political involvement and the concentration on local affairs seen in participation in new "activist" groups by suburban house owners and housewives.

To say, as it has been said, that Democrats become Republicans and liberals become conservatives the moment they move to the suburbs is, it seems to me, a superficial diagnosis of the political and human phenomena involved here. The deeper problem is the *social* cop-out. Here I agree with Broder and other commentators that it is essential to bring these millions of suburbanites back into the reality of America.

Any consideration of the problem of suburban alienation must take into account the racial aspect of it. This new dimension of the suburban matter involves the question whether the legal concept of school desegregation—established as the law of the land by the Supreme Court in 1954—may or should be enforced by busing black or white children between the cities and the suburbs.

Busing *within* the confines of a city has lost much of the emotional effect it had some years ago. Despite protests, demonstrations, occasional violence, and countless law suits (and despite

•

President Nixon's order in late 1972 to HEW to slow down the whole process), the notion of busing as a means of desegregating schools and creating a reasonable racial balance in them has in most communities been generally accepted. Back in 1970, for example, school buses in Denver were blown up just before the start of the school year, and there was widespread concern, from New Orleans in the South to Detroit in the North, that enforced busing would result in virtual civil strife. During my trip around the country in 1970, I found that the busing issue was an over-whelming preoccupation in Tennessee and North Carolina—to mention two states where I tried to look into this problem with special attention—and a major issue in that year's midterm con-gressional elections.*

However, as I was to find in time, Americans tend to accept new social developments on a long-term evolutive basis. First it was the question of simple school desegregation, and it took

*Among other southern flag-waving issues (gun control, school prayers, and the controversy over Nixon's unsuccessful nominations of Judges Haynsworth and Carswell to the Supreme Court), busing unquestionably was a significant factor in the defeat of Albert Gore, a fairly liberal senator, in his bid for a fourth term from Tennessee. When I was in Memphis and Nashville, Bill Brock, his Republican challenger, was satu-rating the state with radio spots proclaiming, "No child ever got an edu-cation riding on a bus." I thought it downright silly as I listened to them on my car radio, but evidently the electorate did not share my opinion. Later, Brock came up with radio and TV statements declaring, "On bus-ing of school children Tennesseans said No, but Albert Gore said Yes. . . . Isn't it about time that Tennesseans said No to Albert Gore?" At that point in history, Tennessee was already part of the new and increasingly prosperous South, but the state's old-fashioned Rooseveltian liberalism shifted to the Right under the influence of this very prosperity. In November, Brock beat Gore. The defeated senator, whom I knew slightly but pleasantly over the years, subsequently analyzed his downfall in his book *Let the Glory Out,* remarking accurately that the Republican catch-phrase accusing the Democrats of advocating "forced integration of the suburbs" became "code words for racism."

pretty close to fifteen years before this idea was by and large accepted. I imagine that the emergence of a new generation of young parents in the 1960s had a lot to do with this maturing of white attitudes. (Still, as late as June 1973 the United States Court of Appeals had to issue an order directing further enforcement of school and college desegregation in Pennsylvania and sixteen southern and border states. Interestingly, the reason was that HEW was, in the court's opinion, "actively supplying segregated educational institutions with Federal funds, contrary to the expressed purposes of Congress." The court ruled that HEW lacked the right to seek voluntary compliance with the 1964 Civil Rights Act through a policy of channeling "Federal funds to defaulting schools." This situation, it appeared, existed in ten college systems and two hundred elementary and secondary school districts in the seventeen states. To be sure, the offending systems and districts were a minority in the overall educational facilities in these states, but the court's action was a useful reminder that school segregation had not yet vanished altogether.)

The next great controversy was busing inside the cities. Again, there were protests, threats, and the direst of predictions. Then the new racial issue, involving city and suburb, savagely erupted in January 1972, when U.S. District Judge Robert R. Merhige, a Virginian sitting in Richmond, approved a consolidation plan providing for a merger between Richmond's 70 per cent black school system with the 90 per cent white systems in the suburban counties of Henrico and Chesterfield. This was quite a bombshell, for what Judge Merhige did went far beyond the simple notion of school integration. Given the fact that Richmond, the Confederacy's capital in the Civil War, is roughly 50 per cent black and that the whites are rushing to the suburbs in one of the most massive land grabs in the American South, the judge ruled, in effect, that the city and the suburban counties should be reintegrated as administrative units. One interpretation of Judge

Merhige's action was that it would, as a practical matter, break down the boundaries between Richmond and the suburban counties. Perhaps it is not surprising that suits for similar school-integration plans cutting across county lines were instituted in Atlanta, Boston, Buffalo, Dayton, Detroit, Durham, Grand Rapids, Hartford, Indianapolis, Louisville, and Wilmington.

The outcry against the Richmond decision, not surprisingly, was deafening, for the rich (white) suburbs wanted to retain their isolation and independence. Cities like Chicago, where the school population is 43 per cent black (it is 90 per cent white in the surrounding Cook County suburbs), were under pressure to join pending lawsuits for countywide integration while the suburbanites mobilized against it. As a Richmond city councilman told a newsman, the best way to get elected in Henrico and Chesterfield counties "is to run against the city of Richmond." In a sense, then, open warfare broke out between the poor cities and the rich suburbs.

To the immense relief of suburbanites, Judge Merhige was overruled in May 1972 by the Fourth U.S. Circuit Court of Appeals. Late in May 1973, the U.S. Supreme Court split 4–4 on the issue, thus letting the appellate court's decision stand. (It was the same Supreme Court that a few months earlier, responding to the general social mood of the Nixon administration, threw out the Chicano school-tax case in San Antonio, Texas.) The sanctity of the American suburb—at least in Virginia—was thus upheld for the time by the highest court in the land.

Having discussed this whole matter at length with jurists and political leaders, I am not sure in my own mind whether Judge Merhige was entirely wise in his original Richmond ruling, inasmuch as I have reservations about artificial solutions to deep social problems. But, I fear, the outcome of the Richmond case has been to reinforce temporarily the suburban sense of detachment from national or even urban problems. I say "temporarily" because less than a month after the Supreme Court ruling, the U.S. Court of Appeals in Detroit came to a totally opposite conclusion. In this instance, the ruling was that black children from Detroit must be bused out to the white suburbs, and white suburban students must ride buses to schools in the city so that overall racial balance may be achieved.

The original Detroit decision had been made in 1971 by a federal judge who had argued that since the city's student body was predominantly black, no effective integration could take place in its school system. If effective segregation was to end, busing between city and suburbs was required. In upholding him two years later, the appeals court found that even if segregation practices in Michigan "were a bit more subtle than the compulsory segregation statutes of Southern states," they were "nonetheless effective." Hitting at the heart of the controversy, the appeals court's majority decision said, "We see no validity to an argument which asserts that the constitutional right to equality before the law is hemmed in by the boundaries of a school district."

The Michigan appellate decision did not, of course, change the status quo in Virginia, nor was the Supreme Court action in the Richmond suit applicable to Detroit. Each was a specific and separate ruling. But what the Michigan Court of Appeals did was to reopen the whole question of how far state and local governments may or may not move in dealing with racial discrimination in education. In the end, the Supreme Court may be forced to render a basic decision on this point, binding on the whole country, and in so doing it would presumably be judging not only the enforcement of the Civil Rights Act but also the social and political realities of an America split between city and suburb.

The suburb can be a virtually self-sufficient fortress. The commuting head of the family usually (though not always) works five days a week in the city, but as a rule he cannot be bothered about anything happening in the *urbs* unless it inconveniences him personally—in terms of, say, transportation or surroundings at work. His and his family's life is truly centered on the home.

It is a pattern that the merchants of America perceived early in the game. There is virtually no major American city whose department stores have not opened multiple suburban branches or shifted to the suburbs altogether. Put realistically, the department stores do not expect to make money from blacks, Chicanos, or Puerto Ricans, and, accordingly, they have pursued the carriage trade. (This obviously affects urban job markets and city tax revenues, but, as an executive of a nationwide chain of department stores told me recently, "the hell with 'em.") In the suburbs, the department stores and other merchants join forces to form huge shopping centers—some of them connected and covered, air-conditioned in the summer and heated in the winter —where the housewife can buy anything from a can of beans to a Pucci dress. Alone or with the family, she can eat lunch and, if she so desires, taste the first bloody mary or martini of the day. All she has to do is to park her car on the sprawling lot, remember where it is, and happily proceed to shop until fatigue overcomes her. But it is an intriguing question what the energy crisis will do to this new culture.

Aesthetically, the suburban woman shopper leaves something to be desired—at least to my old-fashioned eyes. And she is at her worst in the warm months. To go to a shopping center in the summer is to be surrounded by women with curlers in their hair (not always disguised by scarves), dressed in halters, shorts, sloppy housedresses. The *femella genus americana* seems to be a new and totally uniform breed of the suburban woman. They all look alike to me, the blondes and the brunettes, and I keep wondering why they allow themselves to be seen looking so unattractive in the daytime, before embarking on the great late-afternoon effort to beautify themselves for husbands, lovers, friends, neighbors, and cocktail-party acquaintances. (Male chauvinist or not, I believe deeply in the aesthetic appearance of a woman at all times. Possibly, I have been spoiled by my wife who, to the best of my knowledge, has never left the house looking unattractive or slovenly. More subtly, I tend to think of Lowell's line: " 'Twas just a womanly presence, an influence unexprest.") But perhaps this is related to the pervasive sense of ennui or downright boredom affecting the lives of so many affluent suburban wives. The worst off, I believe, is the suburban housewife with a college education and no way to make proper use of it.

I am very sympathetic to the idea that women should be liberated, emancipated, or whatever current word applies. But observation indicates that the American suburban wife is virtually a prisoner of her milieu. To be sure, more and more of them work —for money or as volunteers—but the majority seem to be tied down to the repetitive cycle of serving breakfast, sending off husband to work and kids to school, perhaps driving in a school car pool, cleaning house (alone or with a maid), fixing dinner, watching television, and going to bed with or without sex as the case with the tired commuter-husband may be. The safari to the shopping center will then be a central adventure. I have raised the awkward question of "What do you do with your time?" with dozens of suburban wives, and the cycle described above is the usual answer, sometimes adorned with mention of a cocktail party or dinner given or attended, an evening trip to the big city, or a PTA meeting. The city wife, I am pretty sure, leads a less confined, more interesting life.

Boredom and other tensions peculiar to suburbia are creating a major alcoholism problem among suburban women, not to mention the fact that the structure of suburban life in general encourages a considerable amount of drinking among adults and teen-agers. Researchers on alcoholism say that throughout the

United States the ratio of male to female alcoholics has changed from five to one ten years ago to two to one. A recent article in the *The New York Times* quoted the director of the Alcoholism Guidance Center in Westport, Connecticut (believed to be the wettest town in America), as saying, "In a community like ours, it's easier to cover up. . . . There's money for liquor, for psychiatry, for a housekeeper, all of which may work against coming to grips with the reality of alcoholism."

I'm obviously not professionally competent to discuss alcoholism patterns among American women. But my own observation has been that women alcoholics are most commonly found in city ghettos, for reasons of despair with the hopelessness of their lives, and in the affluent suburbs, presumably for the opposite reasons of ennui.

What of the traditional amenities of nonrural life—restaurants, big-city newspapers, and so on? The exodus to the suburbs has done extraordinary things to some great and not-so-great urban institutions. A major victim is the newspaper. The flight to the suburbs has led in many cases to a drop not only in circulation and readership but in advertising revenues; the decline in the urban job market has cut down on the Help Wanted columns, a significant portion of advertising lineage. At a time when most big-city newspapers are in trouble anyway because of brutally rising production costs, these developments have hurt badly. Moreover, the big-city newspaper is increasingly challenged in what used to be its natural suburban circulation area by a proliferation of local daily or weekly publications. Most of these have been highly successful, given the inward turn of the suburbanite and the way his interest centers on local events—and local advertising. A case in point is *Newsday* on Long Island, a troublesome rival to *The New York Times,* which traditionally regarded the area as its fief. *The Washington Post* has been able to hold its own more or less because it intensively covers Maryland and Virginia affairs in its news columns, provides general news essential to the commuting Washington bureaucrat and politician, and benefits from suburban shopping-center advertising. *The New York Times* has been trying to compete with a special Long Island-Queens-Brooklyn section and the recent addition of a section of New Jersey news and advertising inserted in the papers sent to that state. Television, whose impact has been further increased by the development of cable TV, is also making inroads among the less-motivated suburban citizens. (It is easier to watch the evening network news than to read a newspaper, unless one commutes by train and might just as well do the latter. But there are fewer and fewer train commuters.)

Other institutions, if this is the proper word, are also moving to the suburbs. There is an enormous growth in the number of suburban restaurants; is this one reason why so many first-rate New York eating places have been closing down? The comparatively new phenomenon of "singles bars" has cropped up in the suburbs, indicating a new influx there of divorced or widowed (or simply unmarried) men and women. Finally, "massage parlors," a new euphemism for a very ancient institution, have appeared in droves in the suburbs, flushed with their urban success and catering to bored or lonely husbands, wives, or "singles." They are one of the less attractive by-products of our sexual revolution, but they make the point that there is almost nothing unique left in the cities to attract the suburbanite.

Once upon a time, the notion of "living in the country" meant fresh air, elbow room, and a home of one's own with a half-acre of land or so around it. In a word: privacy. Or so it sounded in A. C. Spectorsky's *The Exurbanites* in 1955. Nowadays, in 1974, none of this seems possible any longer—and the exceptions that prove the rule may not even be with us in a few more years.

Today the American suburb itself is the victim of overcrowding and pollution, to the point where established suburbanites fight fierce zoning battles to keep out not only new inhabitants but also industries and corporate headquarters looking for a place under the suburban sun. This is a second phase of the national war to protect the environment. Areas that not so long ago went out of their way to attract industry and encourage "industrial parks" in their midst to gain more local jobs and tax money now fight these incursions tooth and nail. It has finally dawned on the suburbanites that they are inviting pollution, crowding, higher taxes, and all the other ills from which they fled in the first place.

Greenwich, Connecticut, for example, defeated the Xerox Corporation in its request to build a huge corporate headquarters on the town's outskirts. With some hundred corporate offices in the high-income Greenwich area—the most recent big arrival was American Can—the town no longer wants businessmen and their offices. The concept of "environmental pollution" has been used in this zoning battle, and the Greenwich Environmental Action Group announced in 1973 its discovery that "the demand for housing which will ultimately be created by the staggering one million square feet of office space we've already added in three or four years will be upon us before long, causing heavy tax demands." Another local activist predicted that if Xerox and others were permitted to come, "Greenwich will become a gilded mill town"—which is what much of Westchester, Fairfield County, and northern New Jersey already could be called.

Similar battles against new industries and headquarters are being fought across America. Waterford, Connecticut, a suburb of New London, is on the warpath against a utility planning to build a second and third nuclear power plant there. The first plant was welcome in 1966 because of its tax contribution: now, however, Waterford sees it all getting out of hand. Yonkers, in Westchester, is engaged in a fight over a proposed 118-acre, $49 million shopping center in a nearby wooded area. In Oregon, the government is frankly discouraging California-based industries from opening plants. In New York, environmentalists won their battle against a bridge over Long Island Sound. These controversies over industrial zoning and related growth in the suburbs are among the most constant themes in local newspapers. (In some cases, those opposing industry are frank to say that they fear the plants will bring black, Puerto Rican, or Chicano workers from the cities in a reverse commuter trend. So the racial dimension is ever-present.)

Land pollution, another newfangled expression, is the result of the wild land speculation and development schemes that have marked America's suburbs since the mid-1960s. What the suburbanites find most offensive is the new trend for constructing apartment high-rises and "townhouse" condominium complexes in and around their once tranquil fringe communities. The tall buildings especially disturb the visual attractiveness of the countryside, either because they look so improbable and ugly, rising out of a rural landscape, or because they threaten to become nuclei for future high-rise cities in the suburbs. For some time I have collected newspaper ads for these new high-rises because, I thought, they conveyed perfectly what the developers have in mind for the latest generation of suburbanites. Here, for example, are excerpts from a full-page ad for the Olympus (the name alone tells the story), a sixteen-story apartment building just outside of Alexandria, Virginia, some ten miles from Washington: "Luxury Condominiums. . . . One, Two, and Three Bedroom Apartments from $29,950. . . . Living at the Olympus is living as close to transportation, shopping and entertainment as you'd like. It's relaxing at your own Olympic size pool, playing on your own private tennis courts and entertaining in the spacious Party Room. . . . This is what luxury living is really all about: fully carpeted apartments with individually controlled heating and air conditioning; private, protected indoor parking; solar-bronze glass throughout; 10-light bronze and crystal chandelier in each dining room; telephone and TV antenna outlets in every room that you'd want them in. . . . Yes, the Olympus is everything you need to reach the height of sophisticated living."

A friend of mine has lived for some years in just such a building in a Maryland suburb, and I have visited him on a few occasions. I had no difficulty in finding him because his building sticks out as the only tall structure for miles around. I have discovered that several square miles around the building belong to the same developer (who also owns the shopping center, the gas station, and a mini-country club), and there are plans afoot for similar high-rises there.

All over the country, the suburban high-rise concept is spreading, not only because of the scarcity of land and such facilities as roads and sewage systems required by one-family-home communities, but also because of the rising cost of land and, simultaneously, the immense profits derived by high-rise developers. These skyrocketing land values (and the ever-rising cost of mortgages) would seem to make life in the suburbs almost impossible for newcomers. In Waterford, Connecticut, for instance, acreage went up from $1500 in 1963 to $25,000 in 1973. In Virginia's Fairfax County, the average median cost for a home rose from $18,700 in 1960 to $41,500 in 1972. The county's Mason District, which had 58,000 inhabitants in 1973, carried a total real-estate tax assessment of 1.23 billion dollars, which is immense on a per capita basis, with the true market value probably well in excess of two billion. (Mason, needless to say, is 97 per cent white.)

But Fairfax, the fastest growing county in the United States (its population rose from around 130,000 in 1953 to 533,000 in 1970 and is projected at 1.3 million by 1980), simply froze all growth for 1974 and 1975 after a savage battle with land developers and the state of Virginia. In Montgomery, America's most affluent county, a "sewer moratorium"—meaning that no new housing permits would be issued until additional sewer connections were installed—sent the cost of homes even higher.* (A man of my acquaintance, for instance, bought a relatively modest house just across the D.C. line for some $35,000 in 1961 and resold it easily for $92,000 in 1973.) Fauquier County, in rural Virginia, stretching toward the West Virginia mountains, imposed a six-month moratorium on subdivision rezonings to halt the invasion from Washington until a plan could be evolved relating building permits to the adequacy of available services. (The town of Ramapo, in New York, was the pioneer of this idea.) The Maryland House of Delegates and Senate virtually agreed in the spring of 1973 on a land-use control bill under which the state would have the last word in developing land. The debate was a classical encounter, complete with lobbyists and political pressures, between environmentalists, led by Governor Marvin Mandel, and the building interests. Similar debates are occurring across the United States. In Florida, the city of Boca Raton, an enclave of millionaires, imposed in 1972 a legal limit of 100,000 on its population. It stood in 1973 at 41,000 people, some of whom paid over $100,000 for waterfront apartment condominiums.

In general, the land shortage, the enormous rise in building

*The sewerage problem is one of the most severe ones affecting suburbia. In fact, the suburbs may drown in their own sewage. Fairfax County realized it in April 1973, when a rainstorm knocked out the Lower Potomac sewage treatment plant and 1.24 million gallons of raw sewage were poured during a few hours into Pohick Creek. Delaware's beach resorts —Rehoboth and Bethany—are unable to develop sewage systems to keep pace with what a local real-estate editor called the recent "unprecedented land scramble." Virginia Beach, America's fastest growing city, is paralyzed by its sewage problem. In Yorktown, New York, a plan to build 168 apartments with septic tanks on the shores of Lake Mohegan was blocked at the last moment by the State Supreme Court to prevent the lake's pollution.

materials and labor costs, the sewerage moratoriums, and other factors have been responsible for increasing the value of homes in the United States (mostly in the suburbs) by 91.7 per cent between 1952 and 1972, according to the Bureau of Labor Statistics. (This compares with a 61.2 per cent rise in food costs during the same period.) Economists believe that this spectacular jump in prices is also related in part, particularly in recent years, to massive real-estate investments as a hedge against inflation. The boom began slowing down late in 1973 as mortgage money became scarce and the fuel crisis began to lead to second thoughts about suburban life.

In fact, in the abrupt manner in which trends and patterns shift in America, the building boom began turning into bust at the end of 1973 and early 1974. 1972 was the year when the largest number of houses, mostly suburban, were built in American history: 2,378,500 of them, or more, statistically speaking, than one house for every hundred inhabitants. But the economic crises of 1973 brought this number down to 2,046,000 that year, a drop of 14 per cent, and the estimate for 1974 was for a further drop of 22 per cent. The big drop was in the cities. This decline made it absolutely certain that Lyndon Johnson's goal of 26 million new dwelling units by 1978 could not be even remotely reached. Above all, the housing for the poor would be dealt a crippling blow. Even in 1973, only 200,000 units of subsidized low-income housing were built as compared with 250,000 vacation homes for the affluent. This is why (and because a similar ratio applied in earlier years) even at its height the construction boom was essentially oriented toward the rich, with the urban poor virtually ignored. Societally, then, it did not really matter to the American poor whether the construction industry was booming or busting.

Other problems inhibiting further growth in the suburbs include a significant rise in the crime rate. In New York's Westchester County, for example, a 1973 study found that 78 per cent of local crime was committed by residents rather than outsiders. Though most of the crime originated in the poorer sections of the county, "an area plagued by youth crime might do well to look first at its own children." Similarly, a survey by *The Washington Post* showed that violent crime in the Virginia and Maryland suburbs rose by 620 per cent between 1960 and 1971, while the increase in Washington itself was 392 per cent. A Montgomery County police official said that "growth itself begets crime." Others believe that the proliferation of suburban shopping centers open until late at night attracts criminals from the city in a "spillover" phenomenon. Still another police view is that the emphasis on civil rights has emboldened black criminals to shift to the suburbs.

Finally, reports from suburbia uniformly tell of a spectacular rise in drug and alcohol use and in venereal disease among white middle-class students.

All these problems stemming from growth have, as I have said, led suburbanites increasingly to adopt "no-growth" policies, in some cases extreme ones. In a speech early in 1973, Oregon's Governor Tom McCall said, "We are facing a shameless threat to the whole quality of our life—unfettered despoiling of the land. We find speculators subdividing the waterless desert and embarking on shoreline construction projects in a process we now call 'condomania.' Subdividers are chopping and thrashing away, making hamburger out of the magnificent landscape of Oregon." Wolf Von Eckardt wrote recently that "it makes no sense to replace blind faith in growth with equally blind faith in no-growth. Development is essential and inevitable. The challenge is to channel the new mood into constructive political action on behalf of sensibly planned development, a national urban growth policy, and a radically new approach to real estate property rights and land use. Continued urban growth is essential because the American population keeps growing not only in numbers but also in its appetite for modern conveniences and its demands for social justice."

Similarly, this point underlay a conclusion in a 1973 report by a federal task force on Land Use and Urban Growth. Historically, "Americans have thought of urbanization rights as coming from the land itself, 'up from the bottom' like minerals or crops. It is equally possible to view them as coming 'down from the top,' as being created by society and allocated by it to each land parcel." The report stressed that henceforth "development rights" on private property must be vested in the community rather than in the fact of ownership.

Obviously, we have come to a crossroads. Soon, I believe, we must make basic decisions about the relationship between city and suburb.

During 1973, the Congress had before it once more a bill on Land Use Policy and Planning Assistance designed to set forth long-range guidelines on the use of land, and to establish related federal assistance for highways, airports, and land-water conservation programs. This may be the only possible instrument for an intelligent handling of the American growth phenomenon. The point was made sharply by Senator Henry Jackson of Washington, when he remarked that during the 1970–73 period (he first introduced land legislation in 1970) there has been more "waste, inefficiency and environmental damage than took place in the first hundred years of our existence as a nation." What I have seen throughout the country during those three years certainly bears out Jackson's assertion: it was a time of national insanity, when land developers went berserk and the population happily and uncritically accompanied and accommodated them.

5

A fascinating attempt to resolve the tensions between American cities and suburbs is the effort to construct "planned communities," or "new towns." A relatively new phenomenon, the "new towns" are something of a compromise between the two extremes of metropolitan life. There are still only a few of them around, too young and too new for conclusions to be drawn as to what they really represent, but they may just provide a partial answer to our anguished urban questions.

Brand new cities, carefully preplanned, are not a wholly new idea. Brasilia, Canberra, and Islamabad are prime early examples. They were designed, however, as national capitals and built to government order on a more-or-less grandiose scale. America's "new towns" are based on a totally different, more modest concept. They were born of land-development schemes concocted by private entrepreneurs and intended for financial profit, but curiously in some cases seemed to respond to certain basic social needs. (One early case in point was Long Island's Levittown, built in the early postwar years.)

The most interesting of the two dozen or so American "new towns" is Columbia, Maryland, roughly halfway between Washington and Baltimore in what used to be an entirely rural county (Howard). The essential difference between Columbia—which in 1974, seven years after ground was broken for the first houses, had 33,000 inhabitants, a junior college, eighteen schools, and a newspaper—and some of the smaller planned communities is that it is a *functioning town,* not simply a king-size and rather exclusive country club. It is not only a commuter bedroom community but also a provider of some eight thousand local jobs.

Howard County itself, in pre-Columbia days chiefly dedicated to farming, had only sixteen thousand inhabitants in 1950. Now it has about a hundred thousand and is among the most affluent counties in the country. The significant thing about Columbia, however, is that it is home to the middle class rather than to the very rich. It is also, probably, the most racially integrated of the new towns. (Dale City, in Virginia's Prince William County, also presents a racial mix, but it is a less successful planned community.) The week I visited Columbia, in the spring of 1973, the first black-owned real-estate office opened for business, with a black staff of thirteen, at Century Plaza Building, Columbia's principal office building. The Columbia *Times* quoted the president of the firm as saying, "Columbia has come of age as an integrated community. We expect its growth to continue for many years to come as a major city, a comprehensive response to the aspirations of a free society. It is a city where people—all kinds of people—can enjoy life together."

I made a point of driving to several outlying neighborhoods to see Columbia children coming home from school. The neighborhoods I picked were not the most expensive in Columbia, but they displayed rows of attractive three- or four-family townhouses curving gently along wide, clean streets and tree-shaded courts. That access to housing was defined by the purely economic potential of individual families rather than by racial considerations was evident as I watched black and white children in roughly equal proportion entering the same townhouses after walking together from the bus stops. I received an astonished stare when I asked a real-estate salesman whether the presence of blacks tended to bring down real-estate values. "Here? In Columbia? You've gotta be kidding," he said.

No drop in housing values occurs when black families move

into the best Columbia neighborhoods (I have no idea how many black families already live in the most expensive areas), but I think the important point is that the ancient myth of blacks destroying property values simply did not apply in a well-planned community. By 1974, the town was getting almost too rich for its own good. With a median family income of $19,000 for whites and *$20,000* for blacks, poorer people were being phased out. Plans for 10 per cent of low-income housing are being abandoned.

Columbia, as a matter of fact, was invented by people who were out to make money on housing in a new and unorthodox fashion. (They pretentiously chose to sweeten the package by calling it "the Next America.") The idea originated with James Wilson Rouse, a rather unusual Maryland-born mortgage banker, housing specialist, and Presbyterian elder who advised President Eisenhower on housing programs, spent two years as president of the American Council to Improve Our Neighborhoods, and co-authored a book titled *No Slum in Ten Years*. Rouse, who is president of his own real-estate company, acquired 15,600 acres of Howard County land in the mid-1960s through 169 separate purchases costing him a total of $23 million as he secretly planned to build Columbia. The secrecy was necessary to avoid driving up prices, and Rouse operated through a series of dummy corporations. Even so, he had to pay over $75,000 to do away with a gasoline station that was in his way. His experience touched importantly on the new doctrine, enunciated six years later in the Land Use and Urban Growth report, that community interests must prevail over the fact of private ownership. As Henry Aaron pointed out in his book, the existing law of eminent domain may compel private owners to sell land for a "fair" price for "public purposes," but this concept remains ill-defined and it is unclear whether it is applicable to developers "even though their projects may be socially beneficial."

In any event, Rouse circumvented this problem through his secret operations. Subsequently, he attracted three New York City banks and two insurance companies as fellow investors. By 1973, $650 million had already been invested. Inasmuch as Columbia was conceived as an entirely private-enterprise operation, Rouse let a number of construction and development companies do their own building and selling in the seven villages clustered around a futuristic downtown area. (His plans are for a private investment of $2 billion by the time the town is fully completed in 1981 and reaches the planned population of 110,000.)

Politically, Columbia is an unincorporated town governed by the Howard County Executive and the five members of the County Council. Columbia is thus not wholly self-governing, and there have been quite a few complaints about this. But some of the councilmen are elected from the Columbia villages, and each village has an elected school board (together they form the Columbia Combined Board). So there is a nucleus of self-government, its real political force deriving from Columbia's overwhelming importance in Howard County.

The week I was in Columbia, the politics centered on a proposal, based on a bill approved by the Maryland Senate and endorsed by the Columbia Democratic Club, that all county officials publicly disclose their real-estate holdings. This idea has a certain relevance in a boom area where nearly everyone in power has some stake in real-estate development. But a councilman named William Hanna, himself a real-estate broker, protested at a council meeting that it would force officials to "give up your land and holdings and your wealth and your women." This, he said, "sounds like communism." Columbia, too, has its ultra-conservatives.

On the whole, I found Columbia a pleasant and comfortable place to live, full of green open spaces and free of serious air pollution (though some of it is beginning to seep in from the industrial park on the town's outskirts and from heavy traffic on Route 29, which bisects the community as the main traffic corridor to Washington and Baltimore). Someday, I presume, the courts will have to rule on whether towns can limit their population; there are obvious constitutional implications in such actions, affecting as they do the free movement of citizens. For the time being, the current controversy is whether a 685-acre land tract between Columbia and Ellicott City should be turned into a separate luxury community or into a county park.

Meanwhile, Columbia is full of innovations. It has an artificial lake bordering on the small "downtown" section—a few office buildings, a hotel, restaurants (one specializes in French crêpes), and shops are located there—and one of the most impressive shopping centers I have ever seen. Its vast mall is carpeted, air-conditioned, full of flowers and living trees rising up to its glass roof. On a tiny island on a pond on the ground floor, a musician softly plays the organ and tired shoppers sit around the pond relaxing and listening. It is all very tranquil, if artificial.

Columbia's latest sensation was a giant polyvinyl bubble covering 180 square feet of meadow and sitting on telescopic legs; this extraordinary-looking thing served as the portable campus for the 110-student branch of Antioch College in Columbia. The idea was that the bubble would simply introduce the concept of entirely new cities covered by a megastructure roof, but the Antioch bubble became a major controversy. An architectural critic wrote recently that the "pneumatic campus" was like "the belly of a stranded whale." Nobody knows what the future of the bubble will be, but Columbians are willing to put it down to experience.

Columbia, along with other planned communities, is also the subject of a wider controversy. Late in 1972, a visitor from the Institute of Urban and Regional Development at the University of California attacked the whole concept of new towns at a Washington meeting of the American Association for the Advancement of Science. The speaker, Chester McGuire, made it clear he preferred improved suburbia, because "whereas new towns are most difficult to bring about, these suburbia are undeniably there, growing and multiplying. They absorb most of the population growth, and a vast and increasing share of employment and shopping." But even though the inhabitants of the new towns are beginning to lose their first enthusiasm, most of them still prefer their homes to any in the classical suburbs.

Reston, eighteen miles west of Washington in Fairfax County, is a good example of a planned community emphasizing exclusivism—a country-club new town.

Developed by Gulf-Reston Inc., a subsidiary of the Gulf Oil Company (an interesting example of diversification by an oil company, in the good old days when gasoline was plentiful and a land investment of this sort meant more cars and more gas sales), Reston was always meant as a community for affluent people. The very fact that it was built in Fairfax County suggests the clientele the Gulf people had in mind. Having reached 22,000 inhabitants in 1973—almost ten years after plans were approved for the new town's construction—Reston had an assessed tax property value of $161 million, and its inhabitants were paying the county more in taxes than it cost to provide essential services.

The plans are for Reston to reach a controlled population of 78,000 by 1982, and present estimates are that property value will soar to close to $800 million. But anti-growth sentiment in the county, where officials are more and more frequently elected on anti-growth platforms, and in Reston, where the original settlers would just as soon keep out newcomers, may in the end affect the planned expansion. When I spent some time in Reston, a furious battle was raging in the Fairfax Board of Supervisors over Gulf-Reston's request to rezone 623 additional acres—the area oc-

cupied by Reston in 1973 was 7400 acres—so that a new neighborhood could be developed for 8000 more inhabitants. The county
and Gulf also became involved in a controversy over a $45-
million building the company had built for the U.S. Geological
Survey; briefly, construction had to be stopped. The ban was
subsequently lifted—the building was a *fait accompli* anyway—
suggesting that in the long run there may be no way of slowing
down Reston's growth no matter what the county officials may
desire.

Aesthetically and architecturally, Reston has it well over Columbia. With lakes, sprawling golf-courses, bridle paths, swimming pools, tennis courts, and elegant one-family homes, condominiums, and apartment buildings, Reston is reminiscent of a
well-heeled vacation resort rather than of a full-fledged town.
The inhabitants are a mix of Washington commuters—lawyers
and businessmen or senior government officials who can afford
around $50,000 for a house (some homes come much higher, but
condominium apartments can be had from $35,000)—and
wealthy retired persons. Evidently, quite a few Restonites are
employed at the CIA headquarters in Langley, because the morning and afternoon buses between Reston and Washington have
scheduled stops at the intelligence agency's gate. Around three
thousand Restonites work locally: aside from real-estate firms,
banks, stores, and community services, Reston is the home of a
facility of the Pentagon's Defense Communications Agency and
of branches of General Electric and Litton Industries. The controversial Geological Survey Center will provide about 2500 additional jobs for Restonites and people living elsewhere.

Reston has its own Cable TV system, a newspaper, branch
campuses of three Virginia colleges, eleven places of worship
including a synagogue (Columbia has one interfaith center), a
museum, art galleries, a ballet and theater company, and Democratic and Republican clubs. A bulletin board at the Lake Anne

village center—a tasteful collection of stores, rather than the standard shopping center—told early in 1973 of a forthcoming Reston Singles Spring Party (singles activities are an increasingly important thing in the suburbs and the new towns) and of a planned jet charter flight to Amsterdam arranged by the Reston Housewives Association at $198 per head, round trip. Reston also has a famous unsolved murder—that of a seventeen-year-old girl mysteriously killed in the spring of 1972. The community offers a $2500 reward for information leading to an arrest.

The town is divided into two main sections separated by the highway leading to Dulles International Airport. The area north of the highway, with Lake Anne as its center, is the most elegant and expensive. The southern section, known as Hunters Woods Village Center, is more of a middle-class preserve. To live in south Reston is a bit like living on the wrong side of the tracks, in a middle-class sort of way.

One of the most offensive decisions in recent years, speaking of thoughtless growth and damage to environment, came in the spring of 1973 when the Board of Supervisors of Prince William County in Virginia, another Washington bedroom suburb, authorized the Marriott Corporation to erect a huge amusement park—Great America—next to the Manassas National Battlefield Park.

Marriott is the owner of a hotel and motel chain and a food caterer to national and international airlines. It just so happened that the company's fortunes rose spectacularly after President Nixon assumed office in 1969—his brother, Donald, was a Marriott vice-president—and it has been expanding in every direction ever since. In 1972, Marriott conceived the idea of the amusement park, and its first thought was to establish it in Maryland, not far from Columbia. Howard County, however, had the sense to turn it down, and presently the company set its sights on the Manassas area, directly south of Reston.

Prince William County jumped at the chance of a new source of tax revenues (probably $500,000 annually) and agreed to re-zone 513 acres of land adjacent to the battlefield for Marriott's amusement park. It did so despite violent opposition from the Virginia state government—which was disturbed both by the idea that the battlefield environment would be spoiled by the amusement center and by the drastic shortage of sewer facilities in the area—and from historical and environment groups.

Manassas, of course, is where the two Battles of Bull Run occurred in 1861 and 1862 and the Union suffered some of its worst defeats. This is a region I know quite well, being a bit of a Civil War buff and having driven innumerable times through Manassas on my way to western Virginia along Route 66. The National Park Service has maintained the battlefield in beautiful, clean, and pristine condition, and has thoughtfully provided markers describing precisely what happened when and where in the two great battles. Using as my guide the *Diary* of William Howard Russell, the London *Times* correspondent (in my opinion still the greatest war correspondent ever), I have often tried to reconstruct where the battle lines were drawn, where the Army of the Potomac stood before the Confederates sent it fleeing in panic toward Washington. I have touched base at Fairfax Courthouse and Centreville and made my way many times across the fields of Manassas. I think I found the ridge from which Russell and thousands of Washingtonians in a picnic mood watched the battle below them, before the Union army and the onlookers were forced into rout. I thought about Russell's account of how he set out from Washington on the morning of July 21 to observe the long anticipated battle: "I swallowed a cup of tea and a morsel of bread, put the remainder of the tea into a bottle, got a flask of light Bordeaux, a bottle of water, a paper of sandwiches, and having replenished my small flask with brandy, stowed them all away in the bottom of the gig." I must confess that one fine summer morning in 1963, I did just that: I took off for Manassas with a flask of light Bordeaux and some sandwiches, to sit atop Russell's ridge and imagine the Battle of Bull Run.

Anyway, with all this in mind, it was something of a shock to learn about the Marriott amusement park right next door to Bull Run. The concept of "Great America," oddly Nixonian, did not make me feel better: under that rubric the amusement park is planned to have features of the Great Southwest, New England, and New Orleans, a county fair, the Yukon, rural America, live entertainment (presumably Blue Grass music), rides, and hamburger stands. It sounds so contrived, so cheap! But an explanation was readily available from Marriott's public-relations director in a newspaper interview I read with mounting horror: "We're going into this because we see an opportunity to make money. That's what this system is all about: You give people what they want and you're not afraid to take a profit from it."

Now I take this to be true of, say, Disneyland in California or Disney World in Florida. Obviously, nobody is forced to go to either place against his will, and unquestionably there is a need for such fantasy worlds of entertainment. And the country is peppered with fake commercial historical sites—almost every town between Nebraska and Wyoming has its phony Buffalo Bill fort and some even have regularly scheduled shoot-outs in which bored "sheriffs" and "badmen" fire blanks at each other—and "Indian villages." I have seen them in Florida ("Seminoles") and Oklahoma ("Comanches"), but if you've seen one, you've seen them all. Still, whatever else one may think of this effort to commercialize history (and Americans seem to go for it in a big way), one has to admit that it is generally harmless. As entertainment, it does not approach a circus, which I happen to adore, or a country music festival. But neither Coney Island in New York nor Disneyland nor the Indian villages and the circuses encroach upon actual and already well visited historic sites, as Marriott proposed to do at Manassas.

I mention the Marriott plan because there evidently is a relation between the new towns and such enterprises, since the planned communities provide something of a captive audience in the vicinity. This is probably why Marriott first tried the Columbia area and finally settled for Manassas, not far from Reston. Also, they are two aspects of the same controversy over protecting the land against developers. But among the fierce battles raging on *that* front, one of the most important has centered over the fate of the Adirondack State Park forest preserve, in northeastern New York State. This is one of the most beautiful sections of the American Northeast, touching on Lake Champlain and Lake George in the east and encompassing Lake Placid, Saranac Lake, and Tupper Lake. I visited the Adirondacks during the winter a great many years ago and drove through the preserve in the summer of 1970. Though more and more vacation homes have been built there, the Adirondacks remain basically noble, clean, and underpopulated.

In 1971 the Horizon Corporation purchased 25,345 acres of Adirondacks land from private owners. The Horizon developers appeared to have it in mind to erect a summertime community (a variation on the "new town" concept) near the town of Colton, in the northwestern corner of the Adirondacks. Colton had a population of 1200 in 1973, but under the Horizon plan, providing for five to ten thousand homes and shopping centers and golf links, there would be 20,000 to 40,000 part-time inhabitants. A smaller development by another firm is being planned for four thousand homes in Altamont, near Tupper Lake. Horizon's acreage reaches east to Elizabethtown, a sleepy community famous for the fact that John Brown's body lay in state there in 1859 before burial at Lake Placid, where much of the opposition to the Horizon plan centered, although anti-growth sentiment was just as strong in Plattsburgh and Saranac Lake.

The opposition was based, of course, on classical conservationist and environmentalist grounds. But the Adirondacks people were also concerned that the planned communities would attract unwanted motels and cheap restaurants, as was the case in Lake George township many years ago; others feared that large numbers of outside workers would be brought to the Adirondacks for the planned construction, leading to mobile-home parks, temporary housing, and so on. Finally, there was the ever-worrisome problem of sewerage and water supply.

The Adirondacks State Park has six million acres. Of it, 2.3 million acres belong to the state of New York and, under the state constitution, must remain "forever wild." But the way land ownership has developed over the years, state and private land are intermixed, suggesting that rational development may be impossible. The state is considering a land-use bill and, if it is approved, it may wish to buy up private land to protect the entire area. But if Peter Berle, a state assemblyman from New York City, correctly interpreted the feelings of many property owners, the real confrontation is over the basic issue of private land ownership. Berle told the Adirondack Conference in June 1973 that the Horizon development plan "represents a real thought-out means of enhancing the value of the Adirondacks rather than destroying them or destroying private property."

The success of Columbia and Reston inevitably encouraged developers everywhere to imitate their example. In some cases the results have been mixed; in others, plans are still on the drawing board. Near Washington, there is Dale City, an ill-planned community of some 24,000 people. Lysander, near Syracuse, New York, is a new community, planned for 20,000 inhabitants around 1990, under the auspices of the Urban Development Corporation, a public-benefit corporation. The UDC had also planned nine new towns in Westchester, but local protests forced it to drop the projects. Early in 1973, Lysander was just beginning to rise from the ground: roads were being opened, water and sewage connections were being established, and an industrial project—a plant still without a tenant—was being built.

In Southbury, Connecticut, a private developer built in the late 1960s a planned community of 1500 houses, and its success led him in 1973 to buy four hundred acres of land on the northern shore of Long Island, near Asharoken, for a township for the very rich. The site was bought from Henry S. Morgan, the son of the financier John Pierpont Morgan; he retained his mansion and forty acres around it, but sold the land that stretched along 10,000 feet of beach on Long Island Sound. The builders estimated in 1973 that houses would cost from $80,000 up—which should give an idea of what the Morgan community is likely to be.

Levitt and Sons, Inc., the people who have built all the Levittowns in the world, want to put together a new town of 12,000 inhabitants in Virginia's rural Loudoun County. Loudoun, which has already lost the battle against growth, had a population of 40,000 in 1973, up from 21,000 in 1950. The site of some of the better fox hunts in Virginia, Loudoun is expected to have a population of 60,000 by 1976, even without the Levitt project, and there is strong local opposition to the Levitt plan. And in Staten Island, the Rouse Company, builders of Columbia, tried to erect a major new town—the talk was of 420,000 new residents and an overall $6.5 billion investment—with New York City going to the lengths of proposing that the state legislature create a South Richmond Development Corporation. But a howl went up from Staten Island's real-estate interests and, in the end, the project died.

In New Jersey, however, plans have not yet halted for something slightly more novel. In 1973 General Electric announced that it would assign its staff scientists who had once worked exclusively on space projects to plan a new town to be known as Seabrook Farmington and to be built by a developers' company on a six-thousand-acre tract. The proposed South Jersey community was intended to provide housing for employees of General Electric's re-entry and environmental systems divisions, and for anyone else who wanted to move away from nearby Philadelphia. The idea was that this new town would ultimately house 45,000, but half the land would be left for open space and farms. (Before the developers bought the land for $9 million, it was the site of one of America's largest vegetable-growing and -processing operations.) I have seen some of the blueprints, and if the space scientists are given a free hand they may well come up with truly interesting results.

Big corporations, incidentally, are increasingly going into this kind of land development. International Telephone and Telegraph, for example, is investing $750 million in a new community it calls the Palm Coast, on Florida's east coast between Daytona and Saint Augustine. ITT's plans are best expressed in its brochure for potential land buyers: "To keep from crowding houses together, we've limited dwellings to an average of 2.7 per acre. That's less density than the millionaire community of Beverly Hills. With our protective zoning, you'll never look out your window at any honky-tonky pizza stand, gas station, or neon jungle." The Palm Coast yacht club, completed in 1973, cost ITT around $600,000. But the prospectus also carries a dire warning: "The Florida Division of Health requires a homesite to have either a septic tank or central sewerage. At this time neither can be assured on all lots."

As I noted earlier, most of the new towns are basically huge country clubs. Prices automatically exclude poor people and, usually, racial minorities. For this reason, I found it interesting and encouraging that the Washington Episcopal Diocese is planning to build an integrated new town for eight thousand people on a site it owns near Bowie, Maryland. The diocese explains that it will be a "new type of village designed to provide its residents —young and old, rich and poor, single and married, white and black—a chance to live in a meaningful and peaceful relationship one with the other in a wholesome environment close to the land and nature where they would be afforded limitless opportunities to fulfill their emotional, social and spiritual needs." I know this sounds like another promotional brochure, but I've had many dealings with the Washington Episcopal Diocese, largely through my son who for years belonged to a young people's forum organized by the cathedral, and I take the diocese people at their word. By and large, they are remarkably advanced socially and politically and quite understanding of the needs of young and old parishioners and anyone else who comes into contact with them. Seventy miles north of Phoenix, Arizona, atop a desert mesa, a "city of the future" is being built under the direction of Paolo Soleri, an Italian-born architect, who invented the term "arcology" to combine the concepts of architecture and ecology. This latest new town calls itself Arcosanti, and the construction work is being done by students who actually pay for the privilege of working six weeks for Soleri. (I have not visited Arcosanti, so my impressions are secondhand.) The centerpiece of Arcosanti, as I understand it, is a thirty-story structure that will comprise apartments and offices. Soleri is said to believe in vertical building, even in the desert, to preserve a maximum of open space. When completed, the community will be home to some three thousand people. (Arcosanti is near Scottsdale, where the population grew by 576 per cent in a recent ten-year period and is now well over 70,000 inhabitants.)

I know it is premature to render general judgments about the new towns, but what is important, I think, is that new ideas, some good and some bad, are percolating, as our society strives for solutions to the urban crisis. The vast majority of the new schemes aim at a collective-living environment, but there are individuals, too, who reach out for personal solutions. I have a friend, a retired newspaperman, who decided to live in a Fuller geodesic dome in the tiny community of Shell Knob, Missouri, in the heart of the Ozarks. Another friend built himself a country cottage on the Housatonic River in Connecticut, using his skills as architect and physicist. Still another refashioned an old Virginia mill, built by Thomas Jefferson's father, into an artist's studio. I visited him often, and we would sit at dusk watching the water cascading down a fall on the James River.

At the same time, urban experts are beginning to rethink the whole concept of cities. Dr. Peter C. Goldmark, an inventor in the field of electronics, has been commissioned by the government to study the future of urban populations. Goldmark's notion is that Americans will return to rural and semi-rural (or semi-urban, small-town) life if conditions are made right for them. Among those conditions, he says, are communications facilities allowing people to live pleasantly in rural areas but assured through television and other systems of access to theaters, concerts, museums, and sports events. "When people started moving to the suburbs they thought they would be going far enough," he said in a recent interview. "They were afraid to go farther away because they wanted to have the advantages of the nearby big cities and the rural charm of the suburbs. Today they have neither. The city doesn't have the amenities, and there is little of the rural charm left in the suburbs. . . . The paradox of communications is that the closer together people live, the harder they find it to communicate. . . . Clearly we are already experiencing a decomposition of our social fiber in this situation where 80 per cent of the population is crowded into less than 10 per cent of the land."

Among the special phenomena of American urban and suburban life are the "military cities," communities that derive much—or most—of their revenues from nearby major military installations and from the presence of retired military personnel in their midst. I draw a distinction between these military towns and other towns and communities in the United States whose economies are aided to a larger or lesser extent by nearby air, naval, or army bases. Though the bases and camps are important to these communities—I remember the outcry early in 1973 when Elliot Richardson's principal action during his very short tenure as Defense Secretary was to close down scores of bases for economy reasons—they can generally survive without them.

My own concept of an American military town embraces cities like Colorado Springs, the Norfolk-Virginia Beach area, San Diego, and to a lesser degree, Omaha—cities where the local defense establishments, and the tens of thousands of retired military families, are the economic mainstay. Inevitably, they show the social, political, and cultural effects of an overwhelming military influence, and in every case the armed forces have brought them considerable wealth as well as significant political conservatism—even though many of them are to be found in regions that otherwise are less than affluent.

One of San Diego's principal industries is the U.S. Navy base, the most important on the Pacific Coast, and related naval facilities. It is also a retirement home for admirals and petty officers alike—given its superb California climate and the prevalent sense of camaraderie with those still on active duty. Navy families whose fathers serve with the Pacific Fleet find it convenient to live in and around San Diego—it also is a question of service families' friendships when the husbands and fathers are at sea —and they, too, are a source of income for the city. Tens of thousands of San Diego civilians have navy-related jobs, and the navy is the city's most important employer and local commercial client. San Diego, to be sure, is large and important in other sectors —non-naval industry, commerce, civilian retirement, and tourism—but should the navy pack up and go someday, San Diego would be dealt a powerful body blow.

I visited San Diego only once—many years ago—and my personal impressions are rather limited. But I have spent some time in Colorado Springs and Virginia Beach, both incredible examples of urban growth related to the military, and in Omaha. These trips made it possible for me to catch some of the flavor of the military town. (My first visit to Colorado Springs was in 1970, when I became aware of the city's involvement with the air force and the army. But I returned in April 1971, as a guest of the Air Force Academy for a week's stay, and this gave me a chance to study better the local military culture.)

To measure the importance of the military to Colorado Springs, it must be first noted that in 1973 there were about 50,000 uniformed servicemen and their families living in the metropolitan area (not just the city itself, but all of El Paso County) out of a total population of around 250,000. Nobody seems to know how many retired military personnel live in the area (a chamber-of-commerce official told me this is "a frequently asked question, but unanswerable"); local civic boosters claim that Colorado Springs "has more retired generals and admirals per square mile than any place in the U.S.," a statement that both San Diego and Virginia Beach may dispute. My own guess is that the figure is around 15,000, including families.

The principal military centers are the army's Fort Carson installation, south of the city (a full division is stationed there); the Air Force Academy, situated on an eighteen-thousand-acre reservation ten miles north; and the North American Air Defense Command (NORAD), deep inside Cheyenne Mountain at the southernmost end of town. In addition to the military payroll (pay and allowances for 40,000 servicemen totaling almost $315 million in 1970), these three installations also provide direct employment to close to 8000 civilians (who earned $56 million in the same year). According to a survey by the chamber of commerce, total military expenditures in Colorado Springs Metro Area exceeded $400 million in 1970, the Air Force Academy, which opened its doors in 1958, contributing about $240 million. Tourism, the second-biggest income producer, brought Colorado Springs $90 million.

Of course, most of Colorado is a boom area. The climate, the extraordinary natural beauty of the Rockies and their foothills, ever-improving skiing and other sports facilities, good colleges and universities, and the consequent desire of big-city people from both coasts to "get away from it all" are quickly changing its face and character. It is no wonder that the population of the city of Colorado Springs rose by 104 per cent between 1960 and 1970 to 135,000, or that Lakewood, just north of Denver, jumped 480 per cent—from 20,000 to 94,000—during the same decade. Since then, the boom has been intensified by individuals and corporations going back to gold mining (or, at least, prospecting), as the world price of the yellow metal quadrupled. Gold was Colorado's original attraction, and to this day much of its wealth, folklore, and legend relates to gold. Current estimates are that Colorado's known gold reserves are worth $700 million, so the gold rush is once again on. In Cripple Creek, just over the Rockies west of Colorado Springs, where the first gold strike was made in 1891, a 2.7-acre piece of land, worth forty dollars only a few years before, was suddenly up for sale in 1973 for $125,000.

The wealth gained by Colorado Springs from the military and

tourism brought relative prosperity to much of El Paso County. One-quarter of the population had annual incomes over $10,000 in 1970: this was not as good as Denver, the state's biggest city, where almost a third of the population was in this bracket, but better than half of Colorado's other counties. And Colorado Springs' downtown section—a busy commercial center—shows the city's wealth. I counted fourteen brokerage offices, some of them representing the nation's biggest houses, as well as three expensive art galleries, a number of quality jewelers, and some fine restaurants. When I took my family to Colorado Springs in the summer of 1970, I recall that we had an exceptionally fine dinner at a steak house on East Pikes Peak Avenue downtown. The restaurant was done up in turn-of-the-century red velvet and polished oak—the style of the fabulous Gold Rush days. It made me think of the photographs I had seen of the elegant and opulent bordellos of the era. The nearest thing to *them* that Colorado Springs has these days are bars and restaurants on Southern Nevada Avenue featuring "Topless Matinée Shows" and "Baby Dolls." The clientele are off-duty soldiers and, I must say, none of it has much sparkle or class.

But Colorado Springs has always aspired to have class, perhaps even more so than San Francisco or Saratoga, or for that matter, Tuxedo, Newport, or Southampton in the East. The city's history dates back to 1859 when it was founded by a group of Kansas gold prospectors as El Dorado—its first foray into pretentiousness. But El Dorado was a failure and ten years later it reappeared on the map with the name of Colorado City. This early period is recorded in local history as one of "brawls and shooting affairs," hangings of horse thieves in nearby cottonwoods. But eventually, more righteous citizens came on the scene and established a mile away a township they called Fountain Colony because of its location on Fountain Creek, which traverses the area. While bordellos, saloons, and gambling houses were confined to Colorado City,

Fountain Colony was designed to attract people of "good moral character and strict temperance habits." The man behind this notion was General William J. Palmer, promoter of the Denver and Rio Grande Western Railroad, who presently linked Fountain Colony and Denver by a narrow-gauge railroad.

By the early 1870s, Fountain Colony was the hallmark of elegance. It was wealthy, attractive, and the dry, sunny climate was a magnet for people from all over the world. So many young Englishmen came to live there that the town began referring to itself as Little London. In the midst of the Wild West with gold prospectors, cowboys, thieves, and lawmen shooting each other up, the foppish young people of Fountain Colony played golf, cricket, and polo and went in for fox hunting. The city's official history remarks with dry humor, "The opening of the Antlers Hotel in 1882 was a gala occasion, but the new opera house got off to a poor start with *Camille*—a dismal choice for a large proportion of the audience, who were [lung] health seekers."

In 1891, Colorado Springs, now known as such, was graced by the arrival of a Silesian count named James de Pourtales and his wife, Countess Bertha. Pourtales, who appears in contemporary photographs as a slightly rakish gentleman with a short beard, a nondescript hat, and a pipe clenched in his teeth, built a casino almost at the foot of Cheyenne Mountain. The structure was modeled after great mansions of Potsdam, but the city fathers quickly outlawed gambling as well as drinking and Pourtales vanished from view. But the great Cripple Creek gold strike in the same year threw more fortunes to the happy people of Colorado Springs. The city gained a Millionaire Row, a short block of palatial homes, and Spencer Penrose, one of the millionaires, erected the Broadmoor Hotel, roughly on the site of Pourtales' old casino. The hotel promptly burned down, but Penrose replaced it with a new structure and added parks and an artificial lake. Surrounding land was bought out for private mansions and a class of Colorado Springs citizens still known as the "Broadmoor people" became the local aristocracy. ("Broadmoor people" had a lot to do with the air force's decision to build the Academy in El Paso County.)

The great Victorian gingerbread hotel, done in white and pink, still stands proudly in the shadow of Cheyenne Mountain, where American, British, and Canadian officers plot and monitor all flights approaching the North American continent around the clock. A flash from the underground NORAD headquarters that enemy planes or missiles may be approaching will activate North America's air defenses from the scrambling of the Continental Air Command's jet fighters to the alerting of the airborne patrols of nuclear-equipped B-52 bombers of the Strategic Air Command, Polaris and Poseidon submarines, the Minutemen missiles in their hardened silos in North Dakota and their protective antiballistic missiles' defenses. It will alert the White House and Pentagon war rooms and apprise the President of the United States that he may have to order nuclear retaliation at once. Finally, the nation's radio and television stations will instantly become a coordinated civil-defense network. Actually, such an alert to the broadcasting stations, ordering them to halt all programs and await federal orders, was erroneously sent out from Cheyenne Mountain on February 20, 1971, when a teletype operator of the National Emergency Warning Center fed the wrong tape into the circuit. It took forty minutes to unscramble the ensuing confusion, but it was an interesting commentary on the psychology of American broadcasters in the third decade of the nuclear age that most of them failed to obey the alert in the first place. (NORAD was a key instrument in the worldwide military alert ordered by the White House in October 1973, at the height of the Middle East crisis).

I pondered all these improbable juxtapositions and ironies of the atomic age as I sat at the oak bar of the Broadmoor Hotel one

April Sunday afternoon about two months after that first false alert. I had just finished my lecturing stint at the Air Force Academy and I wanted to savor a bit the elegant aspects of Colorado Springs life. It was just after brunch and the other customers in the combination bar and grill (decorated with faded photographs of Count Pourtales and his casino) were rich tourists who had just finished a round of golf, or retired senior military officers and their oddly faded wives.

On my previous visit to Colorado Springs, I had gone to visit Marshal Sprague, a historian of the West who had lived long enough in Colorado Springs to become an authority on local mores. As we sipped drinks in his garden, I asked Sprague to tell me about the armed forces in Colorado Springs' life.

"You don't feel the military here as an overwhelming social force at all," he told me. "It's as though they were kind of stuck off by themselves and out of the way, and you only feel it through the money that you know they are spending and the civilians who live off of serving the military. You see, they've got Fort Carson: it is out of town, a vast land area, thirty or forty miles long, running down toward Pueblo. . . . Then there's NORAD. . . . It's inside the mountain but it's partly in town. Before, it was all in the east part of town in the area that had grown so tremendously, this incredible growth of the residential population and the stores and things out that way. . . . Then there's the Air Force Academy and we have a few generals out there. But all those things don't seem to change our society much. We go around with the generals, their wives are all very charming people, and they fit into things, but they also have their own society so they could get along without us fine. They are used to running around with one another. . . .

"The powers in a town like this, the large money powers, are two or three large lumps of money. One of them is the Broadmoor group, the hotel people and the foundation that they control.

. . . If the Broadmoor Hotel hadn't been here we wouldn't have gotten a lot of the military we've got because when this brass came out looking for various kinds of things, the hotel has just been magnificent in handling them. . . . Penrose [the Broadmoor founder] invested a quarter of a million dollars in fine wines and cognac in 1917, before the Prohibition, because he was afraid he might not be able to get a drink. When he died in 1939, a great deal of that liquor went to the hotel cellar. The managers of the Broadmoor and their friends and their social set were very conscious from the first of the military. They liked them, they liked to entertain these generals and their wives. That's why we've got so many retired generals here. We're just loaded with retired generals. . . . So when a lot of these fellows came out originally to scout for NORAD and for Fort Carson, and even the Air Force Academy, some of them were impressed by the Broadmoor hospitality."

After a week around Colorado Springs I could understand Sprague's point about how little the military *visibly* affected the city, except that the city's visible new wealth is largely due to their spending. Except during weekends at the Broadmoor and one or two other places, the air force and army people keep to themselves. Close to forty thousand of them live on base—at the Fort Carson complex or the Air Force Academy—and they have no need or time to be involved with the town. On an occasional evening, a soldier who had too much to drink may be seen picked up by Military or Air Police patrols. But Fort Carson and the area immediately surrounding it are sufficient for the soldiers. The Air Force Academy is such an immense reservation that it is rare for officers or airmen to come to Colorado Springs. If they venture off the base, chances are that they would go to Denver and live it up in the "big city." And of course both Fort Carson and the Academy have Post Exchanges, commissaries, and other shopping facilities (where it is much cheaper to buy goods than in the average American store), along with swimming pools, athletic

fields, cinemas, and every other conceivable community require-
ment. Psychologically, there is little difference between military
installations in the Colorado Springs area and U.S. military bases
in Japan, Germany, or Spain. Fort Carson and the Academy are,
of course, bigger and more opulent than the overseas bases, but
the same spirit reigns. As Marshal Sprague noted, the generals
and their wives make the local social circuit for civic-relations
reasons but otherwise live in splendid isolation.

And splendid, by the way, *is* the word for contemporary military life in America, nowhere more so than around Colorado
Springs. At Fort Carson, the army, eager to attract volunteers, has
converted the barracks into quarters that are more like bachelor
apartments or suites in expensive college dormitories. A study of
soldiers' needs prepared for the army concluded that a man
needs storage space, room to read, good lighting and, as an expert
remarked, "he likes to have doors on toilets." There are lounges
for watching television and playing cards and pool. All living
units are air-conditioned, carpeted, and equipped not only with
bathrooms but with drapes.

Officers' quarters both at Fort Carson and the Academy are
correspondingly luxurious. During my stay at the Academy, I
was the guest of young colonels and their families at cocktails
and dinners at splendidly decorated homes, each with a garden.
It was like being in an exclusive suburb in Virginia or Westchester. Generals at the Academy (as generals and admirals everywhere in the United States) entertain with the assistance of enlisted men and noncommissioned officers who are permanently
attached to them as drivers, butlers, and cooks. (This practice
may be on its way out because Congress, to say nothing of the
men themselves, takes a dim view of the taxpayer footing the bill
for personal servants of flag officers and their wives. Besides, the
sentiment is growing that such a use or abuse of manpower is
undignified in a "democratic" defense establishment.)

For all its wealth and military splendor, Colorado Springs suffers from racial problems as other American cities do. Chicanos and Colorado Indians (mostly Utes) there still suffer from job and housing discrimination, despite their relatively large numbers, just as the several thousand black families do. As I mentioned earlier, the local sensation during my 1970 visit to Colorado Springs was the murder of Roosevelt Hill, a respected black educator from Denver, by an off-duty Fort Carson soldier during an altercation over credit cards at a gas station. But the soldier was found not guilty by the coroner's jury and, as far as I know, was returned to military jurisdiction without further action. Most of the Colorado Springs citizens with whom I raised the subject preferred not to talk about it. The following year, I did not find a single officer at the Air Force Academy who could even recall the incident.

There is a strong, functional link between Colorado Springs and Omaha: a signal from Cheyenne Mountain to the Strategic Air Command Headquarters in Nebraska could send B-52 bombers with their nuclear loads toward enemy targets. As home of SAC, Omaha is a military-oriented community—and proud of it. The SAC connection gives Omahans a feeling of belonging to a wider world than the midwestern plain, and it also probably enhances local patriotic sentiments. Driving along Route 6 toward Omaha, I happened to notice a sign over a hamburger joint proclaiming, *God Bless America—Think About It!*

Although there is no operational SAC base in the Omaha area —SAC bombers are stationed at bases on the two coasts, and in Puerto Rico, Guam, and Thailand—the headquarters, including its underground command posts, play a significant role in the affairs of the city. Perhaps most important, SAC became a major local employer at a time when meat-packing plants moved to smaller Nebraska towns with cheaper labor and operational costs, creating a degree of unemployment in the late 1960s that both SAC and several new electronics plants have helped to keep in check.

Actually, SAC is centered in its own private community, Bellevue, some ten miles from Omaha. The news editor at an Omaha television station, discussing SAC's activities in the area, told me, "The SAC role is pretty well evident to everybody, but it is not played up for a whole lot." He did not think SAC affected Omaha very visibly—the same story as Colorado Springs—except financially and in the strengthening of the city's conservative politics. But, of course, Omaha has always been strongly conservative what with its great insurance business and farm tradition. (In 1970, when the Vietnam war and the Cambodian incursion were a major national controversy, the overwhelming Omaha sentiment was with the Nixon administration even though the nationwide student unrest did not spare Nebraska universities.)

"You will find that the top commanders do make an effort to get involved in the Omaha community, especially on the social side," the TV news editor said. "In recent summers there have been efforts by people at SAC to take kids out of the ghetto. They used air force property—they have a very nice recreation area with a lake and so on—to give the kids a recreation program and that sort of thing. But I think SAC pretty much minds its own business. . . . We have an interesting thing on the Omaha campus [of the University of Nebraska]. For years and years, they have had what they call the Bootstrap program—military officers are put on detached service from the army and the air force to come here to finish their education. I'd judge that at any given time there are probably a couple of hundred of them on the campus, and this is a campus of ten thousand or so. . . . The antiwar people tried to draw them into their debates with very little success, except for this one incident: it was after Kent State and all that, and it was the only time I saw these Bootstrappers go out, take the microphone, and make statements. They didn't attempt to shout down anybody or discredit anything. It was a very democratic thing."

Sociologically, Virginia Beach is to the East Coast what Colorado Springs is to the Rockies. As in Colorado Springs, a military establishment, retired military personnel and civilians, and hordes of tourists have joined forces to make a turn-of-the-century resort into one of the nation's biggest boom areas and the scene of a breathless land grab.

Whereas Colorado Springs is largely supported by the army and the air force, Virginia Beach is strictly navy country. It stretches along the Atlantic Ocean immediately east of the vast defense complex formed by the Fifth Naval District, the headquarters of the U.S. Atlantic Fleet. Norfolk, Newport News, Portsmouth, and Hampton are the great navy installations in the region, and Virginia Beach is both a bedroom town and a retirement spot for the navy's people. The Norfolk-Virginia Beach-Portsmouth Metropolitan Area had a permanent military population of 95,000 in 1973, and federal employment, chiefly military, accounted for three out of every four basic jobs in the area. (Pentagon figures also show that in 1972, the state of Virginia received $1 billion in military contracts and $1.8 billion in military payrolls—the third-highest payroll for any state of the Union—and most of it went to the navy, although the air force's Tactical Air Command at Langley Air Force Base in the same area received its share.)

Virginia Beach itself—a sprawling city with a population of over 200,000 and an area of 301 square miles—has four major military installations within its limits: the Oceana Naval Air Station just west of the town is the largest master-jet aircraft base on the East Coast; the Little Creek Naval Amphibious Training Base to the northwest is the largest of its kind in the world and it is the preserve of the marine corps; Dam Neck, to the south, is the headquarters of the U.S. Atlantic Fleet's Combat

Direction Systems Training Center; and Fort Story is a facility of the Army Transportation Training Command. Unlike Colorado Springs, however, Virginia Beach is immensely aware of the military presence. From Ocean View Avenue, a two-and-a-half-mile string of hotels, motels, and old-fashioned beach cottages, one can watch warships steaming to and from Hampton Roads, the entrance from Chesapeake Bay to the Newport News and Norfolk harbors. Overhead, blue navy jets scream, sometimes at altitudes of a few hundred feet, on their daily exercises. Navy helicopters roar over Virginia Beach as they come and go between Dam Neck and inshore installations. The navy is so proud of its facilities that a Virginia Beach tourist brochure informs tourists that "From the Jet Observation Point at Oceana Naval Air Station visitors may watch take-offs and landings of the nation's most spectacular aircraft. . . . There are three jet planes on display which can be inspected close-up." The Naval Amphibious Base is open on weekend afternoons "during which time visitors may go aboard an 'open house' ship and visit the Amphibious Museum."

My wife and I spent a weekend in Virginia Beach in 1972 not so much to observe the naval activity as to see for ourselves what made the city grow to such extraordinary proportions in such a relatively short time. The navy and its support of Virginia Beach were one of the obvious reasons for this growth. So we saw the modest houses of active and retired navy personnel; but what made the greatest impression was the Birdneck Point community, a *very* exclusive home of retired admirals and (presumably) civilian millionaires. Birdneck Point, several miles inland along Great Neck Creek, is built around a beautiful golf course. It is, in effect, a country club, where signs warn that the fine for littering is $2500—the highest I have seen anywhere in the country. Former admirals, I take it, like their preserve to be spotless: it must be the tradition of the scrubbed deck.

Virginia Beach, I found out, became so big in size and population after it incorporated the whole of adjoining Princess Anne County, originally rural, in 1963. In area, it is now one of the ten largest cities in the United States. In 1940, the population of Virginia Beach was only 20,000. In those days, according to old residents, it was an easygoing but elegant resort, famous for its châteaulike Cavalier Hotel (the style of Colorado Springs' Broadmoor), old mansions, and seaside cottages, and a lovely unpolluted beach. It had, in fact, been just that for over half a century, since 1880, when Norfolk sportsmen built an oceanside hunting and fishing lodge. Within seven years a railroad line linked Virginia Beach to Norfolk and the new resort was off to its fame. Actually, the town traces its lineage back to 1607 when Captain Christopher Newport and 104 companions landed at Cape Henry, now the city's northernmost point, and moved toward the mouth of James River. Virginia Beach's boosters claim that their city is as old as America. Between 1940 and 1960, Virginia Beach's permanent population more than doubled to 85,000. After gobbling up Princess Anne County, the figure went up to over 200,000 late in 1972. By this time, land developers and real-estate operators had gone berserk. Not only had the number of housing units doubled in ten years, but the value of new construction doubled in just *one* year, from 1970 ($68 million) to 1971 ($137 million). Advertisements in the *Virginia Beach Sun,* the local weekly, gave a flavor of what was happening. Thus the Walker Realty Company proudly announced that "The Walker Men Strike Again with Another Fantastic Sales Month" and that its top salesman, a Harry Kohlberg, sold $240,612 worth of property in October 1972. "We Need Listings! Any Location or Price Range," the ad said. Oglesby & Barclift, Inc., another realtor, could only claim $71,844 in October for its man, Gene Winebarger, but it noted that he was a member of the "Million-Dollar Sales Club." A woman of our acquaintance bought a house for $27,000 in 1970 (it was priced at $18,000 in 1969) and was offered $60,000 for it late in 1972.

It was obvious from driving around Virginia Beach that the city fathers were blissfully unaware of the perils of uncontrolled growth, though a headline in the *Sun* reported: "Planners Concerned with Orderly Development of City." And well they might be. With the over-inflated population, the 1.2 million tourists in 1972 alone, and the building craze, Virginia Beach was turning into something akin to Miami Beach, Atlantic City, or Ocean City. The motel culture had captured Virginia Beach with a vengeance. They seemed to be everywhere and the City Council just kept approving new applications for more and more. In October 1972, the Council approved ("Despite strong opposition," the local paper said) the application of a single developer for two hundred motel units on Pacific Avenue (a block from the beach) and promised that four hundred more would be allowed in the future. On the same day, the Terry Corporation, believed to be the biggest landowner in Virginia Beach, was granted approval for erecting 207 townhouses. The Terry Corporation, I was told, is a company with ties to developers in Flushing, New York, and its political power in Virginia Beach is said to be unsurpassed. In tune with its development pattern, Virginia Beach was also faced with the problem of how to deal with topless go-go dancers. But it did not seem to trouble the City Council as it reviewed applications for go-go permits. Councilman George R. Ferrell seemed to sum up the official attitude when he told the Council that "I don't mind looking at them, but I think we ought to tax them more than we do." Meanwhile, the beaches were eroding (partly because of an ocean flood) and there was only clay instead of sand. There were insufficient sewer hookups and a shortage of drinking water. Despite the city's wealth (the median annual family income was close to $11,000), there were not enough schools to accommodate the children.

Throughout all this, the navy families tended to their traditional recreational pursuits. Bingo was played weekly at the Fort Story Officers Club, the local chapter of the Navy Wives Clubs of America held its lunches featuring skits about the role of Waves aboard warships (the navy had just authorized Waves to be assigned to ships), and the Tidewater Central Church of the Nazarene held a "God and Country Rally" to hear Lee Hayes, a sailor from the intelligence-gathering ship *Pueblo,* describe his eleven-month captivity in North Korea. In nearby Norfolk, the Jewish Community Center held a Sunday bagels-and-lox brunch for Jewish sailors, while the navy YMCA offered an Astrology for Fun session.

As we drove out of Virginia Beach, this incongruous mixture of modern military power and civilian greed and ostentation, we passed the "First Landing Cross" which marks the spot at Cape Henry where the Jamestown settlers landed 365 years earlier. It seemed like the proper place to ask again what in God's name was America doing to herself?

Every American generation since the Jamestown and Plymouth settlers has held strong views as to how Americans should live and govern themselves. Even in today's frantic culture we have left room for the ancient life styles of the Amish people and the Mennonites. And we have not failed to produce our own new experiments in living. In the 1960s and 1970s, these were the communes and collectives. Communal experimentation reached its highest and most extensive stage during 1971 in Berkeley, California, always noted for its sense of innovation if not down-right eccentricity, and I spent some time there visiting my daughter and her husband. As it turned out, the Berkeley experiment in somewhat radical self-government was not repeated elsewhere on a meaningful scale—though at one time the rebel generation believed it would be imitated in other university communities—but I think it is worth recording. For one thing, it is still alive!

It was probably logical that Berkeley, the cradle of much of the student protest then sweeping the country and mecca of the American youth culture (or subculture), should have been the first community in the United States to vote into office a City Council in which young left-wing radicals exercised considerable political influence. This was the result of elections on April 6, 1971, when radicals captured half of the Council seats and prepared to push for an absolute majority in the 1973 elections. (This bid failed and in 1973 the radicals became in a minority on the Council.)

The battle for Berkeley, an affluent and beautiful city on the eastern shore of San Francisco Bay, was something quite new in American politics. The radicals who won their share of power with the votes of their intellectual, student, black, and "freak" constituents, were challenging the system all along the line, even including the American flag. They wanted not just the kind of cautious reforms that liberal politicians promise voters, but a basic alteration in the city's economic, social, and political structure. They wanted to control the police so that it would be responsive to "the people"; do away with the city manager; create "people's alternative institutions" to care for the poor, the old, the infirm, the helpless young, and the heroin addicts; discharge the community's economic profit motive in favor of investments in beautifying the city and assisting the arts; and let every Berkeleyan be totally free in politics, education, life style, sex, and all else. As their electoral platform put it, "We, the citizens of Berkeley, intend to reassert control over our own lives."

None of this was, of course, tolerable to the Establishment. California's Governor Ronald Reagan set the tone for its response when he announced that the Berkeley election showed that "it can happen here." The conservatives and the comfortable liberals from the "Hill" overlooking the city and the Bay had dire misgivings about the future. They foresaw chaos, licentiousness, "communism," economic ruin, and a breakdown in law and order if the radicals and their "freak" allies went unchecked. As it was, the political agitation in Berkeley did in fact go quite deep. Bank of America branches were bombed and the FBI had to assign an inordinate number of agents to the city to look for Weathermen in hiding and other wanted "subversives." I was told of wealthy, middle-class, and other "patriotic" persons—the latter being chiefly university and municipal employees—moving out to safer Bay Area towns and commuting to work. Expensive "Hill" homes were increasingly for sale, and I remember seeing a sign to that effect on the gate of a lovely Florentine mansion across the street from the staid old Claremont Hotel. Berkeley's 277-man police department had already lost nine experienced officers and more resignations were expected. A ranking city official, at odds with the radicals on the City Council, bitterly spoke of the young people's "hate for the professional" and compared their attitudes to that of the little boys in *Lord of the Flies*. The issue, he said, was "how much anarchy is tolerable."

For their part, the radicals on the Council were darkly hinting that they would use their voting power to block the budget, particularly the police budget, if their demands were not met. Establishment spokesmen countered with threats of petitioning the state of California for law-enforcement assistance—a form of intervention—if the Berkeley Police Department was "emasculated."

The logic of the 1971 Berkeley phenomenon was grounded in the long history of that incredibly vibrant, creative, and tolerant city, as well as in the traditions of the local campus of the University of California, considered along with Harvard to be one of the best colleges in the United States. In 1911, at the height of an earlier period of American political unrest, Berkeleyans had elected what turned out to be a highly successful socialist government under Mayor J. Stitt Wilson. (Interestingly, it was Wilson who equipped Berkeley with its first city-wide police communications system.) The Free Speech Movement erupted victoriously there in 1964. "Free community" institutions—the so-called Alternative Institutions of which the Berkeley people are so proud—were pioneered shortly afterward. In May 1969, a youth named James Rector was killed by Alameda County deputy sheriffs during the bloody battle for the "People's Park," a piece of land in the city's South Campus section, owned by the university, where students and "freaks" had established a recreational area for the neighborhood residents without securing the proper permission. The California National Guard occupied Berkeley for several days and a Guard helicopter bombarded the crowds with tear gas. The first waves of student protest against the Vietnam war rolled from the Berkeley campus.

The radical grab for power came when a new leadership, the April Coalition, found ways of channeling Berkeley's enormous energy, militancy, and political-social consciousness into the electoral process. Almost everybody at the university and in the "free community" was drawn into it: white liberals, militant blacks, left-wing intellectuals, street people, "freaks" engaged in community projects and "political education" about the "Third World" and the perils of American "imperialism," the Gay Women's Workshop, the Gay Men's Liberation Front, and a multitude of other Berkeley organizations, some permanent, some ephemeral. A vast effort went into registering and canvassing voters. On April 6, three of the four April Coalition candidates for the Council were elected, along with a mayor who ran as an independent but was basically in sympathy with their aims.

The Police Community Control Plan, however, a separate proposition on the ballot, was defeated. It called for the division of Berkeley into three areas—the campus and adjoining downtown section, the "Hill," and the black community—and the creation of autonomous police forces in each of them. Elected commissioners would run each police force and coordinate their operations. Even some of the plan's authors admitted later that they had not thought it through adequately. The proposition was turned down by a two-to-one margin, largely because its opponents succeeded in convincing the black community that the plan was "segregationist." But the chief point the April Coalition set out to make had been made: radicals (a term defying precise definition even in Berkeley, where left-wing politics run the full gamut from anarchism and Maoism to an Old Left of the early anti-fascist vintage and liberal left-of-center positions) and anti-Establishment forces in general can capture power under certain conditions through the electoral process.

To be sure, the April election meant to some of the more advanced radicals simply a "tactical" stage in a long-range "revolutionary struggle for power." Their basic suspicion of well-meaning liberals had not changed—they continued to regard them as a more dangerous enemy than the "reactionary Pig Establishment"—and they still proclaimed their underlying contempt for "system politics." A leading Berkeley radical told me during a long conversation in his tastefully furnished bachelor apartment on the "Hill," with soft jazz floating from the record player and incense burning in a tall holder on the coffee table, that the importance of the April Coalition was not simply in having done so well in the election, but in having created a "revolutionary political movement" that must be kept alive at all costs. His conversation was rich in revolutionary rhetoric. A poster portrait of Angela Davis, the black communist philosophy instructor then in prison awaiting trial on conspiracy charges, stared down at us. So the Berkeley election was meant as a step in the social and cultural "revolution" through the ballot. The Coalition's electoral platform summarized the radical program:

"We have seen our government destroy beautiful parks and homes while our people cannot get adequate housing or jobs. We have seen our waters polluted and our fellow citizens choked on smog and teargas, and beaten in the streets.

"And yet, despite our oppression, the people of Berkeley continue to work and love. In our public schools we continue to work both for racial harmony and self-determination; and in our families and our free schools we continue to devise new ways to bring up children and to relate to one another as free human beings. We have struggled to create a new consciousness of our womanhood and manhood.

"We try, with our limited means, to overcome the heartlessness of our economic system, by sharing our food and our homes, and by setting up clinics for our sick—all without the help of the established powers.

"And in the jaws of a government which cares more for the speculations and profits of the rich than for the health and safety of its people, we have brought forth a new birth of direct community democracy.

"Now, through an open process that has confidence in all the people, we come together to draw up our program; to choose the representatives who will help us to implement that program; and to encourage all our fellow citizens to assume the human responsibility and privilege of self-government."

The detailed program following this hyperbolic preamble

called, among other things, for far-ranging tax and rent-law reforms, the naming of municipal judges "endorsed by a people's convention," low-priced public transportation, city-supported youth hostels and child-care centers, the end of discrimination in municipal employment against women, minorities, homosexuals, and the lowering to ten of the legal age for drinking alcohol and smoking. It specifically bound the candidates to "peace and solidarity between the people of Berkeley and the people of Vietnam" and proclaimed that "no citizens of the city of Berkeley should serve with the armed forces of the United States in Southeast Asia."

Now the majority of Berkeley's *young* citizens truly believed in this program and fully expected it to be implemented. Impractical and idealistic as they might have been, they seemed to share a sense of caring for one another. Their often strident militancy was mellowed by a human warmth rarely found in American cities (Oakland, the sprawling ghetto-ridden city adjoining Berkeley, had just voted down a proposal to earmark 2 *per cent* of the municipal budget for poverty programs). In the words of a busy "freak" who helped to run the Free Clinic, the main thing about Berkeley was "this whole business of caring about people."

The so-called radical bloc on the eight-member Council was formed of D'Army Bailey and Ira T. Simmons, both black lawyers, and Mrs. Ilona Hancock, a white housewife. For all practical purposes, the radicals commanded a fourth vote—that of Warren Widener, the new black mayor and a left-of-center liberal. On the other side of the fence were four councilmen whose views ranged from moderate to conservative. They were the three holdovers from the 1969–71 Council: Wilmont Sweeney, a black politician who had been a councilman for ten years and was narrowly defeated by Widener in the mayoralty race; Borden Price, a white Republican; and Tom McClaren, a white conservative. The fourth was Edward E. Kallgren, a white liberal. The

Council was stalemated because it could not agree among themselves on the statutory ninth member.

The radicals had the advantage of youth and exceptional education and background. D'Army Bailey, then twenty-nine years old, is a native of Memphis, Tennessee, who went through the whole struggle of the civil-rights movement in the early 1960s, got himself expelled from college in Louisiana, became radicalized through his friendship with Abbie Hoffman in Worcester, Massachusetts, attended law school at Boston University, and received a law degree from Yale in 1967. He served as director of the Law Students' Civil Rights Research Council of the American Civil Liberties Union in New York and came to Berkeley late in 1968 to become a member of the Neighborhood Legal Services Program. He spent the summer of 1970 traveling around the country to acquaint himself with the "new thoughts" and returned to Berkeley to enter local politics and help launch the Coalition.

Ira Simmons, then twenty-eight, came from Florida to Howard University in Washington, D.C., to earn his law degree. He worked on Robert F. Kennedy's presidential campaign as an advance man and settled in Berkeley in the winter of 1968, serving as executive director of the Oakland Lawyers' Committee for Civil Rights Under the Law. "Lonie" Hancock, then thirty, an attractive New Yorker, a Cornell graduate and mother of two children, came to Berkeley with her biologist husband who taught plant pathology at the University of California.

Shortly before the 1971 election, the April Coalition presented a "guerrilla theater" play depicting Berkeley as a "people's city" isolated from the outside world by hostile surrounding communities blocking its food supplies. In the closing scene, assistance to Berkeley comes by air from North Vietnam and China. A radical student at the university, pessimistic about the Coalition's experiment, asked me, "How can a free territory survive in a sea of fascism?" This was a year before Watergate, and I for one tended to dismiss such rhetoric as nonsense. I did not know about the secret "domestic intelligence" plans of the Nixon administration or how seriously and hostilely it was taking all this radicalism of the young.

On May 15, just after the new Council was sworn in, Berkeley had a lively Saturday-afternoon riot, when hundreds of students and "freaks" attempted to tear down the steel-link fence around the "People's Park" to commemorate the second anniversary of the bloody encounter there two years before. They tore down part of the fence, damaged several buildings on Telegraph Avenue, set piles of plywood and garbage on fire on the avenue, and attacked the police with rocks and bottles. The officers responded with clubs, tear gas, pepper gas, and salvos of clay pellets fired from shotguns, and by the end of the afternoon called for help from Alameda County sheriffs (known as "Blue Meanies") and the Oakland police ("Black Counselors"). Forty-three people were arrested and released on bail. My daughter was in the thick of the affray; I had a hard time keeping my son, who had never seen a riot before, by my side.

Actually, this particular affair proved embarrassing to all sides, and served to illustrate the problems facing the Berkeley factions. Widener and the radicals neither welcomed nor expected the riot. (The mayor, Bailey, and Simmons were away at a meeting in Carmel, and only Mrs. Hancock was on hand to visit the jail that evening to check on the booking procedures.) The police did not want a clash either, and they acted with unusual restraint until provoked. In short order, the new Council found itself caught in the crossfire between its extremist allies and the Establishment. At a special meeting at the Berkeley Little Theatre called to try to choose the ninth member of the Council, Council members faced a standing-room-only audience of roaring, chanting, whistling, foot-stamping, and cat-calling young people. When City Manager William C. Hanley appeared briefly on the stage to deliver documents to Mayor Widener, he was greeted with a chorus of insults. Then, nearly twenty speakers, including several middle-aged liberals, took turns nominating a young radical student for the vacant seat. But when a conservative, a former councilman named Charles V. Hughes, appearing "straight" with a crew-cut and in suit and tie, proposed a candidate who "would be proud to salute the flag," all hell broke loose. The youths shouted obscenities at him and rose with their arms extended in a mock-Nazi salute, chanting rhythmically, "Sieg Heil! Sieg Heil!" Smiling weakly, Hughes returned to his seat in a group of older people who had clustered on the right side of the aisle. Sweeney, the black conservative, was booed by young blacks who called out to him, "Boy!" and "Uncle Tom!" The evening at the Little Theater was a demonstration of sorts of "participatory democracy," but as a long-time observer of the Berkeley scene said to me as we watched, "Everybody here is trapped."

The new Council faced mounting pressures from the outside as well. To be sure, the radicals lost no time antagonizing other California politicians: when they were sworn in on May 4, Bailey, Simmons, and Mrs. Hancock refused to take the pledge of allegiance to the flag, and the Council abolished the procedure altogether by a five-to-two vote (only Sweeney and McClaren opposed the move) although the Stars and Stripes remained in its chamber and in Widener's office. The mayor also signed on the city's behalf the "People's Peace Treaty" with North Vietnam, a document drafted in Hanoi by Vietnamese students and a visiting American group.

Immediately, the City Council in Albany, a nearby community, began taking *two* pledges of allegiance: one for Albany and one for Berkeley. The *San Diego Union* and several other California newspapers printed the text of the pledge and urged readers to mail it along with protest letters to the Berkeley City Council.

Within ten days, the Council clerk reported the receipt of hundreds of such letters. (One letter addressed to the radicals proposed to "remove you to a faraway island until you recover your senses.")

I confess I had difficulty in Berkeley in dealing with the semantics of the situation. For one thing, there hardly were two persons adopting exactly the same ideological label. (Certainly, Berkeleyites chose to *look* alike—the men usually sporting beards and long hair, the women letting their hair fall loose, and both sexes affecting a studied sartorial neglect faintly suggestive of *guerrilleros* or old-fashioned revolutionaries. Representative Ronald V. Dellums, a black politician elected in 1970 as a Democrat from California's Seventh District, comprising Berkeley and Oakland —a hero of the April Coalition, which he helped to hammer together, and of the campus crowds deliriously applauding him when he denounced the Indochina war and spouted radical rhetorics—is a flamboyant dresser given to wearing artistic capes and colorful sports shirts; his attire has nothing in common with the "freak" uniform. When the City Council convened, Widener, Bailey, and Simmons were by far the best and most meticulous dressers in the chamber. Mayor Widener was elegant in a mod-cut brown suit, Simmons quietly conservative in a dark suit with a vest, and Bailey just as ceremonial and sober. Mrs. Hancock wore a dress with a high collar. These excellently dressed people were the city's leading political radicals, while their more right-wing colleagues looked casual in rumpled business suits, and the audience was all sweatshirts and old army jackets. Do clothes make the man?) I made a point of asking a number of people generally identified as radicals to give me their definition of the term. Widener first snapped impatiently, "I don't put myself in any bag," then said that a radical is "for change and has the energy and the nerve to go out and say that we need change. . . . This is in a constructive progressive sense." Mrs. Hancock, who admitted to slight liberal hang-ups, described radicalism as "imagination and nerve which the liberals lack." Bailey, when asked about radicalism, put it this way: "Liberal Democrats aren't worth a shit. . . . So I raised my politics to relevant politics. . . . The liberals didn't endorse us and they lost."

One way of getting at a definition of radical Berkeley politics is to understand its history and ingredients. Its beginning was probably the unsuccessful congressional bid in 1966 by Robert Scheer, then an editor of *Ramparts* magazine. Scheer was the first to seek a political constituency in the "free community." In 1968, the Berkeley people, tired of traditional politics, formed the Committee for New Politics. The following year, the Committee helped elect Dellums to the City Council, but Mrs. Hancock lost by 150 votes. The "new politics" went into high gear in the spring of 1970 when Dellums successfully challenged Jeffrey Cohelan, a six-term white liberal, in the primaries for the Democratic nomination from the Seventh Congressional District. Dellums' growing political organization brought in the "free community" and the campus to register voters in mass to assure him of victory over his Republican opponent in November. By January 1971, the Dellums electoral operation grew into what was to become the April Coalition. It succeeded in registering ten thousand more voters for the Council election than had registered for Dellums' congressional race, a rarity in American politics. Active members of the Coalition were the Berkeley New Democratic Caucus, the Berkeley Black Caucus, the students' April Sixth Movement, the Black Panthers, the National Committee to Combat Fascism (an Old Left group), the Red Family, Chicano organizations, the unorganized but enthusiastic street people from Telegraph Avenue, high-school students, Women's and Men's Gay Liberation Fronts, the new "Wobblies" of Berkeley, and assorted Trotskyites, orthodox communists, socialists, anarchists, Maoists, self-styled Ché Guevarists, veterans of the Venceremos

Brigades who worked in Cuba, "Third World People," Friends of the National Liberation Front (Vietcong), and those simply escaping any known political or ideological label.

But in Berkeley, life style came first and political identification later. Any explanation of Berkeley politics must be cultural and sociological. Of the city's 116,000 inhabitants—the 1970 Census showed a population increase of only 5500 over 1960—about 28,000 were blacks. By relative standards, particularly relative to Oakland, Berkeley blacks were fairly well-off and on the whole tended to be conservative. The university—economically, socially, and politically inseparable from the city—had more than 27,000 students, who lived in dormitories, fraternity and sorority houses, private apartments, and collectives all over the town. Another 16,000 persons were employed by the university on the teaching and academic staffs and in various technical and ancillary capacities. Most of the 9000 professors and instructors lived on the "Hill" and were inclined to be moderates or left-of-center liberals. But some of them are radical-minded, such as Anthony Platt, a bearded Englishman with Oxford and California degrees who taught criminology at Berkeley and was one of the authors of the ill-fated police plan. The university employees were generally conservative. They came from downtown, the black community, and the neighboring areas in the county.

What the size was of the permanent and transient "freak" community of Berkeley was anybody's guess. The "freaks" may be the young people engaged in social and political projects or the street people. A vague estimate put the number of "freaks" at around 20,000, but the figure may have been higher, especially during the summer, when the city was invaded by thousands upon thousands of youths "bumming around the country." At first sight, one gained the impression of a vast and basically idle community dedicated to self-indulgence, free sex, pot, and political fantasies. But this was a one-dimensional impression. There was a certain amount of idleness in Berkeley—very few "freaks" ever hold full-time jobs—and there was all the sex, pot, and politics in the world. It was also true that the "free community," verbally and otherwise committed to the "revolution," exacted financial support from the system it purported to destroy. (Faithful to historical precedent, the revolution-minded "freaks" came from affluent families, and thousands of Berkeleyites—some of them college drop-outs and others graduates—lived on monthly checks sent from home by guilt-ridden parents.) Others made ends meet through part-time jobs, food stamps, and general welfare assistance. The number of cars, including European sports models, was incredibly high among the "freaks" and the students. Berkeley was one vast traffic jam. The affluence of the city's youth culture was also illustrated by the crowds filling Berkeley's eating places, including the rather expensive Bernini's on Channing Way and Reza's on Telegraph Avenue. Both have sun-filled terraces and are reminiscent of Saint-Tropez rather than of a radical community.

Yet the "free community" had more purpose than met the casual eye. Behind the apparent idleness and the obvious political rhetorics, it had created a sense of commitment and an impressive "alternate" social structure. The young people of the collectives regarded themselves primarily as a "survival society," seeking to weather the "oppression" of the Establishment until the dawn of a new day. And chaotic and controversial as much of them may have been, the Berkeley "alternative institutions," based almost entirely on volunteer work, were a social phenomenon unparalleled elsewhere in the United States.

The oldest of these institutions was the Free Clinic, whose volunteer young doctors and nurses attended to forty to fifty persons daily and referred others to public and private institutions. Related to it were the Rap Center, where anyone who had a sudden need to talk to another human being was welcomed around the clock, and the Blow Out Center, where young people, usually narcotics addicts, were free to come and just scream their hearts out. There also was the Berkeley Runaway Center to aid juveniles. The Switchboard was designed to answer day-and-night telephone inquiries about a place to spend the night, a free meal, a friend's whereabouts, legal assistance, bail, and almost anything else. Switchboard volunteer operators, who handled suicide and drug cases and gave emergency psychiatric advice, worked out of the Free Church run by the Reverend Dick York.

Smoking marijuana was accepted as a form of political protest against the Establishment, but heroin addiction, which along with venereal disease was Berkeley's most serious health problem, was rejected as a danger to the community. One of the new City Council's first measures was the adoption of a methadone program. But, as a young woman associated with the Free Clinic told me when I visited her collective, the community was unable to handle the heroin problem alone. "This is our greatest failing. We think we can prevent addiction through our social programs, but once a kid is hooked, stoned out of his mind, there is little we can do."

Because the "free community" did not approve of standard education, it established the Free University of Berkeley (FUB) where for a tuition fee of ten dollars (the University of California charged from $350 to $1500) nearly a thousand people enrolled in courses ranging from Absurd Theatrical Happenings to Ecological Living, Bread-baking, Carpentry, Courtroom Tactics, Arc Welding, Creative Writing, Experimental Psychodrama, Happy Music, Hypnosis, Marxism, Hebrew, Kissing, Post-Revolutionary Marriage, Radical Psychiatry, Scrounging, Sculpture, Sexual Paradox, Shakespeare, Very Basic Auto Mechanics, Work Your Ass Off, and Yoga. FUB offered no credits and no degrees, and it listed its courses in a catalogue that was a pornographic comic book.

Berkeley had a number of "free" schools ranging from the People's Community School (a high school) to nurseries. The Red Family Collective, installed in several adjoining houses on Bateman Street (the letter "e" was erased from the street sign to make it into Batman), ran a nursery called the Blue Fairyland. It had an enrollment of seventeen children, a white rabbit, and, on the wall, a child's scrawled drawing proclaiming, *Blue Fairyland is Right On.*

Both Berkeley and Oakland neighborhoods operated "food conspiracies," which bypassed the commercial supermarkets to purchase foodstuffs directly from farmers. This way food came much cheaper and, presumably, fresher and cleaner. The newsletter of an Oakland Food Conspiracy named the "Saturday Morning Bolshevik" warned its readers that "ice-cream may have piperonal, an inexpensive substitute for costly vanilla flavoring, which is also fine for killing lice." The Berkeley "freaks" were, not surprisingly, food, health, and ecology purists. The city abounded in organic food shops. And on warm days, the Charles Lee Tilden Park, a vast wooded area atop the Berkeley hills, swarmed with thousands of adults and children playing baseball, football, or soccer or just throwing Frisbees. Despite all the picnicking, the park remained amazingly clean: "freaks" do not believe in littering.

There seemed to be no end to the alternative institutions. A People's Office provided legal defense and bail funds (on the evening of the May riot, people in scores of collectives rushed to the jail with cash in their hands to bail out their friends); the People's Architects were dedicated to the design of good housing, Ecology Action to protecting the environment, Solidarity Films to producing community movies; there were "free" bookstores; the Telegraph Avenue Liberation Front patrols kept the street people at peace; a tenants' protective association was formed. One of the most recent projects under consideration in Berkeley in 1972 was a Free Credit Union to make low-interest loans to socially significant projects. It had over $30,000 in pledged deposits soon after it started.

The local thirst for up-to-date ideological materials was quenched by the Yenan Bookstore, a red-painted one-story structure, where the *Peking Review,* Chairman Mao's *Thoughts,* and the rest of the Chinese revolutionary literature was available. The Granma Bookshop, around the corner on Telegraph Avenue, distributed free copies of *Granma,* the official Cuban newspaper, and sold all the radical literature the Berkeley soul may desire.

Everybody in Berkeley was thus free to do his thing. Until the April Coalition came along to transmute this extraordinary amount of talent and energy into concerted political action, the community was a pulsating but leaderless conglomerate of life styles, ideas, and individual commitments. Berkeleyites regarded any form of personal leadership with suspicion, and were so opposed to any form of hierarchy and authority that they even came down hard on their own individual leaders for "elitism" and "ego trips."

Three years is a long time in America. Moods and interests change. Commitments vanish or are channeled in different directions. By now, the radicals and their Coalition have lost their hold on the electorate. Their internal divisions and their obsession with leaders' "ego trips" further weakened the movement. The end of the Vietnam war went far to depoliticize the young people—to the point that they could not be attracted even to local issues. The university, too, turned away from politics, and in April 1973 students stayed away from the polls. Out of the Coalition's four candidates, only one won a Council seat. In August, D'Army Bailey, the elegant radical whom I had visited two years earlier in his incense-filled flat, was removed from office in a special recall election, in which he was ousted from the Council by a three-to-two margin, but it should be noted that the election was held during the summer when most students, normally his supporters, were away on vacation. Bailey was replaced by William Rumford, Jr., a black of more moderate persuasion.

To be sure, Berkeley remains a reasonably "free" community. Some of the alternative institutions have survived. The experiment of 1971 was not useless, aborted, or in vain. I believe that the community learned a great deal from it—even from the Coalition's defeat. A great deal of what happened in Berkeley in those days of euphoria was unquestionably positive, and the example of the social commitment of its young people found followers elsewhere.

Yet there are special American ironies here. On the day the radicals were beaten in Berkeley in 1973, Bobby Seale, still in prison on murder charges when the Coalition had its 1971 triumph, barely missed being elected mayor of neighboring Oakland. In Madison, Wisconsin, a twenty-seven-year-old radical lawyer named Paul R. Soglin defeated the incumbent mayor, a conservative Republican, thanks largely to massive support from University of Wisconsin students. (A few months later, word from Madison was that Soglin was acting as "a system politician," not upsetting the applecart.) At the other end of the spectrum, Ann Arbor, home of the University of Michigan, threw out its Democratic mayor in favor of a Republican because students stayed home on election day and the Human Rights party, a radical group, split the Democratic vote. So goes the American experiment: from the Left to the Right and back again. The important thing is that the experimentation must never cease.

Such is our national concern with the cities and the suburbs that in recent years we have tended to lose sight of the problems and realities of American rural life. This is to ignore a vital part of our society: the farmers, the farm workers, the migrants, the rural blacks of the South, the hill folk of Appalachia, the Chicanos, and the American Indians.

The principal phenomenon is of course that our countryside is being rapidly depopulated, a process that began with the industrial revolution and the Civil War in the last century and again picked up momentum after the Second World War. Ways must be found to arrest, if not reverse, this migration if we are to restore stability to our nervous and lopsided society.

Three main and interrelated factors go into the story of the American countryside—factors which I have had occasion to discuss before. The first one, the depopulation of rural areas in general, is shown by the 1970 census figure that just under 54 million Americans lived in rural areas—farm and nonfarm—which is roughly one-quarter of the total population. Absolute figures are meaningless because of the overall growth in population, but in relative terms the cities grew demographically by 13.3 per cent between 1960 and 1970, at the expense of rural America. The percentage drop in the rural population was only 0.3; the apparent disparity between the two figures is explained by high birth rates compensating for the heavy flight from farm areas. In any event, a net population deficit obviously means no growth.

The second factor is the vanishing of *farm* populations. In

1940, 30.5 million Americans (25 per cent) were classified as "farmers," whereas the figure in 1969 dropped to 10.3 million (5 per cent). Still another measurement shows that in 1970 only 6.8 per cent of Americans were engaged in farm work, agriculture, forestry, and fisheries (48.2 per cent were white-collar workers, 35.9 per cent blue-collar workers, 5.5 per cent in public administration, and the balance in the services sector). The total of farmowners, farm managers, farm laborers, and foremen dropped from 2,314,000 in 1960 to 1,384,000 in 1970. In other words, the number of Americans directly engaged in farm work dropped by nearly half.

From Nebraska to Tennessee I have seen empty towns, where only mangy dogs sleep in the sun, and farmhouses and barns are boarded up. I remember the empty vastness I saw driving through western Illinois, Iowa, and Nebraska, for miles on end no sign of human presence except for an occasional tractordriver working on the wheat and corn fields. One day, I recall, I was struck by a news story on my car radio reporting on a study of how great megalopolises were growing along the East and West coasts, crowded by millions upon millions of people. Empty land stretched all around me as far as the eye could reach; how incongruous it all sounded! Once in a while, past and present would invade one's consciousness: somewhere in Iowa, a sign proclaimed that Herbert Hoover's birthplace was to be found in a little town a few miles from the freeway; on a secondary road in Illinois another sign warned the motorist that horse-drawn vehicles used it, too, and one should be careful. At intervals, there would be tall silos for storing grain and new trucks parked alongside. Agriculture was there, all right, but barely a sign of human activity behind it.

By the same token, the number of individual farms in the United States plummeted from 5.9 million in 1947 to 2.8 million at the end of 1972. In the early 1970s, farms were disappearing at an annual rate of 100,000, and it is important to note, I think, that four out of five of the remainder were classified as "commercial" in the sense that each had at least $50,000 in annual sales. The rest were "noncommercial," meaning that each sold between $50 and $49,499 annually in products. Most of the latter, however, hovered around $10,000. To a large extent, this situation stemmed from the consolidation of acreage into vast farms, often by agribusiness corporations, which can operate more economically on a large scale with intensive mechanization and a drastic reduction in human labor. By 1973, agribusiness was a $140 billion combination of farms, cooperatives, and companies producing everything the farmer needs. For these reasons, the farm output on a man-per-hour basis has risen three times faster than in any other industry. It went up 45 per cent between 1960 and 1970.

This brings us to the third main factor in the American rural reality: poverty and unemployment. Although nonfarm employment has risen in rural areas, mainly in the service sector, it has not done so sufficiently to absorb the workers (usually black) displaced from agriculture. In the last ten years, for example, approximately 500,000 crop-share tenants were squeezed out, principally from cotton plantations, and current projections are that some 200,000 part-time harvest jobs will have been lost between 1968 and 1975 in California, Michigan, North Carolina, Oregon, and Texas. The number of migrant workers had already dropped from 400,000 in the mid-1960s to just under 200,000 in August 1970. This was a peak employment month; even so, the annual income for a six-person family with all the members working was $3350. A migrant family's annual income average in 1970 was $1937 for 152 days of work.

I am not arguing, of course, that the institution of the migrant worker should be preserved. The exploitation of migrant workers by farmers and land corporations has for years been a disgrace. The point is that the transformation of the rural society must take them into account; simply to condemn them to idleness and starvation makes no sense.

As matters stood in the early 1970s, poverty was the overwhelming fact of rural life despite the wealth of agribusiness corporations. Three-fifths of all poor American families lived in the country. Whereas 10.7 per cent of all American families were below the poverty line, the percentage in rural areas was between 15 and 16 per cent.

Twelve million blacks, more than half of all blacks in the United States, live in the South, so it is self-explanatory why black destitution was at its worst in the rural South. Again, the Census figures help to make this point. In rural nonfarm areas, roughly half of the resident blacks lived below the poverty line. And the income gap between whites and blacks is widening rather than closing as a result of the social changes and distortions occurring in recent decades in the rural South. Small wonder, then, that blacks were fleeing to the cities. (I think it is also pertinent to note the racial aspects of farm employment. In 1970 blacks accounted for 24 per cent of all farm laborers and foremen; when it came to farmers and farm managers, however, the figure was only 3 per cent.)

So dramatic is the depopulation phenomenon in the American countryside that only six states have more than 10 per cent of their population engaged in farm work. They range from South Dakota with a little over 20 per cent to Idaho, with 11.4 per cent. (Iowa, at the heart of the farm belt, has 12.5 per cent; Kansas 8.2 per cent; and Illinois, the state of the rolling plains, only 2.4 per cent.) This extraordinary lopsidedness poses a tremendous dilemma for America.

It would be foolish, to say the least, to suggest that the government, or somebody, try to reverse what has for long years been a major migratory pattern. Obviously, economic realities make it impossible for big farmers, whether individual or corporate, to abandon mechanization, redivide the land, and go back to manual methods of farming in order to provide employment. But what *can* be done to reduce urban overpopulation and rural underpopulation? I remember asking a young man in New Mexico why he was planning to move to Chicago and his answer was that it was "too God-damned hopeless and boring down here. . . . I am young. . . . I want a piece of the action." This, I believe, summarizes the problem, one of the most complex American problems of the century.

It seems to me, after discussing the subject with scores of experts, that what is required is a major national policy decision to make rural areas attractive and livable. I do not propose policies designed to turn millions of Americans back into farmers or farm hands, but a national program to assist the development of nonfarm rural areas, that is to say, small towns. This would require massive investments by the government and the private sector of the economy in housing, health, and education as well as jobs and cultural facilities.

Under the Nixon administration, however, the policy seemed to be to penalize rural America rather than help her. Whereas the federal budget in the fiscal year 1972 earmarked $7.1 billion in outlays for agriculture and rural development, the estimated total for fiscal year 1974 was only $5.6 billion. In 1973 the administration refused to continue a $1.5 million annual grant—a pittance—for the Rural Housing Alliance pilot project, a program administered by the Office of Economic Opportunity which assisted farm workers, many of them migrants, to build their own houses at thirteen sites in Alabama, Florida, Illinois, Louisiana, Michigan, Missouri, New York, Ohio, Wisconsin, and Texas. Writing in *The Washington Post* in 1973, Colman McCarthy quoted a social worker as saying that the Alliance was the "foremost and perhaps only government authority on migrant and farm-worker housing. . . . They were one of the few Federal groups in the field that the poor did not resent."

Likewise, it appeared, federal food-assistance programs in rural areas were functioning unevenly throughout the country. A 1973 report by the Senate Select Committee on Nutrition said that while the food-stamp program was doing well in some states (30 million Americans are eligible), 280 "hunger counties" remained in the United States. The total bill for food stamps reached $3 billion in 1974. The Committee's definition of a "hunger county" is when over 25 per cent of residents are poor and less than one-third receive federal food stamps. Virginia, for example, had thirty-four "hunger counties" and Arkansas, one of our poorest states, was ill-served by the program. The government had assigned in 1972 over $1.3 million for "black lung" clinic programs in Appalachia—most of the money was for Kentucky miners—but this, too, became a massive rip-off as local lawyers kept the bulk in fees for themselves.

I would not attempt to compete with Robert Coles in describing life in Appalachia and other poverty-stricken rural areas, or the conditions of the migrants. It would fill volumes—and Coles has done just that—to discuss the tragedy of rural America. But I must record my impression during my motor tour of the United States that hamlets I saw from Arkansas to Tennessee and North Carolina could not possibly belong to the same culture and civilization as the rest of the nation. The sight of the shacks and hovels, the barefoot children with empty eyes and distended bellies, made me think I was back in the Brazilian Northeast or India rather than in the world's most affluent country.

The year 1973, of course, was the time when our farm economy became so insanely distorted that chicken farmers chose to kill baby chicks by the hundreds of thousands rather than feed them for the market at what they considered unfairly low prices imposed by government controls. Other farmers and breeders slaughtered pregnant sows to avoid piglets, because feed was too expensive. Cattle breeding was deliberately held back to protect high meat prices (this was after the sharp price increase forced the housewives' meat boycott during April 1973) and, incredibly, the United States was faced by an artificial food shortage on top of the energy shortage. All this was happening when farmers' incomes were higher than ever before—farm prices had risen 35 per cent in 1973 and net annual family farm incomes were averaging over $10,000 in the Corn Belt—but this prosperity was by no means trickling down to the farm hands and migrants.

It was also against this background that César Chávez and his United Farm Workers went on fighting their fierce battle, going back to the mid-1960s, to unionize farm workers, chiefly in the West, against the opposition of big-farm operators, who would prefer no unions at all, and the Teamsters who decided to smash Chávez and take over the fields themselves. The more I learned about Chávez's efforts, the better I realized that what was at stake was much more than a matter of union jurisdiction: the contest was between a terribly underprivileged American group—mostly Chicanos—and the vested interests of corporate growers and those of a greedy and corrupt union. It was no surprise that Chávez induced a clear-cut political polarization. In 1969, when the Chávez-inspired grape boycott was in progress nationwide, no self-respecting liberal would buy grapes unless the boxes carried the black-eagle symbol of Chávez's union. Later, and this was when the Teamsters entered the fray, it was the lettuce boycott; during the 1972 Democratic National Convention nominating speakers urged the lettuce boycott, and at the Republican Convention a month later the lettuce boycott was denounced.

I met briefly Chávez in Washington in 1971; we chatted in a mixture of English and Spanish—it came sort of naturally to both of us. I was rather taken by this intense, totally dedicated, almost fanatical man. I came away with the impression that he was one of those very special Americans who keep our society reasonably honest. I had the same impression late in 1972 with several American Indian leaders I met in Washington when they were occupying the Bureau of Indian Affairs in protest against the treatment they have been receiving from the white man almost ever since Andrew Jackson's Indian Removal Act of 1830 and the decimating wars of the last century. America's greatness is still the heritage of those who fight for their rights against a society that seems to demand conformity, easy compromise, and roughshod disregard of the concepts of justice, decency, and caring.

America is still full of such men and women of courage and principle. They may be Chicano, black, or Indian activists, but they may also be part of the white Establishment—fearless judges, legislators, writers, priests, and just plain people who are serious about American standards. Despite the terrible pressures imposed by the sheer weight of our society and the consequent inequities, I retain the faith that perhaps even in our time, America shall overcome it all.

POWER
IN AMERICA

Power in society is political, economic, and cultural. These three elements mesh together, interact with each other, form a whole of greater or lesser coherence. The American power structure—I mean by this something both more complex and more elusive than simply the skein of instrumentalities managed by the federal government or by great corporate interests—is the cause as well as the result of extremely deep cultural and social strains and pressures.

The point I am making is that in America, perhaps more than anywhere else in the world, the shape and the character of power—and the manner of its exercise—are neither narrow nor absolute. Power is defined and modified by autonomous societal forces, essentially by cultural forces in the broadest sense, that determine where it goes, how it is handled, and, closing the circle, what impact it has on society. This unique American process reveals the profound, frequently divergent cross-currents of our national life which, in turn, make the United States the fascinating revolutionary society it has always been and, hopefully, will remain forever.

The next point, axiomatically, is that this interplay of forces has brought positive as well as totally disastrous results. Let me cite apposite examples in our time.

On the negative, or disastrous, side we have continually and I believe wrongly intervened in foreign situations—Cuba, the Dominican Republic, and, above all, Indochina. We have also witnessed a consistent and alarming assault on our own domestic life as evidenced by the Nixon administration's attempts at surreptitiously constructing something akin to a police state, through the series of connected episodes forming the Watergate scandals, and corrupting our political campaigns and processes.

These were developments in a climate that also produced Lieutenant Calley and the Mylai massacre, blind corporate greed, crime waves, and drug addiction. Certain negative societal-cultural conditions evidently allowed such events to be set in motion. These conditions included a social permissiveness about the violation of ethical standards on the highest level—I do *not* mean the *other* permissiveness associated with the youth rebellion, the sexual revolution, and so on—a sense of non-caring about the life of society, and a refusal to know or recognize what was occurring until it was too late. Perhaps the trauma of Vietnam inured us to it all, made us determinedly deaf and blind.

Having covered Washington as a newspaper correspondent during the Nixon era and having had uncomfortably close professional involvements with various aspects of the Watergate scandals, I think I had a fine vantage point for observing the extraordinary political goings-on, ranging from Indochina policy to Republican-party scandals. All these things seemed to me to be part of a larger but real social context.

But there was a positive side, too. The civil-rights movement, the integrationist legislation, the transmutation of the youth revolt into the antiwar movement, and, finally, the violent reaction against Watergate by the public, the judiciary, and key segments of the Congress had their roots, I believe, in healthier cultural and ethical currents. I like to think that all these responses are part of the self-corrective mechanism of the American society. But, on the other hand, I may have been caught in the trap of my own Jeffersonian optimism and innocence about America.

What we have been witnessing, then, is a clash of cultural currents and pressures. The Old Culture was challenged by the civil-rights and antiwar movements and the whole spectrum of revolutionary social change bursting out in the second half of the century. The challenge came from the New Culture—which was refreshingly closer to the traditional American values than the

Old Culture, as represented by what may be broadly described as the Nixon Establishment, with all its musty and empty rhetoric about work ethic, law and order, national security, and so on. Challenged, the Old Culture responded with aerial terror in Indochina and the nearest thing to repression we have known in the United States.

In Indochina, President Nixon authorized during most of 1972 and for a good part of 1973 some of the most destructive bombings in history. It took a major uprising in Congress, threatening to cut off *all* government moneys, and the refusal by a growing number of B-52 pilots to fly bombing missions against Cambodian peasants, to force Nixon to call off the bombardment of Cambodia in mid-August. The shocking aspect of this, I thought, was that the White House had realized all along that, first, Cambodia could never effectively defend herself alone and, second, that the bombing raids obviously could not be sustained forever. Although Nixon enjoys likening himself to Disraeli and Henry A. Kissinger thinks of himself as a Metternich and Bismarck, the truth—as it began to emerge after the signing of the Vietnam peace accords—was that both of them were infinitely cruel and more pointlessly devious than their historical heroes. This is not a place for a detailed discussion of American diplomacy-cum-bombing, but suffice it to say that what we have been learning of the history of the secret Vietnam negotiations between 1969 and 1973 makes it appallingly clear that the White House succeeded in lying to its North Vietnamese enemy, its Southeast Asian allies, and the American people and Congress—all at the same time.

At home, in the name of *its* concept of law and order, the same government has been violating Constitutional rights, rationalizing official burglary and wiretapping as acts designed to protect "national security," and creating a secret-police apparatus centered at the White House. Its highest figures were overtly or covertly allying themselves with mind-boggling financial scandals linked to political campaigns. The President was a tax-dodger.

This was the Watergate chapter of the 1970s, still running its baffling course two years after the June 1972 raid by White House operatives on the Democratic National Committee headquarters. But a new reaction to the excesses of the Nixon administration did begin, much in the way in which the rising sun blots out the moonlight. This was the New Culture asserting itself through a national mood favoring impeachment proceedings against the President or his resignation; the pressures that forced Spiro Agnew's resignation from the Vice Presidency for, in effect, accepting bribes while in office; the courageous attitudes of Special Watergate Prosecutors Archibald Cox and Leon Jaworski; the attitudes in the courts and in the press. The clash of these two cultural currents—the Nixonian and the anti-Nixonian ones— set in motion the great political conflict in the middle 1970s.

In discussing the travails of American society, I have used the word "culture" in its strict dictionary sense, to wit: "Act of developing by education, discipline, etc., the training or refining of the moral and intellectual nature"; "the enlightenment and refinement of taste acquired by intellectual and aesthetic training; the intellectual content of civilization; refinement in manners, taste, thought"; "a particular state or stage of advancement in civilization or characteristic features of it"; and, finally, "complex of distinctive attainments, beliefs, traditions, etc., constituting the background of a racial, religious or social group." In this broad sense, I speak of morals, ethics, thought, taste, and traditions when I relate culture to the American scene. It is the *humanitas* of the Romans and of Holmes and Brandeis.

The coming together under one roof of such disparate elements as moderate antiwar activists, old-line liberals, radicals, and Black Panthers to cope with racism and the Indochina war

(I am thinking too of what became known with certain derision as "radical chic") was a *cultural* situation. It is, to be sure, an old tradition for intellectuals and creative people to assume the leadership of great national causes. In the 1960s, because they had a national following based on their individual merit (sometimes only on glamour), they became much more than intelligent voices in the wilderness. Why else would Nixon's amazingly insecure White House—psychologically and culturally insecure —have felt the need to tap the telephones of liberal columnists and reporters, as well as those of its own officials, and to place many of them, along with outspoken movie actors, on its childishly secret list of "political enemies"? I, too, had my phone tapped in 1971. It seems so petulant and plain silly.

One theory held in Washington was that this whole cultural insecurity of the White House—affecting such different men as Nixon and Kissinger—was the factor that pushed them toward friendships with celebrities in the entertainment world as well as with the very rich. In the dullness of Nixon's Washington, there seemed to be an envy of the "beautiful people"—real ones and fake ones—who a decade earlier had helped to make the capital so glamorous for the Kennedys. Because most creative and intellectually influential people had turned their backs on Nixon, the friends of the White House became, instead, the evangelists Billy Graham and Oral Roberts; John Kennedy's one-time friend Frank Sinatra (despite his appearances before a congressional committee investigating organized crime); John Wayne (whose *Green Berets* and cowboyesque masculinity so impressed Nixon); Sammy Davis, Jr. (whom his fellow black entertainers cut dead); a collection of very wealthy people, some with strange financial ties; and top leaders of the scandal-ridden Teamsters' Union. White House guest lists tell the story, often when they are matched with contributions' lists. There is nothing wrong, of course, about presidential friendships with millionaires and financiers except that the Watergate scandals have suggested that these friendships had something to do with secret campaign contributions, the "laundering" of campaign money through foreign banks, etc.; some of Nixon's friends and contributors have been indicted on criminal fraud charges. During the Kennedy and Johnson administrations, many Americans made gifts of priceless chandeliers and antiques and famous paintings to the White House to enrich the national heritage. Under Nixon, the White House got a bowling alley from Charles "Bebe" Rebozo, the President's closest personal friend. And this cultural environment of the White House—the spirit of the *nouveau-riche* and the taste of the bargain basement—inevitably molded the manner in which the nation's supreme power was exercised. Most of these friends were tough *hombres* and, not surprisingly, the Presidency was tough and unforgiving with its enemies, foreign and domestic. I remember being struck, as were so many others in Washington, by Nixon's desire (or need) to watch more than once the movie biography of General George S. Patton just before ordering the incursion into Cambodia in the spring of 1970. To Nixon, the man who *always* wears the flag in his lapel, General Patton was evidently the kind of hardened American who would not conceive of losing a war for the United States. I suppose that one should not have been surprised that in those days the President kept telling us in his speeches that he would never let America become a "pitiful giant."

Toughness, or the impression of toughness, was also manifested by Nixon in his public adoration of football, a violent sport, and his growing penchant for discussing public policy in gridiron terminology. (This, by the way, forced many foreign diplomats and journalists in Washington to learn the intricacies of football so that they could readily understand what Nixon was talking about. But one evening, Eugene McCarthy suggested to me that the foreigners should also learn the meaning of the "forward fumble," a play, he insisted, invented by his Minnesota high-school football team.)

The administration, in its cultural impulses, regarded radicals, suspected radicals, and militants of every type as real enemies of the nation. Although the country did go through a period of considerable violence, the government seldom looked for the roots of all this trouble, despite the naming of various presidential inquiry commissions; instead, a disproportionate amount of attention and manpower was devoted to policing the nation. Increasingly, law-enforcement agents were given extraordinary latitude on all levels. Narcotics agents broke into the homes of innocent people and terrorized them at gunpoint. Yet the same administration secretly hired thugs and *provocateurs* against the opposition political party and involved the White House and top national intelligence agencies in burglaries and political spying. Meanwhile, common and organized crime (the latter often enjoying considerable protection at high levels) blossomed, traffic in narcotics prospered, alcoholism rates soared, the courts could not handle the volume of criminal and other cases, defendants spent months if not years awaiting trial, and the American prison system kept degenerating.

Although the White House claimed in 1973 that heroin addiction was finally declining after having doubled between 1965 and 1969, the problem was still casting a ghastly shadow. There were 1735 deaths from narcotic overdose during 1972. Alcoholism jumped to unprecedented levels. Labor reports said that more and more workers needed to hit the bottle at noon to be able to live through the day. A television spot sponsored by Alcoholics Anonymous showed the actor Dana Andrews standing on an overpass over the Santa Monica Freeway in California and announcing dramatically that he was an alcoholic and that one out of five drivers on the road in the afternoon rush hour was drunk.

All these problems—including the conditions in the courts and prisons—are of deep concern to the New Culture. As I have said elsewhere, its influence in the alcohol and narcotics areas has been limited. In the prisons a lot of serious work has been done or attempted to help prisoners and to persuade the government that it was dealing with human beings who needed to be rehabilitated and not with mindless animals. But the New Culture's impact has been greater in other areas of national life, which also means other areas of power.

Advocates of ecological and environmental protection have affected America's economy—and the power of great corporations to do as they please—to an astonishing degree. The automotive industry, for example, found its profits threatened by governmental pressure resulting from demands by environment-minded constituencies for strict emissions controls on all cars. Both the administration and Congress had become acutely aware of the sentiments of such voters and of *their* power at election time. Oil companies, already badly hurt in their public relations by frequent oil spills from tankers in coastal waters, became environment-conscious, if one is to believe their nationwide advertising—television viewers are familiar with the "We-Want-You-to-Know" commercials showing their efforts to protect land and sea environments. And they have lost hundreds of millions of dollars because the courts have blocked for years the building of an Alaska pipeline. Utility companies have been forced to abandon plans for nuclear power plants or to look for new locations. Yet, the energy crisis came to the succor of the corporations. Suddenly, environmental standards were relaxed and Congress authorized the Alaska pipeline.

One of the phenomena that most struck me when I returned to the United States in 1969 was that Americans in general and young Americans in particular had virtually no interest in the space program. I happened to be on Yugoslavia's Adriatic coast the day Neil Armstrong first set foot on the moon, and I remember the excitement as the local people watched his pictures on television being transmitted from the moon and fed into the Eurovision network. That week, Americans were heroes in Yugoslavia. But for reasons that remain unclear to me, Americans never developed a passion for the space program. Perhaps they were overconditioned to it by their familiarity with Flash Gordon and Buck Rogers, and what they were watching on home television seemed like an unreal abstraction. Even the monotonous voice emanating from Mission Control in Houston sounded improbable. And for many people, the space program was a waste of money that could be better spent or, as some of them put it, a diabolical design by the government to turn the people's attentions from real problems on earth. In the summer of 1970, during a trip to Asia with the secretary of state, I discussed this problem with Colonel Michael Collins, who piloted the first mother craft to hover over the moon while Armstrong made his descent. Mike had just become Assistant Secretary of State for Public Affairs and he was taken along on this trip to tell war-ravaged Asians about his space venture—an idea that left something to be desired in terms of common sense. But Mike was telling me about a tour of American campuses he had just made and he was truly hurt that the students could not care less about space. "All they wanted to talk about was the invasion of Cambodia," he said with what was clearly sincere astonishment.

One perhaps should not attach importance to outward appearances of Americans in a time of deep cultural conflict. But, in my judgment, appearance reflects a personal expression of individuality and creativity. This craving for individuality, often inadequate or distorted as it may have been, was behind the new fashions of the 1960s and 1970s, just as it was behind the kind of industrial sabotage—a desperately bored worker damaging a product because the dent would be his personal signature—that on the surface seemed irrational. (I know of at least one corporation—an electronics plant near Chicago—where workers are encouraged to sign their names on each product they finish putting together.)

The New Culture also encouraged an emancipation of the American woman in a deeper sense than the sloganry of Women's Lib would suggest. It has played a crucial role, I believe, in the society's acceptance of legalized abortion—despite the furious opposition of the Roman Catholic church and other groups—and, ultimately, in the Supreme Court's action upholding this legality. It has taken away the last shreds of opprobrium from divorce—there were 800,000 divorces in 1972—and it seems to have finally dawned on a great many people that a good divorce is preferable to a catastrophic marriage. Naturally I do not advocate that marriage and divorce be taken lightly. In my own family, our daughter, Nikki, was divorced after less than three years of marriage; my wife and I (both of us are children of divorced parents, but this page is being written on the eve of our twenty-fifth wedding anniversary) accepted it without any reservations because we were convinced it was the right thing to do. But we all know too many couples who cling to each other in mounting desperation because they lack the courage to face reality. And marriage counselors and Family Court judges have told me that it is rare to save a marriage when it reaches a point of emotional collapse.

Scanning best-seller lists or watching television is one way to take the cultural pulse of a society. Here too we find conflict in tastes and interests. For many years now, books on sex and dieting have led the best-seller lists, presumably indicating that Americans desire to be sexually happy *and* thin. Come to think of it, these two things may work in tandem. Inspirational and even religious books likewise do extremely well at bookstores: this, I surmise, is reflective of the obsessive American need to improve oneself. Little seems to have changed since Dale Carnegie sold millions of copies of *How to Win Friends and Influence People*. But the national guilt over Vietnam has turned a number of recent books about the war and its politics into best-sellers; and this is something new—the start of a real awakening of the national conscience about what we were doing in the jungles of Indochina.

Musically, the new culture gave us rock groups and the deafening noise of electronic amplifiers of voices and guitars. But rock and roll was beginning to fall by the wayside to make room for country music—the bluegrass fiddles—and for our indestructible jazz. Is this a new wave of romanticism and nostalgia, just as a Broadway revival of *No, No, Nanette* displaced the *Hair* and *Oh! Calcutta!* kind of productions, and Lerner and Loewe busied themselves in 1973 rewriting *Gigi* for the stage? *The Sting,* a tale of the 1920s, won the 1974 Academy Award, and *The Great Gatsby* took moviegoers two or three generations back. Scott Joplin and ragtime were rediscovered. Yet, when Bob Dylan reappeared publicly in early 1974, he still had the power to electrify hundreds of thousands of his admirers as no other performer could.

I mentioned earlier the success of religious books. It evidently is related to the larger surge in religiosity in the United States in these troubled times. The phenomenon in itself is not surprising —people have always turned to God and gods in time of need, and Americans have a deep religious streak in their make-up. A Jesuit theologue of my acquaintance disapproves of frenetic Pentecostal revival meetings and certainly even more of the new vogue of Satanism and witchcraft (though he was fascinated by *The Exorcist*), but he does argue that a society living under our kind of technological stress unavoidably seeks emotional and spiritual relief in mysticism. Billy Graham attracts greater and greater throngs to his nationally televised sermons, often held at huge sports stadiums, and "Declarations for Jesus" are made by thousands of people, old and young, stepping forward at the end of the service. There are "Jesus movements" and "Jesus freaks" and "street Christians" along with Oriental cults as people, especially young ones, search for personal truths established churches no longer seem to offer them. Thus old-time Pentecostalism thrives side by side with the Divine Light Mission, an Oriental movement headed by Guru Maharaj Ji, the fifteen-year-old Perfect Master, whose followers filled the vast Houston Astrodome to seek Buddhalike revealed knowledge. I watched recently "Religious America," a beautifully done series on educational television, delving into the mystery of the new religious experiences.

I am not addicted to television, but I do watch it with a certain regularity, and I can truthfully report that as often as not television plays a positive social and cultural role, "Religious America" being a case in point. I am not speaking, of course, of summer reruns of Perry Mason and the mind-bending detective series with their emphasis on every conceivable form of violence. I am bored, to say the least, with Mannix punching his adversaries into a bloody pulp or fat Cannon solving crimes through brain and brawn. But there are programs, even some of the so-called police variety, that deal fairly openly with serious national issues, and I give "Marcus Welby, M.D.," a high rating for bringing out into the open complex human problems; I remember in particular an insightful treatment of epilepsy.

I have learned a lot, I think, from daytime soap operas, especially when it comes to understanding what faces the contemporary American women. I know it is unchic to be a soap-opera devotee, but I honestly think there has been an immense improvement in their quality from the days in the late 1940s when I lived in New York and, because I worked nights, I developed the habit of listening to such pearls of daytime radio as "Mary Noble, Backstage Wife" or "Stella Dallas."

In another dimension, I believe, the networks have shown considerable courage and imagination in producing such specials as "The Selling of the Pentagon," a study of the military establishment's overkill public-relations effort, or "The Rockefellers," a sober study of that great millionaire family. When I was in Colorado Springs in 1970, a man of my acquaintance told me how the air force organized junkets to fly the city's leading citizens to sophisticated military installations around the country to gain their support for the installation of the antiballistic missiles system (ABM), then a hotly contested issue before Congress. If, indeed, similar undertakings were taking place in other American cities, then the Pentagon was guilty of a major self-serving promotion campaign at the taxpayer's expense and the CBS special may have been, if anything, understated. (In 1973, the General Accounting Office reported that the Pentagon failed to list $48 million in public-relations expenditures in the two previous years by excluding such promotional efforts as free civilian tours. The Pentagon actually spent twice as much as it had admitted on self-promotion.) I also thought CBS was imaginative when it conceived the idea, halfway through the Senate Watergate hearings, of reviving the films of the confrontation twenty years earlier between Senator McCarthy and Edward R. Murrow.

All the way up to the full eruption of the Watergate scandals in 1973, the Nixon administration fought the networks tooth-and-nail. The White House uttered threats that licenses of TV network affiliate stations would be lifted if they persisted in accepting the network feeds of programs objectionable to the administration. At the same time, it began cutting down the funds for the Public Broadcasting Corporation, the educational network, and demanded that programming decisions be taken away from individual news directors. This, of course, fitted into the administration's war against the overly outspoken "liberal media" just as the courts, taking advantage of the Supreme

Court's ruling that newsmen must, in effect, disclose their sources to grand juries, began to put recalcitrant reporters behind bars. This was the ebb period for the news media, though the influence of Watergate resulted in at least a temporary shelving of the White House's offensive against the free press.

The Old Culture's vengeful reaction came in many forms, one of them the Supreme Court's five-to-four ruling on June 21, 1973, that states and communities may ban films, plays, and publications if they consider them to be obscene and pornographic—even if they are acceptable in other jurisdictions. This decision, emphasizing again how conservative and culturally retrograde the Supreme Court had become with the advent of Justices appointed by President Nixon, set in motion what may be one of the great cultural controversies of the decade. For one thing, it threw publishers, movie makers, and television producers into total confusion as to what was permissible and where. Whatever standards had been established by the Supreme Court in specific cases in past years—and thus served as precedents—were now out the window. The decision immediately raised First Amendment questions concerning the freedom of speech and of the press (for example, the instant banning of *Playboy* magazine in Virginia's Albermarle County suggested that any official in the country may ban publications that in *his* opinion are obscene) and of course the unanswerable question of how obscenity should be defined. As Chief Justice Burger unhelpfully explained in the majority opinion, the new standards would be applied by "the average person," which sounds as if he were deputizing cultural vigilantes.

Quite clearly, the Court acted to curb the excesses of "hard" pornography that came to life and flourished in recent years as a distorted by-product of the New Culture. Anyone who has visited New York's Times Square in daytime or at night, or downtown San Francisco, is aware of the extraordinary proliferation of pornographic "blue movies," peep shows, "hard-porno" magazines, and various "parlors" where actual sexual acts are performed for the benefit of sweating businessmen and office clerks on their lunch hour or on their way home. There is no question, at least in my mind, that this whole situation had gotten completely out of hand, that greedy pornographers were making fortunes out of it, and that entire urban neighborhoods were polluted by this explosion of pornographic cheap sex. But, it appears to me, what the Supreme Court had done was to throw the baby out with the bath water. The old standard was that the test of "redeeming social values" should be applied before any restraining action was taken against alleged pornography, although there are few people who can agree on what precisely constitutes such "redeeming" qualities. In 1956, for example, John Cleland's eighteenth-century novel *Fanny Hill,* unquestionably a work of pornography, was declared not obscene by the Supreme Court because it had "minimal literary value." Under the 1973 decision, however, the judgment is left to the arbitrary perception of local zealots in communities across the United States. Within two weeks of this decision, hundreds of raids against movie houses and bookstores were carried out from coast to coast.

But what is obscene? I, for one, do not regard *Deep Throat* as a pioneering work of art and I even have reservations about *Last Tango in Paris.* My seventeen-year-old son saw *Tango* and pronounced it boring. But I believe adult Americans should be free to make the choice of whether they wish to attend showings of *Deep Throat* or *Tango.* What I fear, in other words, is a witchhunt directed against movies, books, and magazines that someone happens to dislike. In the cultural climate advocated by Nixon's White House and his Court, the 1973 decision can easily lead to a field day for self-appointed censors. And where is the line to be drawn? At *Playboy* magazine? At *Cosmo?* At *Deep Throat?* At *Tango?* At *Portnoy's Complaint?* At books which include Anglo-

Saxon four-letter words? At Nixon's tapes with "expletives deleted"?

One argument long advanced by self-appointed guardians of American morality—the very same "average" people whom the Chief Justice had just handed the power to censor and ban—is that pornography encourages rapists. It is true that more rapes are occurring every year (as we have had a rise in most other categories of crime). But it is absurd, to put it mildly, to correlate pornography and rape as cause and effect. I am sure that there have been rapists who read *Playboy,* as they may read the *Reader's Digest* or *Popular Mechanics,* but what about rapists who do not read *Playboy,* and *Playboy* readers who are not rapists? The argument is obviously too nonsensical to warrant further discussion, but if the Court is to be consistent it should have also laid the foundations for banning such books as, for example, *The Great Train Robbery* to discourage impressionable people from robbing trains or hijacking planes and *The Man Who Stole Portugal* to keep them from counterfeiting currency. And why not André Gide's *The Counterfeiter* and Dostoievsky's *The Gambler* (the latter on the grounds that gambling is illegal in most of the United States)?

The Court's decision was a backlash expression of the Old Culture, with its enormous potential for political and ideological censorship and mischief, at a time when right-wing parents' groups were already keen on banning books they found objectionable in the schools. It is bound to have political repercussions in a sense of increasing the censorial powers of the government even outside the narrow confines of obscenity statutes. As I keep insisting, political and economic power is intimately related to culture and its trends.

In the narrow sense of the word, power in America is exercised by the Executive branch of the federal government and by state and local governments. But the crucial difficulty is that the power of the American Presidency has grown to an unprecedented and dangerous extent.

The sheer size and weight of our society, the magnitude of our domestic problems, and the undeclared ten-year war in Indochina have combined to create the most centralized federal government in history. This type of centralization axiomatically results in an authoritarian government, particularly if Congress, as has been the case since about 1965, tends to abdicate *its* Constitutional powers and becomes instead a fairly pliant tool of the White House. Franklin D. Roosevelt, guiding the country out of the Great Depression and through the Second World War, had authoritarian inclinations, but the Congress often kept him in check. Lyndon Johnson was the first truly authoritarian President in the postwar period. But it took Richard Nixon, the man whose life prior to his 1968 election was a long string of frustrations, to turn the White House into a virtually impregnable power center—until the Watergate scandals and the related reawakening of Congress.

The Nixon Presidency has also been one of the most isolated in American history. I doubt whether this isolation was entirely attributable to the memories of Dallas and subsequent American political assassinations. Nixon's personal sense of extreme privacy went far beyond the requirements of security imposed by the Secret Service. Ever since he took office in 1969, Nixon has been almost completely unavailable—not only to newsmen (which might be my personal and professional complaint) but to members of his own cabinet and congressional leaders as well. And as years went by, Nixon's obsessions became greater and greater. He virtually eliminated cabinet meetings, reduced the number of news conferences to an absolute minimum, and ruled from the White House (or from his Florida White House at Key Biscayne, the Western White House at San Clemente, or Camp

David in the Maryland mountains) as an invisible President for all practical purposes—except when he demanded time to deliver a television speech. His immediate and totally devoted staff, the men whom he can thank for Watergate, shut him off from the outside world, and only two or three of them (and Kissinger) had immediate access to the President at the Oval Office or at his hideaway suite at the Executive Office Building.

I first met Nixon in 1958 when I traveled with him around South America on the trip made famous by the stones and spit hurled at him in Lima and Caracas. He was then vice-president and, I must say, he made an effort to be pleasant and friendly though one could easily detect in him a sense of insecurity and uncertainty. I remember attending a rather pleasant party given by the Nixons at their home for all those who had accompanied him on the trip. But during the three and a half years I covered Nixon, I did not have a single conversation with him, although I traveled with him on foreign and domestic trips. In fact, I never saw him at close quarters except at his rare news conferences or when he appeared briefly to be photographed with visiting dignitaries. When he was in Florida, newsmen were housed at a downtown Miami hotel and were summoned once or twice a day for briefings by White House Press Secretary Ronald L. Ziegler at a special office across the street. Writing about Nixon but never really seeing him, I developed in time the paranoid suspicion that he did not exist at all. But, then, all kinds of paranoid tendencies were growing among people immediately concerned with Nixon's activities.

I am not sure I ever understood Nixon's political philosophy, assuming he had one. Essentially, he was a pragmatist, an improviser, and a man enamored of power and its trappings. Though the Republican party traditionally stood for a decentralized government, Nixon built the most centralized government in the history of the Republic. To be sure, he paid lip service to decentralization, particularly when he launched his New Federalism (this, too, defies definition) and began distributing federal money to states and municipalities under the revenue-sharing legislation passed by Congress. This was meant to replace to some extent federal welfare programs after Congress quite unnecessarily killed his welfare-reform plan. But, at the same time, Nixon proceeded to impound funds voted by Congress for a variety of projects. Presently, he engaged in epic battles with Congress over Executive Privilege to prevent his advisers from testifying before congressional bodies.

In economic policy, particularly international monetary and trade issues, Nixon specialized in improvisations and dramatic surprises—much of which backfired. Though his greatest pride was foreign policy—the *détente cordiale* with China and the Soviet Union were his great accomplishments—he never had the patience to study foreign policy in depth, leaving it mainly to Kissinger. He rarely read newspapers or magazines, depending, instead, on a daily summary prepared by his staff. Officials in the National Security Council were warned never to send the President memoranda running longer than two pages. When Kissinger finally negotiated the Vietnam peace agreement, it took him a day or so to get Nixon to read the text.

Nixon's constant concern was with the exercise of his power and its perpetuation into the second term. This is why he had no time to read the Vietnam agreement: it was two weeks before the elections and Nixon was worried about the outcome, even though all signs were that he would defeat Senator McGovern by a landslide.

Nixon was obviously in love with power and its panoply. Soon after taking office, he ordered that the White House police be dressed in white uniforms with peaked caps, reminiscent of a Viennese operetta cast. I remember going to the White House lawn one morning to see Nixon receive a foreign chief of state and, to my enormous surprise, I discovered that army heralds in gala uniforms were stationed on the south porch to play the fanfare. It was one of Nixon's ideas, too, I was told.

There is no question in my mind that American corporate interests never fared better in the United States in the last fifty years than under the Nixon administration. For one thing, Nixon, the impoverished son of a California grocer (he never tired of reminding the world of it in the best Horatio Alger fashion), had an immense respect and liking for big money. He had all the traits of the *nouveau riche* who could never come to terms psychologically with the fact that he was no longer poor. For another thing, Nixon had spent six years before his election to the Presidency as a highly paid corporate lawyer in New York. A great many of his associates in the government came from corporate life or big law firms. All Nixon's personal friends— except for Billy Graham—were from the corporate world. Small wonder that the corporations and the rich men of America felt at ease with Nixon. As the Watergate scandals unfolded, it appeared that *quid pro quo*s had been worked out between some corporations and the administration and that campaign contributions were involved. There has been no proof of Nixon's personal involvement in such dealings, but there was ample evidence that his personal lawyer, Herbert W. Kalmbach, and other key figures were deeply enmeshed in campaign solicitations— big corporations were bluntly told they could not afford politically not to contribute—and in "hush money" pay-offs to the men who burgled the Democratic National Committee at the Watergate office building. Despite inflation and Nixon's hopes for balanced budgets, no effort was made to raise corporate taxes; instead, the government tended to look the other way when corporate accounting wizards built tax shelters and invented tax loopholes for the companies and their principals. Corporations like International Telephone and Telegraph (with annual revenues close to $6 billion) were powers unto themselves, trying to influence policy and to pervert antitrust laws with secret pay-offs to the party in power.

Conversely, it was not surprising that organized labor, most blacks, and poor people harbored unkind thoughts about Nixon. His administration's policies helped, I thought, to deepen the social and class conflicts already scarring America. These were further enhanced by inflation and the soaring cost of food as well as the shortages that hit the country late in 1972 and in 1973. (Nixon's few friends in the labor movement included the Teamsters' Union, long tarnished by corruption, whose former president, James Hoffa, won a presidential pardon in 1971 from the prison sentence he was serving for misusing union funds.) At the same time, conditions were allowed to develop under which corporation after corporation could report record earnings and profits during 1973 just as the stock market plummeted, the dollar was losing its value, and wage-earners were mercilessly squeezed by runaway inflation. Yet the President could not bring himself to proclaim a long-term mandatory freeze on prices and wages or propose an excess-profit tax (as was done during World War II) or even, during the energy crisis, to accept as part of new legislation a special windfall-profits tax on the oil corporations and a rollback of crude-oil prices. Instead he lifted all the economic controls in May 1974, at the peak of inflation.

Power in Washington is also exercised by the military-intelligence complex in the name of national security. Put another way, this is the power exerted by the Pentagon and the intelligence community—the Central Intelligence Agency, the Defense Intelligence Agency, and the super-secret National Security Agency—agencies with enormous budgets, bureaucracies, and constituencies.

For fiscal year 1974, the Pentagon had a proposed budget of nearly $88 billion, about one-third of the total national budget. (This included billions of dollars in military retirement pay and allowances.) The intelligence community's funds are hidden in the federal budget, but my educated guess is that they exceed $10 billion. Congress has the power to control military expenditures, but the intelligence people are accountable to nobody except theoretically the President (who probably has no time to study the appropriations) and to a few congressional committees that meet behind closed doors and have learned long ago not to ask too many questions.

The Pentagon's power relates to its ability to pour billions of dollars in contracts to defense plants and subcontractors throughout the country. Uncounted millions go for secret research to perfect weaponry. Other millions go to construct and maintain bases and for payrolls. As the nation's largest single indirect employer (not counting the personnel in the armed forces), the Defense Department can make or break whole cities. Seattle, home of the Boeing Aircraft Company, slides into unemployment and recession when Pentagon orders lag. Saint Louis would be badly hurt if the Douglas-McDonnell Company lost contracts for Phantom jets. Parts of Long Island would be in trouble if the Pentagon took away its orders from the Grumman Company for the new swing-wing jet fighter. And the companies know that the Pentagon is fairly tolerant of cost overruns, despite protests from Congress and individual government officials.

With such power of the purse, the Pentagon has powerful allies in Congress and in industry, even though the mood in general is turning against excessive military expenditures. Senators and representatives from states where the defense industry is vital do not lightly challenge the Pentagon. I remember from my early days in Washington that the conventional wisdom held that South Carolina would keep collecting naval installations so long as L. Mendel Rivers, chairman of the House Armed Services Committee, was alive. He died in 1972 and navy funds for South Carolina began to dry up, but elsewhere, others are aware that $1 billion may be spent on developing a new tank for the army, and that there may be other billions whenever funds are approved for the new nuclear-powered submarine and the B–1 bomber.

From my own observations, however, I tend to doubt whether the military, aside from its inertial economic power, exercises much influence over the formulation of basic national policies. Although the secretary of defense and the chairman of the Joint Chiefs of Staff participate in major decision making, they have rarely called the tune on such issues as the settlement of the Indochina war. It can be obstructive, however: the White House had a difficult time persuading the Joint Chiefs to go along with its negotiating position in the Strategic Arms Limitation Talks (SALT) with the Soviet Union. A friend of mine who took part in the negotiations told me that United States and Soviet military members of their respective delegations were closer to each other than to their civilian fellow negotiators. Obviously, the universal military mind takes a dim view of disarmament. The intelligence community likewise has a limited role in initiating or formulating basic national policies, although it enjoys considerable operational leeway under the supervision of a secret White House committee.

America is an extraordinary society. It seems to thrive on contradiction and self-flagellation. It has a vast reservoir of morality and decency, yet it can allow itself to be dragged into such catastrophic involvements as the Indochina war. It is both soft-hearted and cruel—to itself and to others. It helped to rebuild a war-ravaged world, but it also unleashed an awesome power of destruction over Indochina. It is capable of infinite compassion on some levels—Americans will open their hearts and their checkbooks for almost any cause and, as individuals, they will care for others in need—but has been unwilling or incapable of lifting 25 million of its own members out of dismal poverty. America has failed thus far to solve the problems of her cities and she is not quite certain what to do about her sprawling suburbs.

Americans have deep love for their land and for nature, but they are destroying both through pollution that could be controlled and man-created erosion of the soil. They worry about poor nations on other continents but cannot cope adequately with economic or racial problems at home. They are religious, even devout, but they have a terrifying streak of frontier violence in them. They are devoted to children, whom they generally spoil, but have no patience and little sentiment for the old. We study the lives of other nations—and hold strong opinions about them —but we know little about ourselves. America is so volatile and her processes of change so rapid that we seem to have no time or opportunity for introspection and self-evaluation.

I started writing this book after five years' absence from the United States, at a time when new generations were awakening to a new conscience. I spent three years examining the American society, and I have met with both discouragement and encouragement. I have described the reasons for one and for the other. Is there a final, firm conclusion to be drawn about contemporary America? My own inclination is to avoid sweeping conclusions because they would be inevitably misleading. But I would like to end on a note that is of overwhelming importance to me.

It is my belief that essentially we are a decent society—I see it in my own children and in the children of others. And I think that our evolution and maturing as a nation is indeed made possible, enhanced, by the deep revolutionary strain in our national history. So long as America remains a revolutionary society—

revolutionary in the sense of seeking change and searching for new truths—and so long as we accept that confrontations among us are as inescapable as they are necessary, then I feel certain that We Shall Overcome, and that this will come in our time.

A BRIEF BIBLIOGRAPHY

Aaron, Henry J. *Shelter and Subsidies.* Washington, D.C.: The Brookings Institution, 1972.

Barrett, S. M., ed. *Les Mémoires de Géronimo.* Paris: François Maspero, 1972.

Berrigan, Philip. *Prison Journals of a Priest Revolutionary.* New York: Holt, Rinehart and Winston, 1970.

Bronfenbrenner, Urie. *Two Worlds of Childhood: U.S. and U.S.S.R.* New York: Russell Sage Foundation, 1970.

Brooks, Van Wyck. *Three Essays on America.* New York: E. P. Dutton & Co., 1934.

Clemens, Samuel L. *The Innocents Abroad.* New York: Harper & Brothers, 1869.

Dickens, Charles. *American Notes.* London and Glasgow: Collins' Clear-Type Press, 1842.

Douglass College. *Report of the Commission on Ethnic and Race Relations.* New Brunswick, N.J., 1971.

Goodwin, Leonard. *Do the Poor Want to Work?* Washington, D.C.: The Brookings Institution, 1972.

Gore, Albert. *Let the Glory Out: My South and Its Politics.* New York: The Viking Press, 1972.

Hurwitz, Ken. *Marching Nowhere.* New York: W. W. Norton & Company, 1971.

Levy, Mark R., and Michael S. Kramer. *The Ethnic Factor: How America's Minorities Decide Elections.* New York: Simon and Schuster, 1972.

Marquand, John P. *Life at Happy Knoll.* Boston: Little, Brown and Company, 1954.

Moquin, Wayne, ed. *A Documentary History of the Mexican Americans.* New York: Praeger Publishers, 1971.

Myrdal, Gunnar. *An American Dilemma: The Negro Problem and Modern Democracy,* 20th anniversary ed., postscript by Arnold Rose. 2 vols. New York: Harper & Row, 1962.

Nabokov, Peter. *Tijerina and the Courthouse Raid.* Albuquerque: University of New Mexico Press, 1969.

Newton, Huey P., and Herman Blake. *The Revolutionary Suicide.* New York: Harcourt Brace Jovanovich, 1973.

Ohlin, Lloyd E., ed. *Prisoners in America: Perspectives on Our Correctional System.* Englewood Cliffs, N.J.: Prentice-Hall, 1973.

Reich, Charles A. *The Greening of America.* New York: Random House, 1970.

Report of the Task Force on Juvenile Justice. Bethesda, Md.: John Howard Association, 1973.

Rockland, Michael Aaron, ed. *Sarmiento's Travels in the United States in 1847.* Princeton, N.J.: Princeton University Press, 1970.

Rouse, James Wilson. *No Slum in Ten Years.*

Russell, William Howard. *My Diary, North and South.* New York: Harper & Brothers, 1954.

Spectorsky, A. C. *The Exurbanites.* Philadelphia: J. B. Lippincott Company, 1955.

Tocqueville, Alexis de. *Democracy in America.* New York: Alfred A. Knopf, 1945.

———. *The European Revolution, and Correspondence with Gobineau.* Garden City, N.Y.: Doubleday & Company, 1959.

Tucker, Robert W. *The Radical Left and American Foreign Policy.* Baltimore: Johns Hopkins Press, 1971.

U.S. Commission on Civil Rights. *Understanding Fair Housing.* Washington, D.C., 1973.

U.S. Department of Commerce, Bureau of Census. *1970 Census of Population: General Social and Economic Characteristics, United States Summary.* Washington, D.C., 1972.

U.S. Department of Health, Education and Welfare. *Work in America.* Washington, D.C., 1972.

U.S. Senate Select Committee. *Report on Nutrition and Human Needs.* Washington, D.C., 1973.

Wade, Edward. *Code Relating to the Poor in the State of New York.* Albany, N.Y.: Weed, Parsons and Company, 1870.

Weaver, Peter, et al. *Business and the Consumer.* Washington, D.C.: American University, 1971.

Wright, Nathan, Jr., ed. *What Black Politicians Are Saying.* New York: Hawthorn Books, 1972.

Wylie, Max. *Four Hundred Miles from Harlem: Courts, Crime, and Correction.* New York: The Macmillan Company, 1972.